Origins
Of the
Fourth
World
War
by

J.R. Nyquist

PUBLISHED IN THE UNITED STATES OF AMERICA
BY
BLACK FOREST PRESS
P.O.Box 6342
Chula Vista, CA 91909
1-800- 451-9404

Disclaimer

This document is an original work of the author. It may include reference to information commonly known or freely available to the general public. Any resemblance to other published information is purely coincidental. The author has in no way attempted to use material not of his own origination. Black Forest Press disclaims any association with or responsibility for the ideas, opinions or facts as expressed by the author of this book.

Printed in the United States of America
Library of Congress
Cataloging-in-Publication
Second Edition
ISBN: 1-58275-010-6
Copyright © July,1999 by J. R. Nyquist

This book is dedicated to the memory of
James Angleton.

Acknowledgments:

Editorial Advisors:
James Thornton
Greg Nyquist
William J. Kelso
Zoe Hare
Sarah Foster

Special thanks to Greg Buls

Cover design by
Linda Daly

Contents

Introduction

Many Americans in this post-Cold War era, especially younger people, would be vexed to hear the motto of the old Republic of Venice: "Happy is that city which in time of peace thinks of war." Americans, it seems, and indeed the entire West, have come to a bizarre conclusion that the world has somehow opened an unprecedented chapter in human existence—where a commercial worldview reigns supreme, where peaceful trading in goods and services has replaced national and ideological rivalries, where the peculiar ethnic characteristics of the many peoples of Earth have been erased, and where all humanity has been transformed into contented consumers watching television comedies, listening to rock music, munching fast food, and wearing designer jeans. Those images are rooted in blind hubris, of course, and their vacuity and absurdity match to perfection the peril they engender, as we see in J. R. Nyquist's arresting book, and as we see, for that matter, in even the most cursory review of the history of the world.

The American philosopher Richard M. Weaver notes that our contemporary bourgeois culture invariably places quantity ahead of quality and matter ahead of spirit, as must it do if its materialistic ideals are to be realized. Significantly, it also strives relentlessly to denigrate the memory. In his *Ideas Have Consequences* Weaver writes, "Materialism and success require the 'decomposed eternity' of time for their operation." Elsewhere, in *Visions of Order*, the same author remarks that "the part that consciousness has in our relationship with phenomena is largely a matter of memory. The recollection of uniform lines of cause and effect in the world, the recollection of who we are and of what we are committed to, are equipment for dealing with experience." Weaver notes finally that, "The effective men of the world are not cheerful forgetters but painful rememberers," and he wonders "whether there is not some element of suicidal impulse in the mood" that inclines men to spurn knowledge of their past.

II

This observation by Weaver is pivotal. Were memory of history as acute today in America as with other peoples at other times, we would not now be marching blindly to our destruction. Were it as acute, we would remember the stern admonition of the Father of our Country, George Washington, that, "to be prepared for war is one of the most effectual means of preserving peace." We would note well the grim fate of other nations that forgot their elementary history lessons. Consider the example of France in the third quarter of the nineteenth century. If Americans could remember that example, and draw the proper conclusions, perhaps they would be rather less naive.

During the 1850s and 1860s, the Second French Empire enjoyed enormous prosperity, and the regime of Napoleon III held such overwhelmingly popular support that it seemed as solid and durable as the flamboyant façade of Jean Louis Garnier's new Opera House, the pride of Paris at that time. Militarily, the nation nourished itself on the reputation of the Napoleonic Era, then six decades in the past, though the truth was that France by the late-1860s had already quietly slipped from its former position as a first-rate military power. The handful of perceptive men who saw the dark clouds gathering to the northeast were scorned as pessimists and accused of wanting to turn the country into a barracks; after all, the country was economically strong, so much so that it literally wallowed in luxury.

If sybaritic excess was rampant, corruption and vice were also widespread. So it was that France, decadent, blinded by wealth, engrossed in the chimerical world of gaudy parties, grand balls, frivolities of every description, and endless salon chatter, failed to gird herself for the approaching contest. Sociologist Vilfredo Pareto sagely observed that whereas in Prussia, in those years, the requirements of the army dictated financial policy, in France the financiers dictated military policy. So it was that when the moment of truth came in the summer of 1870, the French army crumpled, its vaunted reputation exploding like a child's overblown balloon. For France, the humiliation, suffering, and destruction, in the context of the time, were simply immense.

Needless to say, the France of that period may be deemed fortunate from the perspective of our poor century. Weapons of mass destruction did not exist in the nineteenth century, warfare generally was not directed towards non-combatants, and the nation-states of Europe were not animated by Procrustean ideologies. Thus, the total obliteration of France, the French government, the French people, and French culture not only would have held no appeal to Bismarck, it would never have occurred to him. The conditions he imposed on vanquished France were, while unpalatable for the French then, extremely moderate in comparison with our contemporary norms. Nevertheless, the experience was one the French remembered for fifty years, through the First World War. We Americans, and our allies, would do well to recollect it now and pray fervently that it not be too late.

I think it noteworthy that Mr. Nyquist does not write in terms of absolute certainty; he has not been bitten by the determinist bug. And we cannot emphasize that too strongly. Likelihood is not the same thing as categorical certitude. Few things that lie in our future may be called inevitable. Almost 150 years ago, Sir Edward S. Creasy wrote as follows: "I am aware that...the reproach of Fatalism is justly incurred by those, who, like the writers of a certain school in a neighboring country, recognize in history nothing more than a series of necessary phenomena, which follow inevitably one upon the other. But when...I speak of probabilities, I speak of human probabilities only. When I speak of Cause and Effect, I speak of those general laws only, by which we perceive the sequence of human affairs to be usually regulated; and in which we recognize emphatically the wisdom and power of the Supreme Lawgiver, the design of the Designer."

On the other hand, wisdom in matters connected to national survival presupposes a cognizance of Sir Edward's "human probabilities" and "general laws." To eschew determinism does not mean to embrace foolhardiness. Disbelief in the ineluctability of history does not necessarily have to be indicative of stone-blindness to agonizing reality. Should a resident of one of the less pacific districts in one of our major American cities be so witless as to leave his doors unlocked at night, we indulge in hyperbole should we call his *likely* doom *inevitable*. In short, ignorance in the era of atom-charged rockets and inflexible ideologies is most decidedly *not* bliss.

—Fr. James Thornton

Author's Preface

You cannot fight an enemy unless you have words for him. But if your enemy, by way of deception, takes those words away, what can you do? The word for our enemy was *Soviet Union*. Another word was *communist.* Yet another word was *KGB*. For seventy years these words accumulated a rich series of meanings, blackened by decades of atrocity and treachery. The creatures designated by these names recognized the weight of their old insignia. Therefore, according to a carefully laid plan, they shed the old names, denounced the crimes associated with those names, and began a fresh start.

But does the murderer cease being a murderer when he calls himself Smith instead of Jones? Does a treacherous oligarchy suddenly become trustworthy by shedding its old ideology and adopting a new one?

This leads us to the question of nature.

What was the *nature* of the Soviet oligarchy which suddenly declared itself to be liberal and democratic? What was the *nature* of the most infamous secret police in the world, before and after its name was changed?

Surely it must be recognized that a name is only a tag. To change a name is not to change the essence of the thing named. This great truth has not been observed with regard to the changes in Eastern Europe and the Soviet Union. We have new names in Russia, but we also have—as Aleksandr Solzhenitsyn pointed out—"the same old faces."

Of course, everyone can see that there has been change in Russia. Everyone can see that the Warsaw Pact is now defunct, that East Germany has merged into West Germany, that the Soviet Union has been replaced by the Commonwealth of Independent States, that communism is daily criticized in the former communist countries. In terms of American security, however, these are not proofs of the ruling oligarchy's well-wishes. The same basic staff runs the Commonwealth of Independent States as ran the Soviet Union. If they hated and envied us before, why should this attitude (deep down) turn to love and well-wishing? After the fall of the Soviet Union, *International Currency Review* published a list of the leaders of the so-called independent republics.[1] The list follows:

Azerbaijan: KGB General Gaidar Aliyev, former Communist Party First Secretary.

Armenia: Levon Ter-Petrosyan, KGB-controlled nationalist leader.

Belarus: Aleksandr Lukashenko and Vyacheslav Kebic, Communist Party Soviet Union Central Committee members, opposed to the USSR breakup.

Estonia: Lennart Meri—assuming things are exactly as they appear, Meri is the only genuine non-communist leader of a former Soviet republic.

Georgia: MVD General Eduard Shevardnadze, USSR Politburo member under Gorbachev, Georgian Communist Party First Secretary, and non-voting member of Brezhnev's Politburo.

Kazakhstan: Nursultan Nazrbayev, USSR Politburo member under Gorbachev, Kazakh Communist Party First Secretary, and President of Kazakhstan S.S.R. Minister under Gorbachev.

Kyrgyzstan: Asar Akayev and Apas Dzhumagulov, Kyrgyzstan Communist Party Central Committee member and Premier of the Krgyzstan S.S.R. respectively.

Latvia: Valdis Birkavs and Anatolijis Gorbunovs, Communist Party Secretary and Latvian Communist Party Secretary for ideology.

Luthuania: Algirdas Brazauskas, First Secretary of the Lithuanian Communist Party.

Moldova: Mircea Snegur. CPSU Central Committee member and CP First Secretary, Moldavia S.S.R.

Russia: Boris Yeltsin, non-voting member, Communist Party Soviet Union Politburo.

---

[1] *International Currency Review:* 22, 3-4.

Tajikistan: Rakhmon Nabiyev, Tajik Communist Party boss.

Turkmenistan: Saparmurat Niyazov, First Secretary of the Turkmen Communist Party, member of Gorbachev's Politburo.

Ukraine: Leonid Kuchma, former communist director of a USSR missile plant.

Uzbekistan: Islam Karimov, Communist Party First Secretary of Uzbekistan.

What this list demonstrates is the continuity of the Communist Party staff under the Commonwealth of Independent States. Therefore it is not surprising that the old GULAG camps are packed with prisoners. It is no wonder that arms limitation and reduction treaties are being violated as nuclear war preparations continue. In this context, Avraham Shifrin, who wrote *The First Guidebook to Prisons and Concentration Camps of the Soviet Union*, penned a letter to Christopher Story on 5 June 1996. In that letter he said "the situation in the camps of Russia, the Ukraine (as well as other parts of the USSR with the exception of the Baltic States) has not changed."

Even the Soviet withdrawal from Afghanistan is a classic deception. Consider the following curious facts: One of the main warlords recently fighting for control of Afghanistan was General Abdul Rashid Dostum, an ethnic Uzbek whose troops entered Afghanistan as part of the Soviet Army. During heavy fighting in the summer of 1997, General Dostum's army received air support from Soviet-made bombers based in "former" Soviet Tajikistan. How did this come about? Dostum's Uzbek troops were declared "mercenaries" in the mid-1980s, dropping out of the Soviet Army by permission of the Soviet leadership, and were subsequently declared "Islamic" prior to the Soviet withdrawal. After Dostum's defeat in 1998, General Masoud took up the fight (with Moscow's help).

This leads me to ask if the West actually won the Cold War? Looking at the communist victories in the Congo and Angola, together with Nelson Mandela's victory in South Africa, the picture is one of unrecognized Western defeats. But nobody remembers that Mandela is a communist.

As Avraham Shifrin said in his letter to Chris Story: "The West believes the Russian lies, as it wants to believe there will be a quiet life, but there won't be."

— J. R. Nyquist

1

Modern Decadence

And they cast dust on their heads, and cried, weeping and wailing, saying,
Alas, alas that great city, wherein were made rich all that had ships in the sea by
reason of her costliness! for in one hour is she made desolate.
— REVELATION 18:19

Alas! There cometh the time when man will no longer give birth to any
star. Alas! There cometh the time of the most despicable man, who can no
longer despise himself.
Lo! I show you *the last man*.
'What is love? What is creation? What is longing? What is a star?' — so
asketh the last man and blinketh.
The earth hath then become small, and on it there hoppeth the last man
who maketh everything small. His species is ineradicable like that of the
ground-flea; the last man liveth longest.
'We have discovered happiness' — say the last men, and blink thereby.
— FRIEDRICH NIETZSCHE

1. *The sociology of decline.* — What goes up, must come down.
Such was my first crude thought in 1987, an idea rendered more
eloquent by Oswald Spengler when he wrote: "The coming of Caesarism
breaks the dictature of money and its political weapon, democracy."[1]
And yet, one need not read Spengler to see that we have entered a
period of decline, to see what Jacob Burckhardt meant when he wrote of
the great advance of capitalism in Europe; of art and science becoming
mere branches "of urban moneymaking" carried away "on the stream of
general unrest." Burckhardt worried about specific symptoms of decay,
about a decline in local as well as national patriotism. In exasperation he
asked: "is everything to turn into big business, as in America?"[2] In the

---

[1] Oswald Spengler, *The Decline of the West*, trans. Charles Francis Atkinson (New York: Oxford
University Press, 1991), p. 414.

[2] Jacob Burckhardt, *Reflections On History*, trans. M. D. Hottinger (Indianapolis: Liberty

historian's mind, the great danger was not money itself, but the destructive effect it might produce on the pre-capitalist foundations of society. In this context it was Friedrich Nietzsche, one of Burckhardt's fellow professors at Basel University, who gave voice to the insight that the capitalists are politically inadequate, possessing the wrong instincts; that the urban bourgeoisie is nothing but fodder for the future "masters of the earth." Along these same lines Joseph Schumpeter suggested that capitalism is the last senile stage of feudalism. In truth, the leaders of commercial society are the opposite of political visionaries. Max Weber pointed out long ago that "The nub of the social and political problem is not the *economic* situation of the *ruled*, but rather the *political* qualifications of the *ruling* classes and those classes which are *rising* to power."[3] The destiny of a society, and perhaps the survival of civilization itself, depends on the nature of its ruling class. Taking a closer look, it might be argued that Karl Marx's whole project was a sly attempt to exploit weaknesses in the emerging ruling groups, which were then being born out of capitalism. In other words, given the political inadequacies of the capitalists, Marx sought to fashion an anti-capitalist ruling class by setting down new laws and by formulating new tasks under the guise of "socialism" (a nebulous term, perhaps signifying nothing but hostility to bourgeois power). Taking the dark side of Marxism seriously, going beyond its explicit ideological categories: Marx anticipated the commercial herd's vulnerability. He laughed at the middle class, all the while respectful of genuine aristocracy, noting that in history "all facts and personages of great importance" occur twice: "the first time as tragedy, the second as farce."[4] In saying this, Marx was suggesting that bourgeois history was a joke, that the bourgeoisie knew little about power, and less how to keep it. As a revolutionist he wished to put an end to economics, the ideology of capitalism, and turn the cycle of farce back into a cycle of tragedy.[5]

Here we come face to face with the Revolution. Marx and Nietzsche, who both influenced Spengler, especially on the matter of Caesarism breaking the dictature of money, knew that liberal democracy would sooner or later collapse. It was this notion of a new Caesarism, lurking in the nineteenth century mind, which puts the communists and fascists of the twentieth-century into proper perspective. In this context,

---

Classics, 1979), pp. 265-266.

[3] Max Weber, *Selections in Translation*, ed. W. G. Runciman, trans. Eric Mathews (New York: Cambridge University Press, 1978), p. 267.

[4] Karl Marx, *The Eighteenth Brumaire of Louis Bonaparte* (New York: International Publishers, 1991), p. 15.

[5] The thing to remember, in this context, is that politics is about three things: In the first instance it is about power; in the second instance it is also about power; and in the third instance, it is power again.

the totalitarian formation was correctly anticipated by farsighted individuals, and therefore it came into the world naturally and logically. If this were not so, then clever people could not have understood it beforehand.

With the First World War and the Bolshevik Revolution these notions finally manifested as a conquering and tyrannical force: not as some bizarre aberration in history, and certainly not as something that would easily collapse; but, rather, as a deep, even metaphysical reaction to the culture-power of money. What emerged from all of this? A new type of warrior aristocracy, the "Vanguard Party" of Marx and Lenin, possessed of intellectual weapons specially designed to cope with the monetary and political influence of the bourgeoisie. The Bolshevik Revolution and the fascist revolutions rejected unfettered capitalism, pronouncing themselves in favor of social discipline. They were militaristic. In this context Burckhardt said that in the nineteenth century culture had triumphed over church and state. In the twentieth century the Bolsheviks would use the state to triumph over church and culture, to trample them down as much as expedience would allow. Nietzsche understood that this was coming when he wrote that "God is dead," and when he stated that Western man had lost the talent for generating authoritative institutions. Only Russia, he warned, had durability and promise in it.[6] Everywhere else in Europe the money power had weakened the political function in its authoritative role. It had transformed the state into the tool of an unchecked market culture, while the church had become a mere business enterprise. Further hedonistic urges were thereby unloosed by capitalism, and ancient institutions were forced to retreat. Disintegration and disorder could not be helped, especially on the most basic level, *in the soul*. The worst would happen. There would be revolutions, civil wars, even world wars. The danger was that this overabundant culture, dominating every other consideration with its passionate economic desires, would, in the words of Joseph Schumpeter, destroy its own "protective strata."

To explain what Schumpeter meant by "protective strata," let us digress: The "steel frame" of modern capitalism, said Schumpeter, depended on "the human material of feudal society." This human material marshalled the army, gave policy to the state, "it functioned as a *classe dirigente*." Yet the middle class wanted complete control. The bourgeoisie grasped political power, and the old aristocracy was suddenly unsure of itself. The bourgeoisie had science, money, and "reason" on its side. The old aristocracy could no longer justify itself before the people, who wanted jobs and money. But the new bourgeois

---

[6] Friedrich Nietzsche, *Twilight of the Idols: Or How to Philosophize with a Hammer*, trans. R. J. Hollingdale (London: Penguin Books, 1990), pp. 103 - 104.

style of political leadership lacked depth. It misunderstood the nature of power. It routinely miscalculated in ways the old aristocracy could not have done. The explanation, said Schumpeter, was that the old aristocracy had warrior traditions. It was bred to stand tall. Mystic glamor and the lordly attitude of command had been its ancient province. On the other side, the bourgeoisie thought only in terms of a balance sheet.[7] The nobles made leadership into an art, the middle class made it into a new kind of following; that is, into democracy. No longer did the West have a class dedicated to defend it against outsiders and infidels, to command its armies and design its policies. The West had only careerists and bureaucrats, mercenaries and MBAs. The money-men felt that everything could be bought, and everything could be sold, that war was something that depended on reserves of cash. But as the great Machiavelli noted: "it is not gold...that constitutes the sinews of war, but good soldiers; for gold does not find good soldiers, but good soldiers are quite capable of finding gold."[8]

And on this false basis, with gold going forth to find good soldiers, the Cold War was fought. Its configuration was made, in advance, to accommodate the money power. That accommodation, in and of itself, soon became the objective. Economic logic suggested that the poor dilapidated Soviet Union, led by Lenin's militant politicians, would admit defeat once it became apparent how well the West was getting on in terms of general prosperity. We, on our side, would combat communism by living better than the masses of the communist bloc. On this second false basis, the international bourgeoisie engaged "the zone of militarism" (as Andrei Navrozov has called the USSR)[9] in a contest to see who could be more comfortable, who could enjoy more amenities, and who could walk on the moon. Such was a contest, or a series of contests, the Soviets had no intention of entering into, regardless of what they said at the time. But as the bourgeoisie remained fixated on economics and the technological byproducts of an economic orientation, it did not notice that another contest had begun: a psycho-strategic duel in which its own

---

[7] Joseph A. Schumpeter, *Capitalism, Socialism and Democracy* (New York: Harpor Torchbooks, 1975), pp. 134-139.

[8] Niccolo Machiavelli, *The Discourses*, trans. Leslie J. Walker, S. J. (England: Penguin Books, 1985), p. 302. For same reference in other trans. see *The Discourses*, 2: 10.

[9] Andrei Navrozov, *The Gingerbread Race* (London: Pan Books Limited, 1993): an important book by an unexpected Russian free-thinker, utterly misunderstood by those who should have appreciated and utilized his unique Russian standpoint, however paranoid it might appear to the Cult of Naiveté. Especially disappointing in this regard, the editor of *National Review*, Mr. John O'Sullivan, dismissed Navrozov as a "conspiracy nut." Adding to the universal critical rejection, Navrozov told me in a January 1996 telephone conversation that his publisher withdrew support for the book in the midst of printing.

illusions were exploited and Russia's weaknesses were simultaneously turned into strengths.

Today, in 1998, we are led to believe that our system triumphed in the Cold War, that the communist dragon was slain. It is a strange thing, is it not? The Party of Lenin and Stalin, according to Khrushchev's statement, would give up communism when "the crab sings." And so the Party crab, which has always moved backwards as a way of moving forward, sang a strangely characteristic song. A group within the Party itself, elevated by KGB Chairman Andropov, inveigled to mothball the Soviet Union with a crabwise maneuver: "One step forward, two steps back." In the final analysis, we must suspect that Vladimir Lenin inspired this maneuver.

> One step forward, two steps back.... It happens in the lives of individuals, and it happens in the history of nations and in the development of parties. It would be the most criminal cowardice to doubt even for a moment the inevitable and complete triumph of the principles of revolutionary Social-Democracy, of proletarian organisation and Party discipline. We have already won a great deal, and we must go on fighting....[10]

The crab sings, the Party divests itself, and the commercial mob celebrates a victory achieved by its own comfortable way of living. In the USSR all names are changed, but the underlying substance is not altered. "The Russian and Soviet 'security organs' have been reorganised and renamed many times in their history without these changes significantly affecting their personnel, their mentality or their operations," wrote KGB defector Anatoliy Golitsyn in a 1993 memorandum to the CIA. "The recent reorganisation and alleged reform of the KGB is no exception."[11]

Russia's courageous investigative journalist, Yevgenia Albats, confirmed this view when she wrote:

> By now, the reader is well aware that there had never been any real question of disbanding the Committee for State Security [KGB]. Oh, a bit of patching had to be done, not so much for the benefit of the Russian public, which was much too busy looking for bread (that hungry autumn, there wasn't a loaf left by noon), as to dazzle the West. And it worked.[12]

---

[10] Vladimir Lenin, *V. I. Lenin: Marx, Engels, Marxism* (Moscow: Progress Publishers, 1968), pp. 138-139.

[11] Anatoliy Golitsyn, *The Perestroika Deception: The World's Slide Towards the 'Second October Revolution ['Weltoktober]* (London and New York: Edward Harle, 1995), p. 215.

[12] Yevgenia Albats, *The State Within a State: The KGB and Its Hold on Russia — Past, Present, and Future*, trans. Catherine A. Fitzpatrick (New York: Farrar, Straus, Giroux, 1994), p. 306.

In Russia, new actors speak new lines. Nonetheless, it is the old theme with the same plot. A performance is given before the world audience. It is meant to dazzle the Americans and West Europeans. The observant journalist tells us that "the notion that the KGB was the instigator of perestroika seems absurd.... Yet, it is not so paradoxical after all, when you consider the KGB's true purpose."[13]

And what is that purpose, aside from sending out spies and policing the Russian people?

Disinformation.

But perestroika, says Albats, was much more than a mere disinformation plot. Tremendous underlying forces were being adjusted by the social engineers of the Party and KGB, because communism had failed economically and psychologically. And these failures were not new. Lenin had long before lamented them in his Report to the Fourth Congress of the Communist International, in which he laid down the reasons for the New Economic Policy (NEP), a calculated return to capitalism for the purpose of reviving a collapsed socialist economy. Lenin characterized this policy as "a possible line of retreat." Then he asked:

> What gave rise to this peculiar and...very unpleasant situation? The reason for it was that...the direct transition to purely socialist forms, to purely socialist distribution, was beyond our available strength, and that if we were unable to effect a retreat...we would face disaster.[14]

In this context, Lenin spoke of "our famous Russian ruble," which was famous because the number then in circulation exceeded one quadrillion. In the hall where Lenin delivered his report, there was laughter. "That is something!" exclaimed Lenin. "It is an astronomical figure." The laughter grew louder: "But we do not think that the figure is so very important even from the point of view of economic science, for the zeroes can always be crossed out."[15]

More laughter.

Oh yes, the "zeroes" would be crossed out. But there was no contrition for the suffering inflicted on the Russian people. The propriety of experimenting with a hundred million lives was never questioned. One quadrillion rubles? Ha ha ha.

But returning to the grand purpose of the KGB: even at the

---

[13] Ibid., p. 169.

[14] V. I. Lenin, *Lenin's Final Fight: Speeches and Writings*, 1922-23 (New York: Pathfinder, 1995), pp. 100 - 101. This citation is for the previous paragraph as well.

[15] Ibid., pp. 101-102.

----

beginning of the Revolution, in terms of this aforementioned "retreat," it was important to dazzle the West. Thus the New Economic Policy was scripted to gain financial advantages while avoiding an internal political explosion from the discontented Russian masses. "The most important thing," said Comrade Lenin, "is trade." And sharing Marx's contempt for the bourgeoisie as a ruling class, he added:

> We have been given no assistance by any of the powerful capitalist countries, which organize their capitalist economy so 'brilliantly' that they do not know to this day which way they are going. By the Treaty of Versailles, they have created a financial system that they themselves cannot make head or tail of.[16]

Lenin would fool the capitalists. He would make them believe that communism had failed and was admitting defeat. In this way he would get loans, he would get foreign assistance for building heavy industry. The risk in these ventures would be entirely on the other side. Lenin explained his method as follows:

> As regards trade, I want to reemphasize that we are trying to found mixed companies, that we are already forming them, i.e., companies in which part of the capital belongs to private capitalists — and foreign capitalists at that — and the other part belongs to the state. First, in this way we are learning how to trade, and this is what we need. Second, we are always in a position to dissolve these companies if we deem it necessary, and do not, therefore, run any risks, so to speak.[17]

Today, Yeltsin's New Economic Policy is no different. The dumb foreigner comes in, invests his money, becomes a partner in a state enterprise—and what does he really own? It is an unequal partnership. The state might seize his share of the business at any time. In fact, it is a threat held over the foreign investor, facilitating further investment. The greater the potential loss to any investor, the greater Moscow's hold on all foolish capitalists. Note Lenin's words of scorn:

> I have said that we have done a host of foolish things, but I must also say a word or two in this respect about our enemies. If our enemies blame us and say that Lenin himself admits that the Bolsheviks have done a host of foolish things, I want to reply to this: yes, but you know, the foolish things we have done are nonetheless very different from yours.[18]

---

[16] Ibid., p. 103.

[17] Ibid., p. 108.

So the West should be careful about celebrating its victory over communism. As Yevgenia Albats has warned us, the foreign intelligence office of the KGB is still at work, "maintaining close contacts...with friends in the West, mainly representatives of Communist parties and various national movements."[19] Indeed, the Western media are constantly duped by the KGB's conspiratorial techniques. "I am not interested in casting aspersions," writes Albats, but then: "Have my colleagues from the other world ever wondered why the KGB and some other institutions were so eager to hold 'exclusive' press conferences for foreign correspondents?"[20]

It is, as she said before, an effort to dazzle the West. That is the bottom line. It is an effort to subvert the truth about Russia and gain benefits on the sly. And where will these "benefits" lead?

What does such an elaborate deception ultimately signify?

"We still do not realize," said the Soviet political scientist Andrei Grachev, "that the postwar stage of world history is now ending, and the prewar stage is now beginning."[21] In this context Sun Tzu wrote:

> All warfare is based on deception. Hence, when able to attack, we must seem unable; when using our forces, we must seem inactive; when we are near, we must make the enemy believe that we are away; when far away, we must make him believe we are near. Hold out baits to entice the enemy. Feign disorder, and crush him.[22]

When history brings us to an erroneous way of life, the Fates provide the mechanism of destruction. Nothing lasts forever, but all things tend toward decay. Oswald Spengler wrote: "*A power can be overthrown only by another power*, not by a principle, and only one power that can confront money is left. Money is overthrown and abolished by blood."[23]

So my first crude thought remains: *What goes up, must come down.* The law of gravity is here applied to politics.

2. Civilizations will fall because all things are eventually brought down by gravity. This is true in politics even as it is true in physics.

In 1990 I gathered some statistics from official records, from the abstracts put out by the United States government. In January 1978

---

[18] Ibid., p. 109.

[19] Albats, *The State Within a State*, pp. 221-222.

[20] Ibid., pp. 233-234.

[21] Cited by Albats, *The State Within a State*, p. 349.

[22] *The Art of War*, cited by B. H. Liddell Hart, *Strategy* (New York: A Signet Book, 1974), p. xi.

[23] Spengler, *The Decline of the West*, p. 414.

America had 156,783 persons awaiting arraignment; by 1986 that figure reached 272,736. In 1974 federal courts convicted 217 persons of corruption in public office; in 1986 that figure reached 1,027. Aggravated assault between 1978 and 1989 increased by 49.6 percent; that same period saw a 20.6 percent increase in forcible rape and an 8.6 percent increase in robbery.

A side note that must be interjected at this juncture: the number of lawyers has tripled since 1960.

Next, consider the following numbers: During the 1930s 1,667 prisoners were executed under civil authority in the United States; in the 1940s, 1,284 prisoners were executed; in the 1950s, 717 were executed. Between 1960 and 1976 no prisoners were executed under civil authority.

Here is gravity pulling something down. Decade after decade the idea of capital punishment grows heavier and heavier. Finally, at long last, there isn't momentum enough for it to remain in the air. Therefore it falls. It crashes.

At the same time, criminality is propelled upward. As the number of executions decrease, the number of criminals and the number of crimes committed increase. Gravity has yet to react on these new social phenomena, though recent statistics suggest that new laws may be working. However, as crime travels upward, it moves in more than one dimension. That is, the peaks of modern criminality are not merely composed of soaring quantities, but of high-flying qualities too. If we imagine that criminality is only a phenomenon of the lower classes, we have seen almost nothing. One has only to look to the highest office in the land, and there one finds the cheap stuffing now being kicked, now being leaked, from a bloated presidential façade.[24]

That which goes up may also become president before it comes down.

Here is an evil moment in the writing of this book, and I hesitate to insert a sharp truth between the ribs of so many tender readers; but the Russian dictator N. S. Khrushchev gave the KGB a new mission; namely, to use organized crime as a weapon with which to penetrate American political and economic institutions. A few years prior,

---

[24] e.g., William Jefferson Clinton, as detailed in the testimony of Larry Nichols, Terry Reed, and the journalistic accounts of Ambrose Evans-Prichard, Christopher Ruddy, and Jim Norman. See, in this context, Floyd G. Brown, *"Slick Willie": Why American Cannot Trust Bill Clinton* (Annapolis, Maryland: Annapolis Publishing Company, Inc., 1992); Deborah J. Stone and Christopher Manion, *"Slick Willie" II: Why America still Cannot Trust Bill Clinton* (Annapolis, Maryland: Annapolis-Washington Publishers, Inc., 1994); as for the laundering of drug money in Arkansas, see Terry Reed and John Cummings, *Compromised: Clinton, Bush and the CIA* (New York: S.P.I. Books, 1994); and for Clinton's connection to Communist front organizations and the criminal left, see David Mark Price, *Secret: FBI Documents Link Bill and Hillary Clinton to Marxist-Terrorist Network* (Wichita, Kansas: Sunset Research Group, 1993).

Chairman Mao had conceived of a "Second Opium War" to be waged against the West. All things considered, Khrushchev's advisors and strategists were more sophisticated. The primary reason for going into the drug business was not to poison the youth, but to infiltrate, even dominate, organized crime. And the main reason for infiltrating organized crime, in the words of one analyst, "was the Soviet belief that high-quality information — information on political corruption, money and business...was to be found in organized crime."[25]

In this context, a method central to the recruitment of secret agents is blackmail: You discover skeletons in a politician's closet, and you force him to join your group. This group does not identify itself as an extension of the KGB. It is, to all outward appearances, a corrupt gang of politically interested and financially motivated persons. This is what might be called "a false flag recruitment." Many agents are only useful when working under a false flag, because they would not commit treason by serving a hostile power; so the aforesaid hostile power hides itself behind ordinary, pedestrian criminality.

3. "Sociopath" refers to a person incapable of loyalty, who is grossly selfish, narcissistic, callous, manipulative, and contemptuous of others.

A recent survey indicates that 93 percent of Americans would cheat on their income tax if they could get away with it. Oddly, 86 percent from this same survey would report their neighbors to the IRS for doing the same.

In this context, David Henry Barnett, a former CIA intelligence officer sold the names of CIA agents deployed in Indonesia for $92,000 each.

Thomas P. Cavanagh offered to sell the stealth bomber secrets to men he thought were Soviet agents.

Lieutenant Christopher M. Cooke, an Air Force officer assigned to a nuclear missile silo, called the Soviet embassy to make a deal.

Seaman Michael R. Murphy wanted to sell submarine secrets. He was detected and given an *honorable* discharge.[26]

4. A 1990 newspaper report states that there were roughly 5,000 communist secret agents in West Germany. This figure was discovered when East German secret police files were inadvertently compromised in

---

[25] Joseph D. Douglass, Jr., *Red Cocaine: The Drugging of America* (Atlanta, Georgia: Clarion House, 1990), p. 11.

[26] Thomas B. Allen and Norman Polmar, *Merchants of Treason: America's Secrets for Sale* (New York: Dell Publishing, 1989), pp. 419-430. This citation constitutes an appendix listing page after page of American traitors, including 43 military officers and 17 Federal Employees of various agencies caught spying for the communists.

1990.[27] This, surely, is a pill for anti-McCarthyism. Is it not probable, given that America was the main target country of the communists during the Cold War, that there were 5,000 spies embedded in our government too? The mere fact that we find this figure ridiculous, that we doubt its veracity, is itself a proof of something. To say that espionage and subversion on this scale is impossible only admits ignorance. In the end, there is nothing impossible about several hundred KGB case officers recruiting and running four or five thousand American-born agents.

Unless we get to the root of this we will not be able to see the truth regarding our country. Instead, we will remain enmeshed in our own national illusions.

5. I began collecting my notes for this book in 1987. That year I realized communism was going to "manage" its own collapse. At first I stupidly dreamed that my writing would alert people to the danger. I read hundreds of books, took thousands of notes. Week after week I put them into my computer, arranged them, rearranged them. Some of these notes are long, others are short. Here is one:

In December 1984 William H. Webster, then FBI Director, said: "We have more people charged with espionage right now than ever before in our history." Rear Admiral William O. Studeman, Director of Naval Intelligence, described the nature of some of this espionage as having "powerful war-winning implications for the Soviet side."[28]

At the end of the 1980s I could write such a note imagining that it proved something, that it demonstrated an important aspect of America's socio-strategic problem. I did not foresee that nearly everyone would dismiss this fact as virtually meaningless. I did not foresee that such insights would one day suggest clinical paranoia.

At this late hour, living on the brink of world catastrophe, there is no footnote that will persuade. Public opinion has so hardened, and is so determined to enforce an erroneous view of Russia, that only a fool would step forth and risk his peace of mind by challenging the error. Thus, my own foolishness appears. What began as an attempt to wake the town and warn the people ends as an academic exercise in sociology.

At any rate, I first saw the shape of the future in the spring of 1987. I took notes and made observations which constitute the bulk of this book. The first clue, the first bit of evidence that got me on this track, was something I ran across while working as a graduate student at the University of California at Irvine. I was reading the works of two Soviet bloc defectors: Jan Sejna and Anatoliy Golitsyn. I realized that these two defectors, one from communist Czechoslovakia and the other from

---

[27] "Germany's Distressing Spy Tales," *Los Angeles Times*, 19 December 1990, p. A1.

[28] Thomas B. Allen and Norman Polmar, *Merchants of Treason*, p. 4.

Soviet Russia, were both writing about a long-range bloc strategy for global domination.

Here are three principal quotes on the subject of the Soviet bloc long-range strategy, setting forth what caught my attention. First, I quote Golitsyn where he writes: "'Liberalization' in Eastern Europe would probably involve the return to power in Czechoslovakia of Dubcek and his associates. If it should be extended to East Germany, demolition of the Berlin Wall might even be contemplated."[29] It is necessary to keep in mind that Major Golitsyn is writing about something that was planned many years ago, for the expressed purpose of dazzling the West.

A little further on Golitsyn mentions the strategic benefits of deceptive liberalization in Eastern Europe:

> The Czechoslovaks, in contrast with their performance in 1968, might well take the initiative, along with the Romanians and Yugoslavs, in proposing (in the CSCE context) the dissolution of the Warsaw Pact in return for the dissolution of NATO. The disappearance of the Warsaw Pact would have little effect on the coordination of the communist bloc, but the dissolution of NATO could well mean the departure of American forces from the European continent and closer European alignment with a 'liberalized' Soviet bloc.

However unlikely Golitsyn's prediction, the Czech general, Jan Sejna, another Soviet bloc defector wrote in 1982:

> The erosion of N.A.T.O. begun in Phase Two [of the plan] would be completed by the withdrawal of the United States from its commitment to the defence of Europe, and by European hostility to military expenditure, generated by economic recession and fanned by the efforts of the 'progressive' movements. To this end we envisaged that it might be necessary to dissolve the Warsaw Pact, in which event we had already prepared a web of bilateral defence arrangements, to be supervised by secret committees of Comecon.[30]

And so began my present madness. I could not get these mutually supporting passages out of my head. Some will suppose that my obsession with this singular conjunction debauched my reason. "....the dissolution of the Warsaw Pact in return for the dissolution of NATO," wrote Major Golitsyn.   "....it might be necessary," echoed General Sejna, "to dissolve the Warsaw Pact." In 1987, having read much, having considered even more, I concluded that the Warsaw Pact would, indeed,

----

[29] Anatoliy Golitsyn, *New Lies for Old: The Communist Strategy of Deception and Disinformation* (New York: Dodd, Mead & Co., 1983), p. 340.

[30] Jan Sejna, *We Will Bury You* (London: Sidgwick & Jackson, 1982), p. 108.

be intentionally dissolved by the Soviet bloc strategists. And crazy as the world is, the Warsaw Pact was, indeed, dissolved three years later, in 1990, while I was in the middle of writing this book. My whole world now revolves around this one coincidence.

"The disappearance of the Warsaw Pact would have little effect on the coordination of the communist bloc," wrote Major Golitsyn; "...to be supervised by secret committees of Comecon," echoed General Sejna.

5. My notes continue thus, one after another:

Senator Malcolm Wallop, a former member of the Senate Intelligence Committee, said: "There are far too many in the intelligence community who either do not understand counterintelligence or who, understanding its concepts, have climbed to the top of their career ladders by opposing [such concepts]." [31]

6. General Jan Sejna defected to the United States in February 1968. He was the highest ranking defector to ever come from the Eastern bloc. Oddly, the CIA was not interested in him. They debriefed him in such a way that he could not tell his story. Later, the CIA set up a residence for him—next door to a Bulgarian diplomat.[32]

(In this context, during his last paranoid days as CIA counterintelligence chief, James Angleton allegedly suspected Directors of Central Intelligence Colby and Schlesinger of being Soviet moles.)[33]

7. Patriotism and paranoia are two words that have been creeping, ever so slowly, even mysteriously, toward one another. We ought to wonder why these two words are becoming one single and discreditable whole. Perhaps this shows more than anything, the indirect effects of an intellectual culture that is hostile to patriotism, and a patriotism that feels an encirclement progressing against it. It may also be something orchestrated, something induced, by play-acting paranoids rendering suspicion as a form of illness.[34]

8. On the subject of American patriotism, especially in the war with

---

[31] Ibid.

[32] Joseph D. Douglass, Jr., *Red Cocaine: The Drugging of America* (Atlanta, Georgia: Clarion House, 1990), pp. 139-164.

[33] See Director of Central Intelligence Robert M. Gates's 1996 "book" on the West's alleged Cold War Victory, *From the Shadows*, (New York: Simon & Schuster, 1996), p. 34. It contains a hearsay story to the effect that Angleton thought DCI Schlesinger was "one of them." See also, David Wise, *Molehunt: How the Search for a Phantom Traitor Shattered the CIA* (New York: Avon Books, 1992), p. 286.

[34] Ibid, p. 260.

Iraq, there remains a tremendous misunderstanding. Patriotism as mere flag-waving is only reflective of arrogance. It says nothing about our willingness to suffer. Undoubtedly there are many fine American heroes who have sacrificed themselves for their country. But today, these are not envied. Instead, they are pitied. And this gives us away. For if such a sacrifice were respected and valued, then pity would seldom be our reaction to it. Consider the matrons of old Rome who were greedy for the military glory of their sons, brothers, and husbands. So greedy, in fact, that grief was often overshadowed by the pride of sacrifice.

9. My next note: The Russians keep careful track of all influential people in the United States government. They do this by recruiting those who have access to official circles on a casual social basis. Take the case of James Sattler, for example: a young political scientist who was recruited by the communists while studying overseas. The KGB told him that his mission was to become *more influential in Washington*. He was expected to report on the policy positions of various important people.

Sattler was a convinced Marxist who wanted to change the world. Untypically, he was exposed. When confronted with his role as a foreign agent, his only regret was that he had hurt his parents. Otherwise he said that the Russians were the winning side.[35]

10. In keeping with the moral decline of the times, the CIA, around 1980, decided to seek out young, aggressive, and *amoral* recruits. If these recruits used drugs, that was fine. If they had numerous liaisons with women, it only meant they were enterprising.

11. *A typical case.* — Not long ago, a sinister individual became manager of an electric-boat yard where nuclear submarines were being built. A routine background check on him revealed that he had been convicted in Greece for money-order fraud. In addition, he lied on his job application. Despite this, after being in his position from 1977 to 1980, he was given a security clearance. In 1981 he fell under suspicion of taking bribes from a sub-contractor and was forced to "retire." In 1982 he was indicted. He has since disappeared.

12. Attempts to reform our society cannot succeed because our reforms are always undermined by the spirit in which they are carried out. And it is this spirit, above all, that makes the reforms necessary to begin with.

13. What we need is an honest critique of Utilitarian Civilization; in

---

[35] Thomas B. Allen and Norman Polmar, *Merchants of Treason*, pp. 344-351.

other words: a critique of the rationalizing, liberal-democratic type of social order in all its aspects; especially with regard to its decadence of form, its declining standards, its contempt for traditions; and today's ultimate tendency towards a breakdown of order altogether. We must come to terms with our general and increasing rudeness, our predilection for anti-aesthetic judgments, our ignorance of history, our inability to introspect, our "education to make stupid," our pacifism with which to bring about the greatest wars, our careerism, our obliviousness; and last but not least, our shallow and feeble optimism.

14. *At the forefront of our mediocrity and laziness?* Liberty and equality.

One gags to hear this accusation against all that we hold dear, but there is no way around this truth. A society of "men created equal" ultimately tends toward moral relativism; and moral relativism eventually brings political anarchy, then dictatorship. The classical solution to this problem was to check the licentious urges of the people with aristocratic or religious institutions, while on their side the people could place a veto on the rapaciousness of the aristocrats. This system was known by the name of mixed government. But under the current ideology we haven't any classes out of which to make a mixed government. We have no patricians and we haven't any plebeians. In our society *all interests are harmonized too well*. Every institution has come to reflect the desires of the people, however licentious these desires may turn out to be. The money interests accelerate this process by encouraging sensuality in order to reap huge profits. The money interests side with the carnal impulses of man. The churches, which once checked the carnal tendency, have been outflanked by the tools of money (i.e., radio and television). Consequently, the social discipline of sex, marriage, and child-rearing has broken down. Honesty in small things has lost its glamour. Cheating and petty theft are becoming rampant. Dirty words are spoken more frequently. Workers have become sloppier in their jobs. Drug abuse and alcoholism are increasing. Students are no longer disciplined, and leave off doing their homework. Teenage pregnancy increases. The jails are filled to overflowing, and the justice system cannot process the incoming wave of criminals. Boys are raping girls *on dates*. Child pornography appears in the open.

This is the pattern, deny it though you may.

15. The illiberal supports of liberalism are gone. The foundations of the capitalist order have been weakened or destroyed by capitalist prosperity. Only one thing can save us from utter degradation, and that is—utter catastrophe.

16. We live as if in a dream. Our sense of self-preservation has nearly left us. All moral limits are gone. Work and play absorb our every moment. Silent time is impossible to bear, while the music remains very loud. The new sin, of course, (besides self-restraint) is thinking. For the first time in history it is possible to "think too much," because thinking, if taken too far, leads to uncomfortableness; and above all, *we* are the Comfortable Ones.

17. *Terribleness first.* — We must speak of terribleness. One ought to cultivate the word *terrible*. Roll it off your tongue. Play with it. Bounce it off these fatted cattle and see what happens. For that is the theme which "last men" mock at. For them, everything terrible must be made unnecessary: Hell, the death penalty, moral standards, war, hunger, poverty, and so on. Theirs is the program of the anti-terrible. In their view, every finger which points to a terror should be hacked off. This very notebook, for example, must invariably appear false and distorted from the perspective of these propagandists of cush.

18. We no longer believe in Hell—*we* successful ones; we the people of the United States, surpassing all previous peoples in comfortableness, well-being, ease, and safety; which have become all too normal, expected, and demanded; not merely the goal of our civilization, but also its point of departure.

19. Necessity was once the backdrop of human politics. Today, a new condition has come about: sensual pleasure as backdrop. No longer do we have a government fearful of bread riots, but a government concerned with smoking, drunk driving, and drug addiction; a government concerned with maladies of abundance; a government involved in problems of malconsumption and over-consumption. Because of this, another ethic rises to dominance—non-fat, non-smoking, and caffeine-free. Instead of the Iron Duke of Wellington we might well remember President Reagan's overweight, chain-smoking drug czar.

20. Moral relativism begins with the premise that there isn't any truth. But is this really true?

21. Today, there is no interest in conversing with one's neighbors; diversity hemmed-in and foredoomed; a flurry of unneeded face-lifts, butt-lifts, nose-jobs, cheek implants, youthful images, diets, suctions, fastings, and purgings—the world falsified according to the rules of sex-appeal. This makes for a new society and a new escapism: an escapism detached from the religious impulses of old; an escapism by way of

----

lowest common denominators. Ergo, an increase in sloth and fat; an increase in reactivity versus activity; a weakening of the moral muscle; a decline in originality coinciding with a thirst for novelty. Mind-set? Jaded. A need arises for the bizarre, the sick, the increasingly hysterical and emotional. We have come to expect a presentation of the world better than the world: more interesting, intense, and engaging—which leads to entertainment instead of church as the path to paradise; eclipsing the whole of *real* existence, even to the point of undercutting the human imagination. Enter television.

22. The average American watches twenty hours of television per week.

23. The essence of our society's connecting fabric is an idiot box. Type of shows? Comedy and drama; especially drama with "happy" endings, non-tragic, without any sense of the inevitable—therefore, no sociological sense either. We now have an entire nation with the same vocabulary of vicarious experiences, with the same unrealistic expectations. Emphasis is on images rather than concepts; therefore, a lessening of mental agility; a shrinking of our vocabulary; the end of eloquence; a decline in reading; also, an increased tendency to characterize one's adversary as evil; violence, terror, bloodshed as a stimulant suggestive of a "snuff" movie.

24. The Russian dissident Igor Shafarevich says that the West has entered a "nihilist era" like the one which Russia experienced prior to the Bolshevik Revolution.

25. Hannah Arendt once wrote: "The philistine is the bourgeois isolated from his own class, the atomized individual who is produced by the breakdown of the bourgeois class itself." Arendt goes on to say that the philistine was the human raw material used by the totalitarian powers to organize their depredations; a raw material only concerned for its career, comfort, and security; a raw material that would sacrifice honor and dignity at the drop of a hat. Arendt says that nothing "proved easier to destroy than the...private morality of people who thought of nothing but safeguarding their private lives." [36]

26. In capitalist upper-middle-class society there is no romance but money, no crusade but double-entry book-keeping, no Heaven but riches, no Hell but the unemployment line. Violence is when you bump into someone at the mall or die from a drug overdose. Besides the thrill of a "good high," there is nothing worth dying for; there is nothing worth

----

[36] Hannah Arendt, *The Origins of Totalitarianism*, 3 vols. (New York: Harvest/HB, 1985), 3: 36.

killing for. There is plenty of everything for everyone if we only get a job and do some clerking, some shuffling, some clever speculating. Therefore, ancient human faculties and hormonal urges are left in the lurch. Physical atrophy and coffee become, at this point, inevitable. Heart attacks increase. Sex and other bodily sensations gain exaggerated importance. The basis for "stimulant society" appears. The body becomes profoundly bored. Under these conditions people discover that smoking dope feels nice, as it tickles the soul. All these phenomena spring from the unique situation of the cost accountant, the new capitalist man; a man without the sublime or the beautiful, whose cosmic purpose assumes the shape, at best, of a question-mark; at worst, of a cliché. Danger, purpose, war, creation, risk, love: all too difficult for the balance sheet. Too unsafe. Therefore, one over-indulges or over-emphasizes the human body—giving birth to the diseases of exaggeration (anorexia, obesity, and AIDS).

At one time: church and knighthood, worship and war. At the present time: drugs, sex, and rock 'n roll. No lords, no aristocrats, no kings, no statesmen, no gods above. We have become uniformly obsessive, bored, morbid, and sickly. We have become an empire of nonentities. None are brave enough to speak their minds, to risk their jobs, to challenge the *real* powers: conformism, mediocrity, and fun.

27. Let us consider Shakespeare's *King Lear*: — The old king is absorbed in satisfying his own private vanity. The characters are largely atomized, much like Arendt's philistine. Shakespeare shows us how, in this situation, treason becomes commonplace: brother turns against brother, daughter betrays father, the guest murders his host even as the wife abuses her husband, and so on. The honest man is banished from the kingdom. The flatterer is elevated. True love is despised and false love is believed. There isn't any motherhood in the play. All the women are barren, implying that the future has been taken away. The old man goes insane. The young man, to survive, must pretend that he's insane. No binding elements are left. Shakespeare has shown us society in its death throes, society in a state of senility—a prophecy which finds its fulfillment *in us*.

28. Our personal relations are becoming highly transient and provisional. How has the public welfare been affected? *It is disintegrating.* But this aforesaid disintegration is difficult to recognize because, as a matter of fact, *we are having so much fun.*

29. Marx said that religion is the opium of the people. But what if the people can get hold of *real* opium? What then?

---

30. War without loss is an immorality. That we have imagined it otherwise merely demonstrates that our thinking has become inverted.

31. To take something seriously is to lower oneself in one's own estimation. And yet, only in seriousness is the human person truly elevated.

32. Today, as never before, the pariah is the only man with the chance to think for himself. Everyone else is relentlessly compelled by peer pressures. Everyone constantly blackmails everyone. The threat of ostracism easily molds the soft democratic soul into fashionable shapes.

The out-of-fashion individual, the outcast (perhaps the only real human being remaining) eats out of some dumpster on the edge of town.

33. *Our law-abiding citizen of today.* —Not moral, but tame, domesticated, lazy, comfortable.

34. The aggressive-destructive impulses of masculinity are currently disorganized—no longer focused on the idea of self-discipline and self control, as epitomized by the father image. A chaotic urge to destroy is subtly beginning to direct the male unconscious.

35. The most commonplace psychiatric pathology of the last twenty-five years is something called "character disorder." This is merely another way of talking about moral decline without using the word *morality*.

36. Today's disordered man may be characterized as empty, seductive, and anxious, with repressed hostility for others. In addition, an intense fear of old age and death is noticeable; a fascination with celebrity; and unsatisfactory relations with the opposite sex.

37. The cult of sensuality is antisensual and the cult of social relations is antisocial. In other words, we ruin the enjoyment of life by our sexual gluttony. We give the appearance of being manipulable in order to manipulate. We believe lies in order to tell them.

38. Since authority has broken down, personality takes its place.

39. *Absolute sadistic power* is the coming battle cry. This can be seen in the youngest of our present-day degenerates.

40. The cult of self-promotion has supplanted the cult of

----

achievement.

41.   Ortega y Gasset once said that the root of our problem is slovenliness. In essence: the state is slovenly towards its citizens, the workers are slovenly toward their work, the parents are slovenly with their children, and the children are slovenly in school where the teachers, too, are slovenly.

42. *At confession.* —She is exceedingly rude, her nose in the air, not yet 23-years-old; knowledgeable about everything one needs to know today, and a college graduate. She is definitely superior, smarter, more important. In a word—in three words—she cannot fail.
"My father always says: 'hold your head up.'"
How does she keep from tripping?
"I don't trip. I took ballet."
She divides humanity into classes: Men who are tall, rich, and attractive versus "disgusting little men."
She lands a job with a major American company. Her boss is five feet tall. Someone says that the boss is a nice man and people think well of him. Her instinctive response: "I don't think of him at all."
Why?
"I don't notice men under five feet five inches."
And she philosophizes profoundly: for example, "My favorite day is the 18th." "I'm dating this guy but I don't think we have a 'relationship' yet." "My father wants to give me a car for my birthday. But I've already got a BMW with hardly any mileage on it." And, "You don't have to understand a business to own a business. You only need to read the ledger sheets."
One day she suddenly talks about religion: "You know those little booths that priests take confession in? Well, if you're the next in line and you listen carefully, you can hear the confession of the person ahead of you."

43. The "last man" is led by peer group pressures. He always compromises and retreats. He expertly maintains the lies put into his custody and congratulates himself on being "practical." As a coward and subjectivist, he secretly thrills to the notion that truth doesn't anywhere exist and that if it did exist it would remain forever unknowable.

44. This hatred of participation, this desire to stand outside as a "spectator," this morbid fear of losing—which is nothing but an incapacity to enjoy life—is overtaking us. We are gradually becoming poor sports precisely because we always *have* to win, and because any loss cuts to our very soul. Thus, there is no talent for learning from

----

defeats; no means to growth and maturity. One finds, in our poor sportsmanship, a spirit that says, "Only sweets, only candy. No solid food."

45. American culture is "economic" in nature. Our system of government was organized so that economic activity, perhaps at the expense of other activities, might thrive. This was a proper orientation for a developing frontier society where life was at first primitive, harsh, and unsettled. But somehow we never managed to evolve beyond these humble beginnings; and as we grew in affluence, we retained our economic fixation, failing to open up other cultural horizons. Today the growth of the economy has become the end-all and be-all. Even our basic view of man is tainted by economism. What defines us now, more than anything else, is our continuing reduction of everything to economics, which we imagine is an entirely rational thing to do. We talk in terms of supply and demand, but we forget that demand is a mystical thing, with its roots going down into the soul.

Our economism also leads us to forget that there are human crises outside the locus of mutual profitability, in which one man's gain *is* another man's loss (i.e., as the fundamental social problem). Question-marks seem to mount. Can economics swallow art, religion, and politics without digestive calamity? Does the multiplication of wants through commercial advertising bring us happiness or have we merely reestablished misery by other means? What happens to the virtues of self-denial and self-control under a regime that sustains itself by breaking these virtues down and by cultivating (especially through television) a regime of self-indulgence?

46. When "success" became a measure of moral worth in our society, the "honest poor" had no leg of self-esteem on which to stand. And this is the origin of our modern rabble.

47. If people want to solve the problems of the inner-city, they must first combat the decadence of the suburbs.

48. The loyalty ethic has declined because too many people have become practiced at feigning loyalty.

49. Our country is prosperous. This prosperity has weakened us morally. Corruption within makes us vulnerable to attack from the outside.

2

Weapons of Mass Destruction

As the mode of production, so the mode of combat.
— FRIEDRICH ENGELS

The appearance of the nuclear rocket weapon radically changed previous concepts of the nature of war. Modern nuclear rocket war in its destructive and death-dealing potential cannot be compared with previous wars. Mass application of nuclear rocket weapons makes it possible within a very short time to force a country from the war, or a number of countries, even those with relatively large territories, well-developed economies, and populations on the order of tens of millions.
— SOVIET MILITARY TEXT [1]

The reason why totalitarian regimes can get so far realizing a fictitious, topsy-turvey world is that the outside world... indulges... in wishful thinking and shirks reality in the face of real insanity....
— HANNAH ARENDT [2]

1.   Weapons of mass destruction can exterminate large human populations, demolish cities, and liquidate whole national economies in a few days or weeks. As such, they are civilization-negating devices that threaten with obsolescence and extinction the social institutions of the Free World. But also, the weapons of mass destruction are civilization-creating devices because they make new socio-political forms inevitable.

2.   Michel de Montaigne wrote that "to study philosophy is to learn to die." He noted that death is unavoidable, that if cowardice could defeat death then cowardice would be a good thing. But cowardice can

---

[1] *Soviet Military Strategy*, ed. Vasilii Sokolovskiy, trans. Harriet Fast Scott (New York: 1975), p. 11.

[2] Arendt, *The Origins of Totalitarianism*, 3: 135.

do nothing except increase the power of death. Therefore, let us disarm death of his novelty and strangeness, says Montaigne: "Let us converse and be familiar with him, and have nothing so frequent in our thoughts as death." And later he adds, "Our very religion itself has no surer human foundation than the contempt of death."[3]

3. Biological weapons yield more death per unit of cost than either thermonuclear or chemical weapons.

Doctor Adam Milkovitch, in a Soviet publication, writes: "From results of comparative studies of deaths from conventional weapons, war poisons, and atomic energy, on the one side, and deaths from biological weapons on the other, it is believed today that a biological war would have the greatest effect of all."[4]

4. By far the greatest catastrophe in human history was the Black Death which killed a third of the people living between Iceland and India in the middle of the fourteenth century. The disease itself came on suddenly, was often fatal, and rapidly swept through the nations of Europe.

5. The manufacture of biological weapons is about as complicated as the manufacture of beer.[5]

6. The most likely type of biological attack, in time of world war, would be aerial spraying. This is effective because human beings breathe. During normal quiet activity a man will inhale about four gallons of air per minute. If a biological agent reaches the alveolar bed, which is the deepest part of the lungs, then the agent becomes as effective as if it were injected directly into tissue. This type of penetration is fairly easy to achieve as long as the biological agent is between one and five microns in diameter. Larger particles tend to get stuck or absorbed in the upper respiratory tract. Smaller particles tend to get exhaled.

7. *Let us compare biological weapons to nerve gas.* — One milligram of the nerve agent "GB" gives you a 50 percent chance to kill a man. This sounds quite lethal, but compared to an infectious dose of a biological agent it is terribly inefficient. Another consideration, too, is that biological agents can multiply in the body. Due to this, biological

---

[3] Michel Eyquem de Montaigne, *The Essays*, Ed. W. Carew Hazlitt, trans. Charles Cotton (Chicago: William Benton, 1952), #19.

[4] Milkovitch, "Prospects for Use of Biological Weapons in Future Wars," *Vojnosanitetski Pregled*, XIII, No. 11-12, Nov. - Dec., 1956.

[5] Joseph D. Douglass, Jr. and Neil C. Livingstone, *America the Vulnerable: The Threat of Chemical and Biological Warfare* (Lexington Massachusetts: Lexington Books, 1987), p. 23.

----

weapons can be effectively used to neutralize hundred-thousand square mile areas; whereas chemical weapons, due to weight and cost, would necessarily be unsuitable for such large-scale operations.

8. A dozen chicken eggs contain enough *Psittacosis* virus to infect everyone on earth.

9. Biological attack by aerial spraying is called a "cloud attack." The agent can be dispersed in either gaseous or aerosol form. The effectiveness of a B/W (biological/warfare) cloud is determined by the cloud's concentration of microorganisms and the length of time it remains in the vicinity of the target personnel. Such B/W clouds are subject to meteorological conditions. For example: turbulence caused by wind or thermal effects can mix the B/W cloud with uncontaminated air and dilute it. The ideal wind for an attack would have a speed of approximately four miles per hour, but even thirty miles per hour would not be an absolute drag on weapon effectiveness.

10. The best time to unleash a biological attack is at night or when the weather is cold. This is because heat and direct sunlight can diminish the effectiveness of many biological agents. The ideal condition for launching a strategic biological attack is found in the meteorological phenomenon known as "polar outbreak." In this situation a stable layer of cold air comes down from the Arctic. It maintains its integrity as it travels. Under normal conditions such an air mass would enter the United States from Canada with a thickness of six thousand feet. It would then sweep across the Midwest, turn East, and exit the country along the New England coast with three thousand feet of thickness remaining. Its speed would be approximately twenty miles per hour. One might conceivably infect forty million people by seeding such an air layer with biological agents.

11. As far as the technical procedures involved, planes may parachute bomblets or disperse the biological agent by spraying it from pressurized hoses. Such hoses can provide absolute control over particle size. Ideally, the agent is sprayed into the atmosphere through a nozzle, sometimes with the aid of a gas such a carbon dioxide or compressed air.

12. Major General Marshal Stubbs, one-time head of the U.S. Army Chemical Corps, stated that an attack of "dry biological material," delivered by no more than ten aircraft, could kill or incapacitate thirty percent of our population.[6]

----

[6] Ibid., p. 37.

13. Possible biological agents include: Encephalitis Japanese B, 30-60 percent fatal, no known effective treatment. With this weapon "insect vectors" can be employed to transmit the disease more readily to target populations. Mass immunization is possible; but, have you had yours? Or try glanders (a.k.a. *Actinobacillus mallei*, a bacterium). Very nasty, very efficient: 90-100 percent fatal if no immunization. Treatment is doubtful even with sulfadiazine. Or how about *Cryptococcosis neoformans*—a fungus? The lethality of the U.S. version, before we destroyed our stockpiles in 1969, was classified. We might guess that this chronic fungal infection was not meant to kill its victims, but only to incapacitate them; for the disease often causes a three-month to six-month debility requiring considerable care and attention. If millions of persons became ill in this way, the nation's economic and military potential would be greatly reduced.

14. Because the United States has practically eliminated so many infectious diseases, it is currently unprepared for a serious epidemic.

15. At Sverdlovsk in Soviet Russia, a military-industrial center 875 miles east of Moscow, hundreds were killed by an outbreak of pulmonary anthrax. An explosion occurred on the night of April 3-4, 1979, at a biological warfare facility just outside the city. Lethal spores were released in the form of a large gas-cloud. Luckily, the wind was blowing away from the city into sparsely populated areas where approximately one thousand people were nevertheless killed. Anthrax, if inhaled, causes fever and paralysis of the bronchial tubes, suffocating its victims to death within three to four days. It tends to be fatal. Four days after the explosion at Russia's Sverdlovsk facility the first victims — military personnel — were sent to the local hospital. They were followed six days later by the first wave of civilian casualties. All those hospitalized died, while hundreds more perished at home.

16. As far back as 1941 the Soviet Union conducted biological warfare experiments on political prisoners in Ulan Bator and other parts of Mongolia. In one incident, political prisoners escaped after having been infected by bubonic plague. This apparently triggered an epidemic among the Mongols in which three to four thousand died.

17. Ricin toxin, a special poison used in assassinations, can be made from castor beans.

18. Approximately one hundred pounds of anthrax in aerosol form can kill half-a-million people.

----

19. Anticrop biological agents are another approach to defeating one's enemies. The microorganisms most desirable in this type of biological attack include the cereal rusts, the late blight of potatoes, and rice blast.

20. Soviet chemical warfare instructors have boasted that special toxins, produced at the Jardin de Orquilles biochemical plant in Cuba, could contaminate a third of America's fresh water if strategically placed in the Mississippi River.[7]

21. The most intriguing weapon of all is the psycho-chemical weapon, which can produce specific delusions in target populations. Advanced chemical substances can produce a sense of contentment and a general breakdown of the will to resist.[8]

22. Psycho-chemical agents, called *beta emitters*, can destroy the target population's short-term memory.

23. Thermonuclear weapons largely have three effects: blast, heat, and radioactive fallout. Though it is difficult to shield oneself from the direct blast effects of a close-proximity hydrogen bomb, it is possible and desirable to protect oneself from radioactive fallout. In the event of a nuclear war, given sufficient fallout shelters, 60 to 70 million lives could be saved.

24. According to General J. K. Singlaub, it would take 438 one-megaton bombs to destroy Los Angeles.[9]

25. The fallout from an airburst thermonuclear weapon is so minor as to be negligible, but ground-burst is another matter. When a thermonuclear weapon explodes at ground level much debris is thrown into the air along with radioactivized metals. These blow downwind, settling in an elliptical pattern 150 to 200 miles long and about fifty miles wide. The radioactivity in this area is quite lethal in the days immediately following a nuclear attack.

26. The radioactivity of fallout will rapidly dwindle to safe levels, diminishing to 1/100th of its original strength within forty-nine hours and 1/10,000th of its original radioactivity by the end of two weeks. Some longer-lived particles will continue to cause trouble, but these particles

---

[7] Ibid., p. 150.

[8] Ibid., p. 75.

[9] Interview with General J. K. Singlaub, *Survive*, May/June, 1982.

only exist in very small quantities and would mostly affect those areas directly impacted by ground-burst weapons.[10]

27.   A lethal dose of radiation for an average human is approximately 450 roentgens in twenty-four hours. Some humans, of course, can survive this 450-roentgen dose; however, recovery would require six months of convalescing. No deaths are to be expected from two hundred roentgens in one day or less, although half the people exposed to this dose will become sick. Any exposure of one hundred roentgens or more can cause sickness.

Symptoms of radiation sickness in order of frequency are: nausea, vomiting, diarrhea, loss of appetite, malaise, loss of hair, tendency to bleed, susceptibility to infections from disease. These effects may have a latency period of up to two weeks. Symptoms can appear in varying degrees of intensity.

28. The weapons described above are unique because they can kill vast numbers of people over wide areas. With such weapons it now becomes possible to alter the demography of entire continents, replace the population explosion with a population implosion, darken or lighten the gene pool, exterminate whole races, religions, and language-groups. It must further be emphasized that racists, communists, or religious zealots might desire one or more of these effects. In fact, ideologies of mass destruction are already influential and have appeared in many countries around the world.

29. *The Civil Defense Question.* — The Russian civil defense system is called the MPVO, or Local Anti-Air Defense. The Russians have also created the Voluntary Society for Assistance to the Army, Air Force, and Navy. In addition, Comsomol (an organization similar to the Boy Scouts) has a civil defense function.

Since 1955 citizens of Russia have been required to pass four courses in the theory and practice of civil defense, including instruction on biological and chemical weapons. Russian citizens have been taught

---

[10] There is, of course, the question of "delayed" fallout, popularized by the novel *On the Beach.* According to Peter Vincent Pry, a CIA expert and author of *Nuclear Wars: Exchanges and Outcomes* (New York: Taylor and Francis New York Inc., 1990), p. 195: "Under worst case conditions, delayed fallout from a nuclear war might increase severalfold the annual number of deaths caused by such diseases as lymphatic cancer, leukemia, and cancer of the thyroid. However, these deaths would probably be far fewer than deaths now resulting from industrial accidents, from smoking (lung cancer), or from automobile fatalities. The number of deaths induced by delayed fallout from nuclear war are well within the capacity of society to tolerate, given the much larger number of deaths from premature causes that are tolerated in peacetime."

----

various countermeasures in the event of war. They know where local shelters are and how to take cover if they cannot reach a shelter. They are taught that nuclear war is not the end of the world and that such a war, though terrible beyond belief, is winnable.

30. It has often been argued that those who die in a nuclear war are the lucky ones. But if we stop and think for a moment, the whole argument supposes an odd reversal: that the living shall envy the dead. The unthinking followers of this school, however, will acknowledge their error when nuclear war actually happens. Then they will scream, "We want to live! We *desperately* want to live!"

31. Many Russian citizens know how to detect chemical-biological agents and how to decontaminate surfaces. A civilian gas mask, model GP-4u, which even helps against fallout, offers a high degree of protection from biological agents and has already been distributed to twenty million people in the former Soviet Union. The rest of the Russian population will receive masks when war is believed to be imminent.

Special suits, capes, hoods, gloves, leggings, boots and other gear are standard issue for the millions of voluntary civil defense workers in the Russian civil defense system. In addition to equipment, the authorities have a sophisticated system of alerts through which they pass instructions to the population. These alerts begin with the announcement of a "threatening situation"; next comes the issuing of gas masks; then vaccinations; after that come announcements on the protection of food, fodder, and water against contamination. Last comes the construction of temporary shelters for the rural population.

32. Strobe Talbott, in his fascinating book *The Master of the Game*, describes President Carter's chief SALT negotiator, Paul Warnke, as someone who was quite outspoken on the issue of civil defense. According to Talbott, Warnke was once asked about the Soviet Union's determination to defend its population in the event of nuclear war. Warnke replied that since he lived so close to Washington D.C., and personally stood little chance of surviving such a war, he wasn't going to worry about it.[11]

33. Shortly after its 1969 border clashes with the Soviet Union, China began constructing an elaborate system of tunnels under all her major cities—Peking, Dairen, Mukden, Huhehot. These were dug in order to protect the populace in the event of thermonuclear war. Also, in

----

[11] Strobe Talbott, *The Master of the Game: Paul Nitze and the Nuclear Peace* (New York: Vintage Books, A Division of Random House, 1988), p. 152.

----

smaller towns similar measures were put into effect.[12]

34. In a typical ten-year period, while spending many hundreds of billions of dollars on "defense," we Americans barely spend even a billion per year on protecting our population from nuclear-bacteriological attack. In relational terms, this roughly equals about four dollars of protection for every man, woman, and child in America per annum. Americans spend far more money on cosmetics, movies, pornography, and illicit narcotics. In fact, if we spent as much on fallout shelters as we do on dangerous drugs we'd have the finest civil defense in the world.

35. A list of arguments against the creation of a shelter program would look something like this: (1) Shelters might lull us into a false sense of security; (2) building shelters could alarm and demoralize the youth; (3) shelters demonstrate a lack of faith in the government; (4) shelters will make the government more reckless; (5) shelters will distract attention from more important things; (6) civil defense won't save anybody because the world ends and Columbus falls off; (7) those who survive will wish they hadn't; (8) why live without loved ones?   (9) shelters might alarm the Russians and increase the risk of war; (10) a shelter won't protect you from a direct hit.

36.   We do have, nevertheless, a cosmetic civil defense establishment staffed by officials who are mostly concerned with floods, earthquakes, and other (smaller-scale) "acts of God." In terms of civil defense, the Federal Emergency Management Agency (FEMA) is not really prepared for war. Call your local civil defense authority and ask one of their experts for the procedures in the event of large-scale biological attack. He will tell you, as he told me, that no such procedures exist.[13]

37. The only long-range difficulty resulting from an all-out nuclear war would be from alpha emitters, which are released during nuclear explosions. The principal alpha emitters are the fissile nuclides, $235U$ and $239Pu$. The most dangerous long-term threat is an isotope called $241Am$, because it can be easily absorbed by the human body and has a half-life of several hundred years. Plutonium, on the other hand, is not as dangerous because even if you ate plutonium it would pass through your digestive tract without being absorbed. Luckily, there is so little $241Am$

---

[12] Seagrave, *Yellow Rain: A Journey Through the Terror of Chemical Warfare* (New York, 1981), p. 221.

[13] See the Federal Emergency Management Agency's handbooks: *In Time of Emergency* (H-14, October 1985) and *Protection in the Nuclear Age* (H-20, June 1985).

produced by nuclear explosions that it constitutes a threat only to those people eating food produced in the immediate area of a ground-burst nuclear detonation. Marine foods can also be contaminated.

38. Inhalation of particles is another principal danger. Alpha emitters can move into the gastrointestinal tract from the lungs and ultimately end up deposited on bone surfaces where they remain. An increase in lung cancers is also indicated. Nevertheless, there is no reason to worry about such rare and localized effects. In an all-out nuclear war the plutonium levels in the atmosphere, believe it or not, would still be within EPA guidelines.

3

East and West

The totalitarian ruler must, at any price, prevent normalization from reaching the point where a new way of life could develop — one which might, after a time, lose its bastard qualities and take its place among the widely differing and contrasting ways of life of the nations of the earth. The moment the revolutionary institutions became a national way of life... totalitarianism would lose its "total" quality and become subject to the law of nations.

— HANNAH ARENDT[1]

Lenin, who spent most of his life in the West and not in Russia, who knew the West much better than Russia, always wrote and said that the Western capitalists would do anything to strengthen the economy of the U.S.S.R. They will compete with each other to sell us cheaper goods and sell them quicker, so that the Soviets will buy from one rather than from the other. He said: They will bring us everything themselves without thinking about their future.

— ALEKSANDR SOLZHENITSYN[2]

1. The totalitarian regime in the East is not defeated. It has only shifted its ground. This is the most difficult fact the West has to learn. And why is it so difficult? The West—the leaders of the West—never understood Russia or totalitarianism in the first place. Sadly, the West was fooled by the August 1991 Potemkin coup, the long-standing fake disarmament, and the reformist governments of Eastern Europe. At three minutes to midnight, on the brink of our thermonuclear doom, we believe that Soviet power is a thing of the past. Yet the Soviet Army, under the guise of demoralization, behind the mask of the Commonwealth of Independent States, remains the largest in the world.

2. Even in its supposed death throes the Soviet relic stands—its missiles poised, its leaders *still* dripping with Afghan blood, its

---

[1] Arendt, *Totalitarianism*, p. 89.

[2] Alexander Solzhenitsyn, *Warning to the West* (New York: Farrar, Straus and Giroux, 1976), p. 13.

espionage networks intact. We look on with amazement at this
Antichrist; at this armored, low-built, cruel, tough, oriental animal that
can drink the sewage of the most stagnant ponds while waiting upon its
prey; not guided by economic rationalism or other Epicurean utilities, but
by ancient, primitive, savage impulses. The Soviet ghost succeeds
precisely because it is "the coldest of all cold monsters" in an age of
lukewarmness; and grows because it devours whatever is on hand. How
can we fail to marvel at a phenomenon so rich in contradiction—so
twinkling with absurdity—as this empire against empires, this slavery in
the name of emancipation? Consider its unaccountable feats: the
establishment of a proletarian state in a land of peasants; literacy and
industrialization through terror and hunger; military victory by shooting
one's own generals and by slaughtering one's own soldiers; a black-
market "communist" economy under a regime of criminal policemen; a
backwardness first in space; the mightiest war machine of all time built
by an economic "basket case"; and now, a democracy of totalitarian
functionaries, a reformist policy that doesn't bring reform, a surrendering
of Eastern Europe, the coughing-up of many rockets and thermonuclear
triggers *so that the entire world might thereby be ensnared.*
    Every defeat, every step backward, every disaster in Soviet history
seems miraculously transformed into success. How is this possible? We
blink. We rub our eyes. We blink again. But the paradoxes continue.
Our seers, sociologists, economists, and historians have never left off
predicting the downfall of this curious monstrosity. In 1920 few experts
thought the communist regime would last. Every respectable social
theory, partnered with an infallible logic, told us that the Soviet Union
crumbled in 1921, that it should have been wiped out by Hitler in 1941,
that it passed away with the death of Stalin in 1953, and finally, that it
went belly-up in 1991. How does one muster hostility against an
adversary whose obituary has already been written? By every indication
this adversary barely has a pulse, and drags out its existence like some
wounded hulk. Thus does the Soviet death-rattle stretch through seven
decades as the most tremendous last gasp in history. A few more such
gasps and communism might endure for a thousand years. But nobody
believes that another gasp is possible. To our way of thinking each gulp
of air is the very last. Our only doubt comes during moments of
immediate crisis, during Russia's "elections"; and even then, after the
crisis passes, the Soviet corpse is said to return to its traditional activity;
that is, of decomposing, of being about to crumble, of coming apart at the
seams. And even when the Communist Empire pronounces its own
collapse with melodramatic flair, as with the advent of Mr. Yeltsin, a new
Russian submarine nonetheless rolls off the stocks, with the muffled cries
of Azerbaijan as background music. "That one may smile, and smile, and

be a villain" is more than possible, especially in the Russian bureaucracy. That one may crumble and grow increasingly dangerous is also possible. But who is wise enough to know this?

During the 1940s Joseph A. Schumpeter characterized the typical American attitude toward Soviet Russia: "Let Russia swallow one or two more countries, what of it? Let her be well supplied with everything she needs and she will cease to frown. After twenty years the Russians will be just as democratic and pacific as are we—and think and feel just as do we. Besides, Stalin will be dead by then."[3]

Each decade, however, has found us rolled back by communist takeovers in places like Vietnam, Cambodia, Cuba, China, Angola, Ethiopia, Nicaragua, Tibet, Afghanistan, Mozambique, Zimbabwe, and now, more recently, Zaire; and by the infallible progress of men like Ho Chi Minh, Fidel Castro, and—dare we say?—Nelson Mandela. Soviet socialism ebbs and flows unlike anything we've seen before. Take for example the year 1941, when Hitler decimated the Red Army. Yet the Red Army rose phoenix-like out of the ashes. One recalls Lenin's political and military disasters, like the Treaty of Brest-Litovsk and the Soviet invasion of Poland. We remember Khrushchev's harebrained scheming, and his break with Maoist China. But each Soviet disaster is transformed, over time, into victory; e.g., the collapse of Brest-Litovsk, the communization of Poland, and finally, a new coziness with China. The Soviet talent for resurgence must be taken into account. To find a resilience as great as this, there is only the example set by the Romans after Cannae.[4] But is Russia, like Rome, destined for world empire? We cannot be sure. All we know is that Russia, whatever comparisons we incline to, proves to be a special entity following a law of development all its own. Perhaps Schumpeter was on to something when he wrote: "The Russian century once started may run its course almost of itself."[5] Why? Because Russian foreign policy has purpose, energy, style, depth; while American foreign policy is rambling, sentimental, and shallow. This gives tremendous advantage to Russia and very little to America. The American people want prosperity, not imperial burdens. At heart we are isolationists. Therefore, the most dangerous event of all is this recent and *apparent* collapse of the Soviet Empire. For should the Soviet Union, as phoenix, once again rise out of the ashes, we shall be compelled to rise out of ashes of our own.

3. With regard to all this, some men have seen the future. Friedrich Nietzsche was one of them. Many people suppose that like other thinkers

---

[3] Schumpeter, *Capitalism, Socialism and Democracy*, p. 402.

[4] At Cannae Hannibal wiped out two Roman armies and killed nearly 60,000 men in a single day.

[5] Schumpeter, *Capitalism, Socialism and Democracy*, p. 402 (see the last sentence of his footnote).

----

he merely prescribed a course of action. But after a closer examination one notices in Nietzsche a cool fatalism that is not at all concerned with telling people what to do. Instead, Nietzsche sought to manipulate posterity by anticipating its intellectual predisposition. Thus, his immoralism does not stand in the center; rather, it symbolizes wariness toward the soon-to-be outmoded; and a flattery, by way of imitation, of tomorrow's immorality. Nietzsche, as a man who wanted to hold philosophical sway over futurity, spoke the language of futurity. He wanted to live "posthumously"; therefore, he had to build a bridge to the twenty-second century. How did he do this? With ingenious sociological inferences; by meditating on human psychology; by understanding the social consequences of philosophy and the philosophical consequences of a certain kind of society. Thus he caught a glimpse of the future. In the preface of *Will to Power*, he writes, "What I relate is the history of the next two centuries." He then admits to having lost his way "in every labyrinth of the future."[6]   And what did he find in these labyrinths? "The end of Christianity—at the hands of its own morality."[7] This means that "we shall have upheavals, a convulsion of earthquakes, a moving of mountains and valleys, the like of which has never been dreamed of. The concept of politics will have merged entirely with a war of spirits; all power structures of the old society will have been exploded... [and] there will be wars the like of which have never yet been seen on earth."[8]   Nietzsche's vision was of a universal revolution, with a new humanity growing out of "terrible and violent beginnings," "faced with the choice of perishing or prevailing." He foresaw the appearance of "the *barbarians* of the twentieth century" who shall "come into view and consolidate themselves only after a tremendous socialist crisis."[9] He described the appearance on earth of the "last man," the commercial man, the complacent man, who would fall under the power of "the Masters of the Earth." These Masters will create "adverse conditions" while promising green-pasture happiness. They will "employ democratic Europe as their most pliant and supple instrument for getting hold of the destinies of the earth, so as to work as artists upon 'man' himself."[10] The "plant" man, said Nietzsche, "has hitherto grown most vigorously" under the worst conditions—"danger, severity, violence, danger in the street as well as in the heart, inequality of rights, concealment, stoicism, the art of experiment, devilry of all kinds, in short the opposite of all the

---

6 Friedrich Nietzsche, *The Will to Power*, trans. Walter Kaufmann and R. J. Hollingdale (New York: Vintage Books, a Division of Random House, 1968), p. ix.

7 Ibid., #1.

8 *Ecce Homo*, (Kaufmann translation) "Why I am a Destiny" part 1.

9 Friedrich Nietzsche, *The Will to Power*, #868.

10 Ibid., #960.

herd thinks desirable, are necessary for the elevation of the type man. A
morality with such reverse intentions, which desires to train men for the
heights, not for comfort and mediocrity, a morality with the intention of
training a ruling cast—the future *masters of the earth*—must, if it is to
be taught, appear in association with the prevailing moral laws, in the
guise of their terms and forms."[11] It is to these masters that Nietzsche
addressed himself. This is the posterity he wished to influence—the
noblemen and legislators of the future;[12] "an audacious ruling race"
developed "on the basis of an extremely intelligent herd mass."[13] "It is
clear," wrote Nietzsche, "what I combat is economic optimism."[14]
Forget shopkeeperdom! Forget prosperity! Men must want to be as
gods, for they have killed God. Cryptically, he wrote: "Englishmen,
Americans, and Russians"—as if to indicate the prospects. Especially he
took notice of the Russians, whom he regarded with affection: "Russia,
the *only* power today which has durability in it, which can wait, which
can still promise something—Russia, the antithesis of that pitiable
European petty-state politics and nervousness." In saying this he hardly
meant the regime of the czars, but referred to Russia's talent for
subordination which alone promises new institutions and forms of
authority to the future. The Russians, he observed, lack the sickness of
the West, which believes itself "in danger of a new slavery" whenever the
word "authority" is so much as mentioned.[15]

Thus, with eerie exactness, in uncanny language, Nietzsche
enumerated much that would happen after his own death. Nietzsche
predicted a "war of spirits" (as in the conflict between totalitarianism and
liberalism); a world of antagonists, each faced with a "choice of perishing
or prevailing." All this stems quite naturally out of the end of
Christianity, the so-called death of God. The English, the Americans,
and the Russians would figure prominently as "masters of the earth,"
which—as coincidence would have it—they conquered in 1945, dividing
it into spheres of influence. The Russians, emerging from a tremendous
socialist crisis, would then gather their forces at the frontiers of the
West—as the barbarians of the twentieth century. They promise green-
pasture happiness to mankind while, in fact, creating "adverse
conditions" under a regime of "reverse intentions."

All these predictions and intuitions have been fulfilled. The only
apparent crack in the Nietzschean edifice is the so-called perestroika of
Gorbachev and its aftermath. This perestroika, it seems, is permeated

[11] Ibid., #957. (Note: The "guise of their terms and forms" suggests socialism).

[12] Ibid., #958.

[13] Ibid., #955.

[14] Ibid., #866.

[15] Friedrich Nietzsche, *Twilight of the Idols*, "Expeditions of an Untimely Man," part 39.

----

with that self-same "economic optimism" which Nietzsche declared himself against and which he insisted was illusory.   And this is interesting to make note of, because a genius who in the year 1889 undoubtedly foresaw the larger trends of history, and who did not stoop to reckon with unimportant zigs and zags, ought to deserve our attention far more than a mere "zig" (i.e., the Commonwealth of Independent States).

So what lies ahead? Nietzsche's vision was of a transitional period, stretching between 1889 and 2089, in which Christendom would be supplanted by a profoundly anti-Christian civilization. Though Nietzsche celebrated the demise of Christianity, his writings paint a grim picture of that which comes *after*. Make no mistake, says Nietzsche, the demise of Christianity means the rise of Caesars, immoralists, mass murderers, and a new slavery. *The demise of Christ means the rise of Antichrist.* Carl Jung, recoiling with horror at this vision, thought to salvage Christianity by declaring its mythical and therapeutic significance. But half measures are useless at this stage. One does not save Christianity by paganizing it. Christianity is not at all well served by becoming a mere "tool" of the spiritualized science of psychology.   Besides, can a bygone paganism impart life to a faltering Christianity?

Whatever the ultimate outcome, it is clear that the spiritual foundation of our civilization has been taken away. One is tempted to ask the arrogant modern man, strutting so proudly on top of the Christian centuries, whether he can deny that today's achievements have not ultimately been made possible by Christ? Is not our civilization, at bottom, a Christian structure with a mere liberal addition on the top floor? Is not our science, our industry, and our humanistic politics ultimately traceable to Christ? What *is* this social fabric, this structure of life, with its limited state bound by laws — "under God"? Wherefore came these modern impulses to decency and humanity out of barbarian Dark Ages? Wherefore now these rising crime rates? Wherefore these wars of unprecedented brutality? Wherefore these new signposts of the future — "Hiroshima" — "rocket war" — "gulag"? Our fashionable liberals may, with Nietzsche, curse the Christian civilization which gave rise to so much freedom and prosperity, but do they seriously expect to thrive in the badlands of the future? Have they not learned that the death knell of Christianity is *their* death knell too?

4. Let us look further at these "adverse conditions" that can elevate a man. A recent commentator on this is Aleksandr I. Solzhenitsyn, who directly experienced such conditions as a forced laborer in the gulag Archipelago; and Solzhenitsyn is grateful to the gulag. It uplifted him and brought him nearer to God. He describes, among other things, a

"silent religious procession" through the labor camps; the story of "unstable people" who "found faith right there in camp" and survived uncorrupted. Solzhenitsyn says about these prison camps: "I nourished my soul there." And he writes, "Bless you, prison, for having been in my life."[16] About the prisoners, the "zeks," he says: "Whenever I recall or encounter a former zek, I find a real personality." In reading this, one is reminded of Nietzsche's maxim: "What does not kill me makes me stronger." In this respect, much of Solzhenitsyn's moral power, which lends greatness to his writings, derives from his life of hardship and his redemption through suffering. Who will quarrel with the proposition that the spirit can be strengthened and polished under a regime of "adverse conditions"?

5. It would be natural to ask what Solzhenitsyn thinks of the West. He did, after all, live here in exile for two decades. Certainly he has a few things to say. For example, he notices a "weakening of human personality" in the West. He says about the Russians: "We have been through a spiritual training far in advance of Western experience." Conditions of hardship and oppression have enriched the Russian personality and have instilled a hunger for "higher things." As for the political-military power of the West, he reminds us that "in the twentieth century Western democracy has not won any major war by itself."[17] And indeed, he is correct. The West has been assisted in its world wars by Russian armies, which have made enormous sacrifices. Solzhenitsyn wonders what would have happened to us without this help. One remembers the rapid capitulation of France and the desperate situation of England prior to Hitler's invasion of Russia. What would have happened to the West without the "Russian cannon-fodder"? Would the Americans have sent twenty million boys to die in their place?

In Korea, with no end in sight, our answer was to oust MacArthur and sue for peace.

Solzhenitsyn has understood us all too well, and he knows that under current circumstances "no weapons, no matter how powerful, can help the West until it overcomes its loss of will power." As long as the West continues to rely strictly on weapons, and on technological solutions rather than spiritual solutions, the West will continue to retreat, surrendering its advantages one by one. In this context we must try to realize that Reagan's Strategic Defense Initiative, however crucial it may be, is largely an attempt to avoid the issue of will power. The fact is, if we were serious about fighting and winning a nuclear war, we would already have an extensive system of fallout shelters. But such

16 Aleksandr I. Solzhenitsyn, *The Gulag Archipelago II*, trans. Thomas P. Whitney (New York: Harpor & Row, 1975), pp. 623 - 624, and 617.

17 Aleksandr I. Solzhenitsyn, *A World Split Apart* (New York, 1978), p. 35.

construction, far from being easy, would require great sacrifices. Fallout shelters would cut into consumer spending, and would be gloomy reminders of man's inhumanity to man. And who wants to be reminded? We prefer our sense of optimism, our false hopes, and our carefree outlook; so we opt for a technological miracle. We want a war in which all the casualties are in Dresden and Tokyo. *Our* cities bombed? We won't have it; so we tell our scientists: "Look here, you're obliged to give us a way out." We don't need moral resolve, conviction, toughness, or— as Solzhenitsyn says—"real personality." We don't want to swallow the vile pill of universal shelter construction. Science murdered God, after all; so the ball is in science's court. The triumph of the will? Humbug! Give us a space shield and we'll be fearless again.

But weapons, says Solzhenitsyn, become a burden for those who are psychologically weak; and the next war, he tells us, might seal our fate forever.[18]

6. Solzhenitsyn says there are striking similarities between the party mob in the East and the commercial mob in the West. Both are boundlessly materialistic and free from religion. Both emphasize social instead of individual responsibility. Both share the scientific approach to human problems rather than the spiritual approach, and both put man at the center. Each has the same basic program; namely, that man should step into God's shoes. This is the reason we find ourselves the victims of ever-increasing government controls. Human arrogance, embodied in the state, now usurps God. And the state, as never before, slowly finds its way into every question. But first there is the matter of how to get rid of God, whose tattered authority yet stands in the way. In Russia we can see that God died violently, murdered with the Czar. In the West He dies by inches, killed in shops and malls. In the former, a coup d'etat; in the latter, a slow poisoning. In both instances, a murder of opportunity. The grimy little Machiavels now want God's office. They scramble for it. They tear out each other's eyes for it. All crimes are permitted if only the criminal can deify himself. This is something Stalin understood. And setting his less successful colleagues before firing squads, he propped himself up as a superman, a man of steel; all wise, all knowing. For power, he said, can do anything. It can transform a mediocrity into a hero. It can make stupidity into genius. But most of all, *it can make evil into good.*

"How shall we comfort ourselves, the murderers of all murderers?" asked Nietzsche. "What was holiest and mightiest of all that the world has yet owned has bled to death under our knives: who will wipe this blood off us?"[19]   Only if we become gods ourselves can the blood be

---
[18] Ibid., p. 45 - 47.

wiped. Thus the state or the dictator must assume the mantle of omnipotence, especially because nature abhors a vacuum. And as the statist creatures surge forward to fill this vacuum, they whisper in one-another's ears: "Ye shall be as gods."

7. To us there isn't any question of a higher purpose than this green-pasture happiness of ours. That is how we differ from the Party mob in the East. They, on the contrary, imagine happiness in so-called internationalist duty and the cultivation of "proletarian consciousness"— through an unselfish devotion to revolutionary values. In other words, this party mob has a reservoir of strength in a willingness to kill and be killed. Our captains of industry know nothing like it. For they still calculate in the same old way—*with money.* In effect, they obey no other law. The only thing which keeps them from crime is what Lenin would sneeringly call their "petit bourgeois" instincts. By which is meant their petty ambitions. Lenin, himself, was anything but petty. He didn't want to invent a better mouse trap. To hell with mice! He wanted a world revolution. He wanted a world proletarian empire. Lenin didn't care about a big bank account. Lenin wanted "real power." The capitalists, on the contrary, are more modest. Instead of deifying themselves, they pay lip service to the consumer. That's who they propose to serve. Many of them, to be sure, draw comfort from the fact that they are smarter than their god; that they can manipulate him. This is the form which arrogance now takes in the West. It is Madison Avenue arrogance; an arrogance which says: "He looks good on his throne. Leave him there. Why take him down? He's our puppet, isn't he?" But the true atheists and revolutionists of the East—theirs is an arrogance that spills blood; not at all the petit bourgeois arrogance we have just mentioned; for rather than worshipping consumers, these communists want to be deified themselves *as the vanguard purifiers of the world.* To be sure, the Western elite believes many of the same things as the Eastern elite; only the goal is different in the West. The orientation is that of hedonistic arrogance rather than demonic arrogance. Naturally, lawlessness increases under both regimes. In the East, a lawlessness from above. In the West, a lawlessness from below. The critical difference here is that the party mob in the East has the courage of its convictions and will take everything in hand, being possessed of the wherewithal to play the part of the Great Destroyer; while the commercial mob in the West really isn't a ruling class at all, but a facilitator of consumption and a manufactory of appetite. In other words: a manufactory of sheep that will soon be ready for the slaughter.

---

[19] Friedrich Nietzsche, *The Gay Science,* trans. Walter Kaufmann (New York: Vintage Books, 1974), #125.

8. Whittaker Chambers was once a communist. He believed that "Communists are that part of mankind which has recovered the power to live or die...for its faith"; that is, for "man's second oldest faith,"[20] namely, that men should be as gods. Thus, Chambers, too, notices in communism a supreme effort to step into God's shoes. There are many striking similarities between Solzhenitsyn's observations and those made by Chambers. They both see the West as weak-willed. They both see the arrogance of the intellectuals and the soulessness of modern life. They both fear that communism cannot be stopped. When Chambers left the communist underground he told his wife that he was leaving "the winning world for the losing world."[21]

9. Mao Zedong once wrote: "Either kill the tiger or be eaten by him—one or the other."[22]   What sort of tiger does Mao propose to kill? Paper tigers, of course. He said: "All reactionaries are paper tigers. In appearance, they are frightening, but in reality their strength is not so great." Mao also said: "The atom bomb is a paper tiger."[23] "We are against overestimating the strength of the enemy." However, he added, "People in all countries of the world are now discussing whether or not a third world war will break out. In regard to this question, we must be psychologically prepared."[24]

Comrade Mao was very wise. He knew all about the weakness of the West. He would, if he were alive, sneer at our fancy new weapons. "The so called theory of 'weapons decide everything,'" he said, "is a mechanistic theory of war, a subjectivist and one-sided view. Our view is contrary to this; we see not only weapons but also the power of man. Weapons are an important factor in war but not the decisive one; it is man and not material that is decisive."[25]

But if Comrade Mao had to choose his favorite weapon, and leave "the power of man" out of it, what weapon would he choose? The good chairman readily answered: "We thank Marx, Engels, Lenin and Stalin for giving us a weapon. This weapon is not a machine gun, but Marxism-Leninism."[26]

And why, exactly, is Chairman Mao destined to triumph with this wonderful weapon which "is not a machine gun"? Because: "We are the

---

[20] Whittaker Chambers, *Witness* (New York: Random House, 1952), p. 9.

[21] Ibid., p. 25.

[22] *Mao Tse-Tung and Lin Piao*, ed. K. Fan (New York, 1972), p. 11.

[23] Ibid., p. 233.

[24] Ibid., pp. 237 - 243.

[25] Ibid., p. 230.

[26] Ibíd., p. 5.

opposite of the political parties of the bourgeoisie. They are afraid to speak of the extinction of classes, state power and parties. We, on the contrary, declare openly that we are striving hard to create the very conditions which will bring about their extinction."[27]

Of course, Chairman Mao has since died.

Long live Comrade Deng!

Comrade Deng has said: "We must not in the least neglect or slacken criticism of bourgeois and petty-bourgeois ideologies, of ultra-individualism and anarchism." Deng continues: "It is absolutely wrong to lose faith in socialism and think that it is inferior to capitalism just because we have made mistakes."[28]

And what does Comrade Deng hate most? That people take him for a capitalist. About this matter Comrade Deng wants to say something for the record. Some Party cadres have "criticized as 'capitalism' some of our current reforms, which are useful to the development of production."[29] Comrade Deng says that this criticism is incorrect. He claims that his goal is "to build a socialist civilization with a high cultural and ideological level, so as to inculcate ideals, morality, knowledge and discipline in all our people....We simply must have discipline....I think we should launch a movement to study the works of Marx, Lenin, and Comrade Mao Zedong." In addition, we must free the army from "decadent bourgeois ideas." Any other attitude, says Deng, is criminal. And then he adds, "Serious crimes and major criminals are to be found not only in the economic but in the political and cultural fields as well."[30]

As liberals, we are appalled by such statements. But to the man who draws a firm line and endorses definitive political and moral standards, it is liberalism which proves appalling.

10. It is my contention that the East has strategic sense and the West does not. And what is strategic sense? First, it is the ability to judge the importance of things in relation to ultimate aims. Secondly, it involves skill in maneuvering, delivering blows, weighing risks, divining intentions. It also involves concealment and subterfuge. Often the strategist must resemble the fictional detective hero, Sherlock Holmes, in his ability to infer a great many things from a small set of clues. The intellect of the strategist combines experience and imagination under the guidance of judgment. It is this which leads many of our finest writers to assume falsely that they are capable of strategy. For writers, too, employ

[27] Ibid., p. 4.

[28] *The Selected Works of Deng Xiaoping (1975-1982)* (Beijing, 1984), pp. 319-320.

[29] Ibid., p. 321.

[30] Ibid., p. 386 - 395.

experience and imagination under judgment. But writing and strategy are fundamentally different activities. Writers aim at winning approval, while strategists aim at winning battles. Writers are, therefore, notoriously superficial in their strategic thinking because they confuse approval with conquest. Also, the writer's world is fundamentally different from the strategist's world. For the writer's world is words on a page, while the strategist's world is violence and subterfuge. The writer's judgment need only extend to the pleasantness of sounds, the exactness of grammar, the flattery of fashionable sentiments. He might drop the context, confuse the relationships between variables, and so on, without immediate consequences. On the other hand, the strategist who did these things would not be accounted a strategist at all, but a loser. In diplomacy, espionage, and war—fine words are merely amusing evidences of cleverness and facility; they are hiding places and psychological disguises. The strategist is obliged to see through such outward shows and flourishes. And as for every prejudice of the moment, every fashion, every conceit—these are dangerous to him. To survive he must stick to the truth while the writer operates under conditions exactly the opposite. For a writer endangers sales when he puts truth ahead of popularity. To avoid this problem he must keep matters within socially prescribed limits. If he messes it up and goes out of bounds, his book becomes a classic, but only after he dies or loses his mind. This outcome is exactly what the typical modern writer hopes to avoid. The strategist, on the other hand, is not endangered by too much truth. The truth is never something he has to communicate to anyone, but merely something he must know for himself. And unlike the writer, he cannot succeed unless he acts on that which is real. Therefore he *must* free himself from preconceptions. He *must* go beneath the commonplace surface of things and never rest until he has found the underlying reality. Add to this the fact that his enemy wants to mislead him. Therefore he doesn't merely battle with nature, but with a cunning human adversary. Thus the strategist has need of wariness, especially where the writer might be careless. The strategist wants only the clearest logic, only the nicest distinctions, only the coldest appreciation of human nature and human weaknesses. He must have a nose for smelling falseness. Like Socrates, his method is often dialectical, but not in terms of language. The dialogue of the strategist is a dialogue of moves and counter-moves; of artillery barrages and night assaults. He learns to measure people and things. He is both psychologist and physical engineer.

The reason for introducing the strategist in this way, as an ideal type, is to point out that Soviet society tends to cultivate such strategists while our society tends to cultivate strategic bunglers. It is a truism of

---

sociology that a money-oriented society inculcates economic thinking and a militarized society inculcates strategic thinking. One only has to see how the Soviets dominate chess to know that something very different is happening in their country. Soviet strategists are given plenty of room to grow, while in America our so-called strategy analysts tend to be manipulators of words, trained rather as scholars than as strategists. One must realize that academics are very often memorizers and imitators. This fact is often lost in the padded obscurity of nearly all academic writing; in jargon and equivocation rendered scientific by the ritualized employment of highly exact statistical measurements; by ridiculously complex explanations where simple explanations would serve as well; and by a morbid careerism and narrowness. Nor can the academic, as strategist, see the big picture. He becomes so easily infatuated by irrelevancies that his mind cannot solve the problem at hand. Trained as a specialist he only respects the judgments of fellow-specialists. Habituated to peer pressures his instincts for approval and survival are ill-fitted for strategy and for the boldness and independence of thought required for it. Strategy demands an aggressive, masculine, spirit. I have known outstanding professors of political science, men of great intellect. But I would never trust them with the conduct of a war or the negotiation of a peace. In evidence for my view I point to Kissinger, a scholar whose advice has unwittingly bolstered our enemies and sunk whole regions of the earth into the bloody mire of totalitarian slavery.

Of course, one shouldn't deny the sudden and unexpected appearance of occasional strategists in American political life. But such men are rarities, with all the odds against them. When they appear, they do not last. The fact is, bureaucratism doesn't cultivate or encourage such men or respect their talents. Clearly, the essence of such people—their hardheadedness, their masculinity—is not appreciated in universities, in big corporations, or in government systems built on groupthink. Sometimes I wonder if commercial society isn't a society with feminine values. Perhaps this explains why the Ulysses S. Grant of tomorrow is currently biding his time as a clerk in some small town.

And we don't recruit the right people into the CIA, either. Straight-talkers, men of iron, suspected loners and other eccentrics are shunned and treated like weeds. We let them languish; tending bar, pumping gas, clerking hardware. Most of the time we prefer to put other kinds of plants in our top pots. We prefer to fashion strategists out of other materials. But the communists, as revolutionaries and doctrinaires, have no fear of hard-nosed types, of brutal simplifiers and working-class Napoleons. One sees in the original Bolshevik crew a group of men with enormous talent for strategy. Naturally, they made of Russia an economic basket-case. But they didn't care about economics. They cared about revolution. And as revolutionists their thinking was zero-sum thinking; in other words, *strategic thinking*. Perhaps the cultural atmosphere of bourgeois society cannot abide the vaguest hint that other perspectives exist. This is not to say that our society fails to promote the "foxes." One must not confuse "foxes" with strategists. Very often the fox is merely a weak and devious person who can manipulate his office "image." He cultivates appearances and is frightened of being found unfashionable. Together with other "foxes" he gangs up against the occasional "lion"—and arranges the early retirement, demotion, or transfer of fearlessness. The fox is a sly coward. And in today's peer-group environment cowardice wins. Thus, the fine-tuned cowardice of the fox is a tremendous help to his ambitions. He treads lightly and carefully. He never stands up to his superiors. He backbites. Therefore, unlike the strategist, he lacks the character to command respect and obedience. Far from being a strategist, the fox is a political hack—the antithesis of a soldier-statesman. I say once again: Do not mistake the fox for a strategist. The fox is a comformist. Go through history and name the greatest generals and statesmen. Were they conformists or individualists? One finds, upon exploring the question, that great military men have always been one step away from ostracism. They've always appeared where peer-group pressures were weakest or emergency considerations strongest. Consider Napoleon, who challenged convention at every step, making his own conventions. Hitler scoffed at "ordinary opinions." Caesar made it a point to flaunt fashion. Alexander the Great went *against* his generals. Nelson defied moral norms. Grant was kicked out of the army for boozing. Patton believed in reincarnation.

11. James Burnham, a former Trotskyist, was one of those rarities— a man with strategic sense. This in itself is interesting: for a man with a background in Trotskyism evidently has an easier time understanding strategy than a man with a background in economics (like Thomas Schelling). This makes Burnham important for us. Like Mao, Mr. Burnham realized that a strict reckoning of strategic problems in terms of mere economic strength is "vulgar materialism." Burnham once wrote: "If human conflicts were in truth decided by superiority in arms, there would have been no history." He wrote that "the resources of the spirit... prove weightier in the scale of history than lumps of matter."[31] He said that our latter-day morality blinds us to the essential amorality of the world; that there is a sense of truth in the communist maxim that humanity still lives in pre-history, with the law of the jungle yet prevailing. Burnham saw that the communists had suspended every moral rule because the age of morality, in their thinking, had not begun.

---

[31] James Burnham, *The War We Are In: The Last Decade and the Next* (New Rochelle, New York: Arlington House, 1967), p. 294.

Such an age, the communists reasoned, would only commence with the world-wide victory of communism. And with that event, the victors might afford a little morality.

12. Burnham objected to our "vague economic determinism inherited both from classic laissez-faire doctrine and from...'vulgar Marxism.'"[32] Communism, he insisted, does not spring from adverse economic conditions. Communism springs from revolutionary agitation. America's Cold War strategy, which based itself on economic determinism, was therefore flawed. The foremost example he cited was Cuba, which had the second highest standard of living in Latin America prior to its communist revolution.

13. Burnham foresaw that we would make use of the Sino-Soviet split "to continue evading the challenge" of communism. "Internal disputes," he wrote, "are not necessarily signs of weakness or decay." And then he gave the example of Islam, which expanded rapidly despite "fierce and bloody internal" cleavages.[33]

14. And speaking of internal cleavages, it was under Khrushchev that these cleavages first appeared. It was also under Khrushchev that weapons of mass destruction were first understood (but only in Russia). This is an important coincidence. It was Khrushchev, the liberalizer, who first explained that the communists would relinquish their goals only when "the crab sings." But who believed him? It was Khrushchev, the world's most powerful communist boss, who said: "The rotten capitalist world is collapsing. Friends, let's drink, let's laugh, let's rejoice." It was Khrushchev, the advocate of peaceful coexistence, who shouted to NATO officials at a party: "Whether you like it or not, history is on our side. We will bury you!"

15. After Khrushchev became head of the Soviet Union a small change was made in the Russian dictionary. The word Khrushch had its definition altered from "a type of beetle deleterious to agriculture" to merely "a type of beetle."

16. On 23 June 1959 Khrushchev met with Averell Harriman, son of "robber baron" Edward Henry Harriman. The meeting was held at Khrushchev's dacha outside Moscow. In attendance were Anastas Mikoyan, Andrei Gromyko, Yuri Zhukov and Frol Kozlov of the Soviet Communist Party. Khrushchev was drinking Armenian cognac, and proposing one toast after another. Throughout the evening, Khrushchev

---

[32] Ibid., p. 320.

[33] Ibid., p. 328 - 333.

----

boasted, lectured, and bullied. He also cracked jokes. What if the Americans interfere in Berlin? "The American tanks will burn. And make no mistake; if you want war, you can have it. But remember: it will be your war. Our rockets will fly automatically." And then, like the chorus from a Greek tragedy, Mikoyan, Gromyko, Zhukov and Kozlov solemnly echoed the refrain: *"Automatically."* Khrushchev then began talking about America: "The United States is completely controlled by a tiny circle of capitalists. The workers haven't any voice in the government." And on and on he went. Harriman, quite in keeping with his naiveté, had the impertinence to ask who these all-powerful capitalists were? Khrushchev pushed his finger into Harriman's arm and said, "You're one of them." Harriman couldn't get over his shock. The Soviet premier then proposed further toasts, appeared to be drunk, and finally said to Harriman: "In five to seven years we will be stronger than you. And at the bargain price of thirty billion dollars we will be able to destroy all of Europe and America. We have this option."[34]

17. But Mr. K had no intention of destroying all of Europe and America. He wanted to try something more devious, involving a "long range strategy." We have information about this because of a defector named Anatoliy Golitsyn, who was employed in a Soviet think tank, and who wrote a book about various things he saw and heard. Golitsyn also attended a significant meeting chaired by Khrushchev's KGB chief, Alexander Shelepin, who reorganized State Security in accordance with the new long-range plan, and who led a discussion on various items connected with this plan. According to Golitsyn, the Soviet aim is world conquest (even now, in the post-Soviet era). The target date for achieving this conquest is the year 2000. The difficulty for Golitsyn was that few in the West wanted to hear what he had to say. James Jesus Angleton was one of the few who listened. It was Angleton, as head of CIA counterintelligence back in the 1960s and 1970s, who was inevitably drummed out of the CIA because of that willingness.

Golitsyn took great pains to establish his credibility. Before he came to the West he had memorized numerous stolen NATO documents which the KGB had acquired through its vast network of moles and double-agents. Golitsyn proved useful in a number of espionage cases for the CIA and the British Secret Service. He also fostered an unacceptable degree of paranoia: fueling suspicions regarding the director of the British Secret Service, Sir Roger Hollis, people in the Soviet Division of the CIA, and top people in French intelligence, as well as a number of lesser fish. According to the accounts of authors Edward J. Epstein and

---

[34] Joseph Finder, *Red Carpet* (Fort Worth, Texas: The American Bureau of Economic Research, 1987), pp. 118 - 121.

Peter Wright, Golitsyn also provided information implicating the KGB in the death of British Labour Party leader Hugh Gaitskell, who contracted a rare lupus infection in 1963 after having tea and cookies at the Soviet Embassy. Before Gaitskell's illness, Golitsyn had reported that the KGB planned a high-level assassination somewhere in Western Europe to advance "their man" to the head of a Western political party. Gaitskell's death put Harold Wilson in the Labor Party's top spot. Wilson had significant ties to East European communists.[35]

More perplexing than this was Epstein's revelation that the Soviets were involved in the Kennedy assassination, something which CIA counterintelligence chief Angleton inferred from information provided by Golitsyn and an intercepted telephone conversation between Lee Harvey Oswald and an officer of the KGB assassinations department, Sergei Kostikov.[36] Angleton believed that the Soviets did not play by the accepted international rules, that they sometimes murdered important people for strategic reasons. Because his views were politically unacceptable Angleton was forced out of the CIA in 1974.

Golitsyn, meanwhile, had been dropped by the CIA in 1969 because he insisted that the Sino-Soviet split was a strategic ploy. Thus, he made himself disliked by the incoming Nixon administration which took the Sino-Soviet split seriously and planned to open relations with China. Golitsyn's knowledge of Soviet long range strategy thereafter served only to discredit him. He became controversial because his knowledge of the KGB's dominance of spycraft threatened every CIA bureaucrat whose career hinged on sunny pictures of promising landscapes. Besides this, Golitsyn's revelations about moles in high places had been devastating to the morale of the intelligence community. The happy results which were expected from his "photographic memory" did not materialize. He was a bearer of bad news who held up a mirror to the West and was despised for it. He lectured the Westerners on their failures, instead of providing them with painless or *easy* successes. Golitsyn's personal manner was also a problem. He was insensitive, arrogant, abrupt, and did not mince words. Those who resented Golitsyn, as well as those who were threatened by what he said or how he said it, sought his removal. A virtual civil war raged within the American intelligence community, with various personalities taking sides. The FBI was so convulsed that J. Edgar Hoover fell out with his own deputy director. With so much animosity unleashed by Golitsyn's controversial statements, things came to a head. The American intelligence community would *not* reform

---

[35] My sources for Golitsyn's activities are: Edward J. Epstein, *Deception: The Invisible War Between the KGB and CIA* (New York: Simon and Schuster, 1989); and Peter Wright, *Spycatcher: The Candid Autobiography of a Senior Intelligence Officer* (New York: Dell Publishing, 1988). For details on Gaitskell's death, see Epstein, pp. 80 - 82 and Wright, pp. 455 - 58.

[36] Epstein, *Deception*, p. 287.

----

itself in the light of all this bad news. It refused to deal realistically with the problem of Soviet penetration. Ours was a liberal-minded unintelligent intelligence community. And besides, witch hunts have a bad name with us, even if, as in this case, the witches need hunting. Also, one has to consider the big picture. It was politically unacceptable to challenge the optimistic assumptions of elected officials. Therefore, for reasons of morale and politics, the word of an unreliable Soviet defector named Nosenko was eventually used to discredit everything that Golitsyn had said. From then on the Western intelligence services would only believe what they wanted to believe.

18. In 1984 Golitsyn wrote a book about Soviet long-range strategy under the title *New Lies For Old*. In the book Golitsyn explained that during 1957 the KGB, under the auspices of General Shelepin, helped to devise a forty-year plan for disarming and conquering the West by means of strategic deception. According to Golitsyn, two principal deception operations would be run: first, false splits within the communist bloc to create the impression of a weakened international communism; second, a false liberalization and democratization of the communist bloc that would lead to Western disarmament. Relying on his knowledge of the overall Soviet plan, Golitsyn predicted sweeping changes which would be carefully staged in communist countries. Golitsyn's predictions were not vague, but specific; and I quote directly from his book, which was written during the period of heightened East-West tensions prior to Gorbachev's ascension:
     —In Poland "it may be expected that a coalition government will be formed, comprising representatives of the communist party, of a revived Solidarity movement, and of the church." Golitsyn also stated that "the next five years will be a period of intensive struggle.... An intensive effort to achieve US nuclear disarmament.... A revival of controlled 'democratization' on the Czechoslovak pattern in Eastern Europe, including Czechoslovakia and the Soviet Union.... Brezhnev's successor may well appear to be a kind of Soviet Dubcek.... The Brezhnev regime and its neo-Stalinistic actions against 'dissidents' and in Afghanistan would be condemned.... In the economic field reforms might be expected to bring Soviet practice more into line with Yugoslav, or even, seemingly, with Western socialist models. Some economic ministries might be dissolved; control would be more decentralized; individual self-managing firms might be created from existing plants and factories; material incentives would be increased; the independent role of technocrats, workers' councils, and trade unions would be enhanced; the party's control over the economy would be apparently diminished.....The picture being deliberately painted now of stagnation and deficiencies in

the Soviet economy.... Political 'liberalization' and 'democratization' would follow.... The 'liberalization' would be spectacular and impressive. Formal pronouncements might be made about a reduction in the communist party's role; its monopoly would be apparently curtailed.... The KGB would be 'reformed.... Dissidents at home would be amnestied; those in exile abroad would be allowed to return, and some would take up positions of leadership in the government or be allowed to teach abroad. The creative arts and cultural and scientific organizations, such as the writers' unions and Academy of Sciences, would become apparently more independent, as would the trade unions. Political clubs would be opened to nonmembers of the communist party. Leading dissidents might form one or more alternative political parties. Censorship would be relaxed; controversial books, plays, films, and art would be published, performed, and exhibited.... There would be greater freedom for Soviet citizens to travel. Western and United Nations observers would be invited to the Soviet Union to witness the reforms in action."

—If liberalization were extended to East Germany, wrote Golitsyn, the "demolition of the Berlin Wall might even be contemplated.... Pressure could well grow for a solution of the German problem in which some form of confederation between East and West Germany would be combined with neutralization of the whole and a treaty of friendship with the Soviet Union.... The Czechoslovaks...might well take the lead...in proposing (in the CSCE context) the dissolution of the Warsaw Pact in return for the dissolution of NATO."[37]

19. General Shelepin, sitting in his office on Dzerzhinsky Square, was given the task of stage-managing the *apparent* collapse of the Soviet Union and the breakup of the communist bloc as something that would be believable to the leaders and masses of the Western World. It was Shelepin's job to set up an apparatus designed to foster, *then exploit*, Western hopes. Nor would this be the first such exploitation. The Soviets have operated similar deceptions before. For example: the Trust and the Monarchist Alliance of Central Russia, created by the communists as false opposition fronts in the 1920s. But Shelepin's plan would dwarf these earlier schemes. Here we have the most ambitious strategic undertaking in history. This ambitiousness protects the Shelepin plan from discovery. For being alien to everything that has happened in history *so far*, few will credit its reality. Since most of us expect that other people think as we do, it is difficult for us to imagine people who would predicate themselves upon a long range strategy which we would be incapable of following even if we wanted to. In fact, it is the seeming sanity of Soviet leaders that keeps us from believing that

---

[37] Golitsyn, *New Lies for Old*, pp. 334 - 341.

---

a Shelepin plan exists. The communists appear to be cool, practical, and down-to-earth. But, as Machiavelli said: "Everyone sees what you appear to be, few experience what you really are. And those few dare not gainsay the many."[38] And as we leave the seminars and think tanks of the American strategy establishment, shaking our heads at the elegant men with their equally elegant but wrongheaded analyses of the Soviet bloc's breakup, we begin to appreciate to what extent we are confronting one of the truly great works of art in the whole of human history. For the Soviet long-range strategy is, if anything, a work of art. And so artful is this work, that if a Western analyst began to believe in its existence, the belief would discredit him as a lowbrow crankish paranoid. This gives us pause to consider the great advantage acruing to those Machiavels whose very lives are monuments to bad taste; and who teach us how easy it is to hide from elegant men a reality which resembles bad fiction. For elegant men will refuse, from the first page onward, to read such a reality and, therefore, will prefer the more tasteful and elegant fictions propagated by the KGB.

20. A local talk-radio personality once said to me: "I don't care *why* Gorbachev is doing what he's doing. All I know is that Russia has new freedom. If it's a conspiracy then I'm in favor of it."

Here one cannot get past the idea that Gorbachev has done good things. Ditto for Yeltsin. One fails to think strategically; *i.e.*, in terms of maneuvering for the kill. One lacks the imagination to penetrate the psychological camouflage.

21. Mikhail Gorbachev, in his book *Perestroika*, describes the United States as a land with "millions of unfortunate people" whose government possesses "an almost missionary passion for preaching about human rights and liberties" while disregarding "those same elementary rights in their own home." He criticizes American notions of freedom as masking attempts to impose the American way of life on others. He says that American propaganda partakes of a "cult of force and violence" as well as "arrogance of power, especially military power" and "constant growth in arms spending."[39]

Elsewhere Gorbachev refers to America's "immoral intention to bleed the Soviet Union white economically." He advises Americans to "get rid of such an approach to our country. Hopes of using any advantages in technology or advanced equipment so as to gain superiority over our country are futile." And he goes on to say: "If the

---

[38] Machiavelli, *The Prince*, trans. George Bull (Great Britain: Penguin Books, 1985), p. 101.

[39] Mikhail Gorbachev, *Perestroika: New Thinking for Our Country and the World* (New York: Harper & Row, 1987), p. 201.

Soviet Union, when it was much weaker than now, was in a position to meet all the challenges that it faced, then indeed only a blind person would be unable to see that our capacity to maintain strong defenses... has enormously increased."[40]

About the future Gorbachev says: "The world revolutionary process is gaining momentum and is advancing steadily towards new revolutionary storms.... The main revolutionary forces of today are the socialist world system." The world's problems can only be resolved by removing obstacles "put up by imperialism." He explains that "only the elimination of imperialist forces" can make the world a better place.[41]

Gorbachev blames America for the Cold War. He writes: "Because of NATO, Europe once again found itself harnessed to a chariot of war, this time loaded with nuclear weapons."[42]

Gorbachev points to the West and says: "We see how strong the positions of the aggressive and militarist part of the ruling class are in the leading capitalist countries." He claims that the United States Army "refuses to give up its privileged position,"[43] and that the United States military is "an instrument of an expansionist foreign policy" that has been "built up over the centuries."[44]

Therefore, in Gorbachev's view, the rulers of America are bad eggs. But what about the communists? "Communism," insists Gorbachev, "has a tremendous potential for humanitarianism.... The Soviet Union rejects terrorism in principle....there isn't a trace of a Soviet presence in South Africa...."[45]

Lies, fables and inversions.

Concerning the Soviet Union's invasion of Afghanistan Mr. Gorbachev is quite candid: The fault lies in the extreme backwardness of the Afghans "largely stemming from British rule." As for the West's aid to the Afghan rebels? It is "simply immoral and totally unjustifiable." In every instance it is the West—not the East—which viciously exploits the developing countries.[46]

In Gorbachev's statements we find the same old lies. In perestroika we find nothing but a fabric of half-truths and guarded admissions. Gorbachev is a dictator, a demagogue, the war leader of the war party, and a hard-liner's hard-liner.

---

[40] Ibid., p. 206.

[41] Ibid., pp. 180 - 83.

[42] Ibid., p. 179.

[43] Ibid., p. 135.

[44] Ibid., p. 175.

[45] Ibid., p. 141.

[46] Ibid., pp. 162 - 4.

----

22. So stupid a nation—*these Americans*—to confuse a communist with a "liberal reformer." But this isn't strange. We once said nice things about Stalin too. We once conceived that Castro and Mao were "agrarian reformers." It's always the same story. The West refuses to focus its eyes.

23. Points to remember about the changes in the Soviet Union:

(a) Mr. Yeltsin came into the Politburo under Mr. Gorbachev, who was the creature of Mr. Andropov who chaired the KGB, and who was appointed to that post during Alexander Shelepin's tenure at the Interior Ministry, which oversees the KGB.

(b) The Soviets were caught cheating on the INF Treaty in the Spring of 1990. They were caught cheating on chemical weapons and biological weapons in 1992, 1993, 1995, and 1997.

(c) Soviet espionage against the West has intensified throughout 1990 and 1991 according to CIA and FBI sources. No doubt, Russian espionage continued into 1992 and 1993. In 1994 we uncovered a Russian spy inside the CIA. His name was Aldrich Ames. In 1996 we uncovered yet another high level KGB mole inside the CIA.

(d) There are, as Golitsyn said, communist-inspired anti-Soviet organizations. For example, in Azerbaijan, such organizations were used to create a pretext for smashing the Azerbaijanis. The *New York Times* of February 19, 1990, page A6, presented evidence that the Communist Party of the Soviet Union helped to create the Azerbaijani Popular Front. I quote the *Times*: "Communist Party officials actively encouraged the growth of a nationalist political movement in Azerbaijan, the Popular Front, and tried for almost a year to turn it toward more chauvinist and militant activities." Further on it says: "Many mysteries remain about the anti-Armenian riots in Baku. Local journalists say they appear to have been organized.... The journalists also say at least some of the roving bands were led by convicted criminals recently released from jail."

(e) In Eastern Europe we find a similar pattern. From the same *Times*, front page article of February 19 we read a Rumanian protester quoted on page A7, saying: "The revolution has been stolen from us by old faces." It seems that the National Salvation Front, the self-appointed government that took power when Ceausescu was toppled, is led by men with close ties to the KGB and the Soviet Communist Party. (Please remember that the Soviet government, years earlier, had plotted unsuccessfully to murder Ceausescu. This time they succeeded.)

(f) From the *Los Angeles Times* of January 17, 1990, A10, in an article concerning the Eastern bloc's new "defensive strategy," there is the following curious passage: "U.S. military intelligence officials have complained that while the Soviets say they are reshaping their forces for defensive operations, they continue to deploy supplies of spare weapons parts and huge ammunition caches near the East-West border, where they could be used by troops in an offensive operation."

(g) The International Security Council, a public-policy group operating out of the District of Columbia, reports that Soviet military expenditures have increased twenty-five percent between 1985 and 1990, while United States military expenditures have *declined* by sixteen percent over the same period. In 1988 the Soviets built and deployed about 250 intercontinental and submarine-launched ballistic missiles, while the United States only deployed nineteen. This may be confirmed by examining other commonly available sources on the military balance. Besides the sheer weight of numbers, the Soviets have improved the accuracy and increased the payload capacity of their missiles while developing their own antimissile defense systems.

In keeping with Soviet traditions, Yeltsin announced a ten percent increase in arms spending during his first year in office.[47]

24. In 1958 KGB Chief Shelepin gave a lecture explaining how staged disputes and faked splits between the nations of the communist bloc could be made to look real. After the lecture was over, Shelepin remarked that China was a perfect candidate for such an operation.[48] Along similar lines, Deng Xiaoping said to his fellow Marxist-Leninists of the CCP Central Committee in 1977 that communism was engaged in something called "the international united front struggle" which was a strategy about which the "American imperialists" know absolutely nothing. "We belong to the Marxist camp," declared Deng, "and can never be so thoughtless that we cannot distinguish friends from enemies." He went on to explain that Nixon, Ford, Carter, and future "American imperialist leaders" were all enemies. Nevertheless, these enemies had momentarily become highly useful because "what we need mainly is scientific and technical knowledge and equipment." Deng emphasized that in the future, due to the United Front strategy, America "will have no way of avoiding defeat by our hands."[49]

25. In 1980, according to the dictates of diplomacy and war, communist Vietnam needed to secure the neutrality of Thailand. Such neutrality would have assured the destruction of Chinese-backed Cambodian forces, preventing Cambodian military sanctuaries from being established in Thai territory. But a curious thing happened.

---

[47] San Diego *Union Tribune*, 24 November 92, "Russia to increase spending on arms".

[48] Epstein, *Deception*, p. 97.

[49] David Nelson Rowe, *The Carter China Policy: Results and Prospects* (New York, 1980), p. 16.

communist Vietnam ordered its troops to cross into Thailand on 23 June 1980, *and there was no military reason for it.* A regiment-sized unit with elements of two divisions in support, penetrated Thai territory, encircling the village of Ban Mak Moon. The Vietnamese troops entrenched themselves and awaited contact with Thai military units. Intelligence sources indicated that the Vietnamese actions were deliberate, and that Vietnamese troops were following orders. On 25 June the ASEAN foreign ministers issued a communique condemning Vietnam's "act of aggression." The ASEAN countries then proceeded to freeze their relations with Hanoi while extending an olive branch to China. Thailand soon formed a defacto alliance with China. More significantly, the Thai government ceased making war on the Chinese-backed Thai communists, who returned to Bangkok.[50]

Because of this, the United Front struggle picked up yet another petit bourgeois ally on the road to socialism, which, as Comrade Gorbachev assures us, is not at all a "straight road."

26. In 1962 Khrushchev advised the government of India that the Chinese would not go to war over disputed borderlands. Shortly thereafter, India suffered a serious military defeat at the hands of the Chinese. Khrushchev called the prime minister of India and expressed his regrets. The Indians, badly shaken, decided to align themselves with Moscow. Today, Indian security arrangements and arms procurement are so inextricably tied to the Soviet Union that it would be difficult for them to break free.

And so the Soviet Union, too, has picked up petit bourgeois allies.

27. The "scissors strategy" is a method by which two parties pretend to disagree about something in order to subvert the position of a third party. When the manipulation proves successful it is said that the two principal blades, while cutting against one another, produce the wonderful effect of slicing the third party to shreds.

28. During the period of democratic reforms, the Soviet living standard fell. Goods became scarcer. Food was rationed in Leningrad and other cities. This indicates that perestroika is not a process of economic liberalization, but a process which smashes the economic power (translate, political power) of the general public. Poor people are easier to rule than rich people. They are, in fact, increasingly dependent on the government. Going along with the system becomes necessary for such people. Therefore, poverty strengthens the oligarchy's position. And far from discrediting socialism, the food shortages under Gorbachev

---

[50] Ton That Thein, *The Foreign Politics of the Communist Party of Vietnam: A Study of Communist Tactics* (New York, 1989), pp. 162-4.

and Yeltsin discredit capitalism, liberalism, and democracy. For it is under the program of privatization, liberalization, and democratization that things have become worse. Even now, the inconveniences suffered by the Russian consumer are laid at the door of Mr. Yeltsin, and some of the people are yearning for the "good-old-days" under Stalinists like Brezhnev. The communists in Russia are preparing to say: "We tried capitalism and it didn't work. We tried democracy and it didn't work. We tried peace and it didn't work."

Besides serving as a kind of domestic propaganda, free-market reform deceives and disarms the West. It alleviates fear by encouraging false hopes for Russian bourgeoisification. Market reform in Russia leads the anti-communists into victory sickness. One should consider the possibility that the old Soviet oligarchy needs a smokescreen behind which to redirect wealth for the sake of further military programs (*i.e.*, secret ones). And what of the Warsaw Pact? The key thing is not conventional armies and shaky alliance blocs, but the weapons of mass destruction. These alone are the reliable agencies of the future. Besides, wouldn't it be nice to have Europe in a nuclear free zone so that after a war with the United States the Russians would have somewhere pleasant to migrate? The important thing is not tank divisions in Czechoslovakia. The important thing is rockets and hydrogen bombs with which to exterminate the Americans and blackmail the rest of the world.

29. Remember how Stalin liked to smile and wink at people only to have them shot on the following day? There is something appealing about this approach; that is, from a strictly psychological point of view, and in terms of the effectiveness of one's terrorism.

30. It is stupid to say that the Soviet Communist Party contains "conservatives" and "liberals." The politics of a closed system knows nothing of these labels, but merely produces mutually antagonistic coalitions of "personalities." And despite what the experts say, the communists are still in control, they still rule, and Yeltsin is their secret creature.

31. *Milking Stalin's Terror.* Gorbachev wrote: "There should be no blank pages in history. It is immoral to pass over in silence large periods in the life of the people." Shortly thereafter, mass graves were unearthed which contained hundreds of thousands of corpses. They were victims of communism by way of Stalin. So the Communist Party suddenly exclaims: "Look what *we* did! Oops! You don't suppose we'd do it again, do you?" — and a sly grin. People appreciate this. Hundreds of thousands of corpses all speaking at once on behalf of Mikhail

----

Gorbachev, saying: "We were enemies of the regime, and look what happened to us." Someone from the Party Central Committee cracks a joke about "socialist legality." The Soviet people, as I said, appreciate this. It permits their cynicism an honest self-respect.

32. The Russian people are always prepared to challenge corruption. But ideology is something that is more difficult for them to oppose. For ideology is even more insidious than gangsterism. Even those who have opposed communism in the West hold many ideas in common with Karl Marx.

33. *To carry our inquiry further.* — Why have the Soviets violated so many treaties, even the most recent ones, on which the ink has barely dried? Why do so many of the so-called opposition parties in Eastern Europe turn out to be headed by former secret police informants and communists? Why does the Soviet Union supply arms to so many terrorist organizations? Why does it continue to maintain a closed border? Why are concentration camps still in operation? What about the KGB?

34. At a meeting on 18 March 1908, Lenin said that two mistakes had ruined the Paris Commune. First, the Commune was stupidly carried away with the idea of establishing justice. Second, the Commune failed to exterminate its enemies, and attempted to influence them by moral example. *Absolutely shameful!*

35. When General Eisenhower met Soviet Marshal Zhukov at the end of the Second World War, they talked about various military problems. Eisenhower complained of the loss of time required to clear minefields. Marshal Zhukov didn't think mine fields were much of a problem. "When we come to a mine field," he said, "our infantry attacks exactly as if it were not there."

36. The Leninist regards morality as intimately bound up in an imaginary harmony of ends and means. This is reflected in Lenin's statement: "Everything that is done in the interest of the proletarian cause is honest." Meanwhile, the Western mind, insofar as it accepts specific political ends at all, often regards the means as something dirty. Consequently, the Westerner sacrifices his ends because his means cannot wear a halo. In other words: as moralizer, he chooses strictly unrealizable goals like perfect peace and freedom. The Western mind cannot imagine that *real* peace and freedom are inconsistent with *ideal* peace and freedom; that freedom necessarily exists only in degree and never absolutely.

Real freedom, which only comes about under specific circumstances, is made possible only by methods which invariably rule out ideal freedom; so the best politics is a politics of mitigation, not perfection. The liberal Western spirit, however, has come to regard any compromise in this area as disgraceful. The *ideal,* therefore, betrays the *real.* This is what happened in Vietnam. The war was not objectionable in itself as long as it remained a humane war, an easy war, and a happy war. But since wars are rarely so wonderful, we eventually lost our nerve and allowed Southeast Asia to be overrun by communist armies. We let the greater evil defeat the lesser evil because we didn't want anything to do with evil. In the Soviet mind there can be no such dilemma. Communist ideology, rather than refusing to employ evil for its ideal ends, throws all caution to the wind. Morality is suspended as means have supplanted ends. Today the Russian rulers are inhuman realists. Communist ideology, thanks to Lenin's instrumentalist vision, has both feet on the ground, though its soul is as black as cinder. Therefore, in the struggle for power, victory is still open to the communists because they know how to subordinate all other considerations for the sake of winning. But look at what wins: total nihilism, total destruction, and a government which crushes all human values under its heel. And what of *our* side? What of the Americans? *We* have an evil eye for victory and place many frivolous considerations high above it. This merely illustrates the danger for those who place phantoms like absolute good and evil, humanity, love, or ideal peace, at the center of their world-view. What never occurs to the absolute moralist is that an unrealizable good, *at the center,* castrates the whole. This can be avoided only if good intends victory by means of a judicious collaboration with lesser evils. Man must adopt a somewhat blemished, compromised standard, which is the best that can be arrived at under the circumstances. And please note that this means, especially, the avoidance of Lenin's extreme instrumentalism, which entirely does away with values and standards altogether. The lesson found in this situation is clear. The noble statesman, who defends an imperfect civilization, must be certain that the good he defends is, at bottom, realizable, and that it is better than the alternatives. Man must avoid the mistakes which both communists and liberals have made in worshipping impossible or absolutist goals, which lead the communist to a victory worse than defeat and the liberal to ineffectuality and inevitable extermination. Man must not slander the instruments of victory nor must he worship them as ends in themselves. It is much better in politics to judge of what is possible and work from there, rather than attempting to bullet-proof oneself with holiness.

37. Soviet leaders liken themselves to metal. The Soviet dictator,

----

Josef Vissarionovich Dzhugashvili, gave himself the name "Stalin" because it literally means "steel" — the man of steel. The founder of the Soviet secret police, Felix Dzerzhinsky, dubbed himself "Iron Feliks." KGB General Alexander Shelepin, founder of the KGB's Department of Disinformation and one of those who deposed Khrushchev, adopted the nickname "Iron Shurik." Gromyko, referring to Gorbachev's smile, was quick to assure everyone that the new party chief had "teeth of iron." As Westerners we would laugh at the idea of "Iron Ike" or "Rock Reagan." Americans want their leaders to be likable persons—nice, happy, affable. It is precisely this aversion to "men of steel" that marks us.

38. *Our Domino History.* — Once upon a time there was a theory that everyone laughed at. It was called the Domino Theory. An old man named Eisenhower gave it to us. Serious people do not advance this notion, especially since it has fallen out of fashion. Yet, why speak of the Domino Theory when we already have a Domino History—that is, in the fall of country after country, over many decades, with a regularity that continues even after the alleged collapse of the Soviet Union? For since that collapse, South Africa and the Congo have fallen to the communists, though nobody has bothered to notice.

39. From studying ancient history the single surest observation is that economically advanced states often suffer defeat at the hands of less advanced states. Thus did Greece triumph over Persia, Sparta over Athens, Macedonia over the rest of Greece, Rome over Carthage, and the barbarians over Rome. Our problem today is that we have seen two centuries of the victory of money, and we have accepted this phenomenon as a new law of history. We ought to consider, instead, what special factors have intervened to give money this temporary edge; namely, that money, for much of the period of its success, was not defended by a money aristocracy (as it is now) but by the "throwback" remnants of feudalism with its warrior traditions. Now that feudalism is flat dead, isn't it logical to assume that raw plutocracy will be eaten by predators?

40. Albert Camus wrote: "The majority of revolutions are shaped by, and derive their originality from, murder. All, or almost all, have been homicidal." [51]

Turning the ant-farm upside-down kills the ants. A tragic situation for ants. And if the decent man cares about his ants, if he refuses to turn the ant-farm upside down, if he does not relish the thought of destruction, then, from a certain perspective, the "decent man" is himself an ant who leaves the leveling to history's bulldozer, Vladimir Lenin & Company.

---

[51] Albert Camus, *The Rebel: An Essay on Man in Revolt* (New York: Vintage Books, 1956), p. 105.

Good old Vladimir was one of those "interesting" boys who wondered what all those stupid little ants would do if he buried them under the rubble of their own hill. Who can deny a certain fascination for a ruined ant-farm?

41. Sometimes Pentagon analysts have whispered to each other about Russia's "Potemkin missiles." Sometimes they have sweated under cool Geneva skies in order to eliminate those missiles for the sake of their children's children. But the zigs and zags of fear and jubilation, of detente and crisis, taught them nothing. Never did they understand the Soviet Union. The cliché most popular, most quoted and least analyzed by this crowd, was Churchill's description of Russia as "a riddle wrapped in a mystery inside an enigma." For people lacking the least trace of common sense Churchill's statement has a certain poignancy. But for anyone who bothers to read Russian history, there isn't any riddle or enigma at all. Russia's tradition is to expand, to push out its frontiers. The only riddle is the weakness of the West. In all actuality, Russia's leaders are the simplest people on earth. They are predicated entirely on power, bent entirely on acquiring slaves and loot. How strange it is to imagine that something so commonplace as the pursuit of power is regarded as a mystery! There is no mystery, but only a misunderstanding. The West has always misunderstood the East. Comrade Stalin, if you remember, was once our "Uncle Joe"—a mass-murdering humanitarian. Khrushchev, who promised to bury us, was called a liberal reformer. Brezhnev, the scourge of Africa and Afghanistan, was thought to be a man of peace. Gorbachev is an impostor too. And now we have the "actor," Yeltsin, and his incredible "democratic" circus!

The explanation for all the confusion about Russia, and all the talk about enigmas and riddles, stem from the fact that totalitarian police states are always telling lies and we are always believing them. In this respect we have adopted a time-honored role—as dupes. Machiavelli once said: "Men are so simple, and so much creatures of circumstance, that the deceiver will always find someone ready to be deceived."[52]

Today's military analyst will never get the sense of Russia as the motherland of deception because he is so much a creature of books and abstractions. The Kremlin has coddled him with ten thousand lies, and he wants to *at least* believe a thousand of them.

Russia is simple, so simple. It has become the greatest destructive force since the Deluge. It makes promises and devours its victims at the first opportunity. It is implacable. One only has to follow the finger of Rosa Luxemburg as she mutters: "That is Lenin. Observe his obstinate

---

[52] Machiavelli, *The Prince*, p. 100.

self-willed skull."[53]

42. Joseph Schumpeter said that the state, "which is the product of the clashes and compromises between feudal lords and bourgeoisie, will form part of the ashes from which the socialist phoenix is to rise."[54]

The current type of the state, which is different from the ancient type, both in its structure and its tendency, is nothing but a cudgel waiting to be taken up by the first opportunist. The framework of this modern instrument initially rested on structures similar to those of the ancient states: religion and aristocracy. Over time, however, the aristocrats developed a common national identity with their chattel. That was when the centralizing and nationalist institution of monarchy began to rise up, and found an ally—and a revenue—in the rising commercial power. A businessman, it turned out, was worth more than many serfs. At first the monarchs tried to squeeze money out of the commercial classes. But in the end, the monarchs found themselves on uneven ground. Gradually it became clear that only parliamentary arrangements would suffice. And once the parliaments were unleashed, the kings were doomed. The Crown held out its hand for money, and Money held out its hand for the crown. In fact, the money power swept the old feudal aristocracy aside, supplanting it with democracy (an "aristocracy of blackguards," as Byron called it). In other words: Money transformed the state.

The ramifications were enormous. But let us start with the central ramification, or the central fact of this process; namely, that the money-man, incubating within the protective strata of feudal patronage, eventually grew strong enough to push out the old virtues, and the old aristocrats. His weapons were not merely money and credit, but growing out of money there came liberty and democracy. The money-egg was hatched by the old order; and as soon as the money-man emerged, he devoured the old order—murdering his own parent. In a well-ordered society built by rank, one finally does away with rank. In a law-abiding society built by virtue and religion, one finally does away with virtue and religion. Therefore equality, democracy, and secular entertainment became the pillars of the state. Whatever one calls this type of state, it is unlike any of its predecessors. In reality it isn't a state at all. It is more like an organized anarchy which is constantly growing, spreading, and colonizing, with money as its supreme ruling principle.

This new situation of money swallowing the state meant that money was bound to swallow all ideas that pertained to the state. Thus "political philosophy" came to be swallowed by "political economy." And every

[53] Louis Fischer, *The Life of Lenin* (New York: Harper & Row, 1965), pp. 58-59.

[54] Schumpeter, *Capitalism, Socialism and Democracy*, p. 169.

related idea — especially *moral* ideas — were put into the service of money; attempting to justify the primacy of money *after the fact*; and in such a way that no moral scruple, no Heavenly caveat, should bar the way to hedonism, to materialism, and to the Epicurean ideology which the wisest ancient philosophers had warned against.

After many decades this Epicurean Revolution was complete. In fact, it was so successful that even thrift fell into ill repute — as an outmoded and cramped throwback, contrary to human comfort and good economics. The leading economic theoretician of his time, John Maynard Keynes, understood all of this when he advocated deficit spending. He understood the spirit of the new god and became thereby an apostle of bad habits, a man who saw to the bottom of the holy scriptures of economics and knew—with intuitive genius—where next the world of money had to turn.

The old bulwark of the strong state, the inward virtue of self-control, then came to be sneered at. Ideas of duty and discipline became passé. To say the word "duty" was to utter an hypocrisy. The new bulwarks, guaranteed to make a weak state, came to the fore. That is, people began to worship permissive and anarchistic gods. These were Freedom, Non-Authoritarianism, and "Rights." If the state once stood for order, it now concerned itself with social engineering, that is, with the breakup of order. Family, community, and race were to be smashed. The only thing to be tolerated was the individual, the atom, the prerequisite of the totalitarian state, the ideal fodder, the ideal informant, the ideal victim, the godless little cog who stood for nothing and would fall for anything.

And here we are, just now discovering, that a society composed purely of atoms is not a society. It is formless clay waiting for a Stalin to mold it into some untoward shape. And among those things which give human clay the power to resist the potter's wheel are race, religion, and nationality. Such things can make atoms into coherent units of attack and defense. But when the general shape has been liberalized to the point of becoming an unthinking mass of disparate atoms, there is nothing but readiness for the leash. The emerging totalitarians have only to divide and conquer something that is already divided and therefore begging to be conquered.

43. Since man turned to science and away from religion, history has been the story of the perfection of efficiency (*i.e.*, the instrumentalist's perfection of means). In 1917 this story broke up into two sub-plots, as one part of the world (the Russian part) embarked on the path of political efficiency, and the other (the American part) embarked on the path of economic efficiency. Each has pursued its form of efficiency with a monomaniacal singleness of mind that defies any admixture of other elements. Both represent pathological episodes. In each case the goal *is*

the means. That is, money as an end in itself, and power as an end in itself.

In this context, the philosopher Nietzsche said that man repeats the same mistake over and over again, of setting up his means as the end, losing track of where he is going altogether. Alas, poor man, with his short span of attention.

44. When Christ said that man does not live by bread alone, he also might have thrown in, for the sake of modern readers, that man does not live by science alone. Bread, Christ was saying, sustains the body, but not the soul. Science, too, is like this. And a scientific society (where science is the basic precept) despiritualizes its constituent elements.

45. Albert Camus believed that (since the death of God) *justice* has primary importance. By justice he meant the question of moral order. But, as God is dead, moral order cannot exist any longer. Man must therefore achieve such an order for himself. He must build it.

But in all of this Camus runs directly into a problem. Man is not up to the task of achieving moral order for himself. The temptations along the way are too great. More importantly, the idea of divine grace *disappears*. And this is disastrous.

In light of the feebleness of our "justice," it appears that Christianity was, without doubt, the most positive movement in all history. This fact, quite at variance with current intellectual fashions, will be the next great discovery of the secular mind: a discovery based on the fact that the grace of God is superior to the justice of man.

46. We notice in this analysis that capitalism, as a system based on the primacy of money, only rules by concession; while communism rules by shedding blood. In other words, capitalism thirsts for agreement and lives off the fat of the land, while communism thirsts for victims and lives off submissions and sacrifices.

Here we see a type of algebra, a logic, with a direction and tendency of its own. It is ironic that the great revolutions to liberate man have come to this: to a choice between these two forms. One which is power in decadence, and the other which is power altogether broken loose from its moorings.

47. In modern democracy the will of the people has replaced God as the wellspring of political-moral legitimacy. In Russia, however, a more traditional and historically successful principle was inserted: aristocracy under the guise of the "vanguard party." Thus Leninism alone retains a higher and more conscious type of politics — pursuing its power interests only as a disciplined elite can.

48. We do not yet grasp this inverted theology of Russian totalitarianism. We do not yet grasp its inheritance from the Church, from the Czar, from the Okhrana, and from the xenophobic instincts of old Russia. Notice the following symptoms of the aforesaid inversion: The Party is infallible, it is sovereign, it is pure. Everything it does is justified. It is all-powerful and all-wise. Consequently, the Party cannot respect any law because that would place it below something else.

Consider the observation of Joseph Schumpeter, who wrote: "Marxism *is* a religion. To the believer it presents, first, a system of ultimate ends that embody the meaning of life and are absolute standards by which to judge events and actions; and, secondly, a guide to those ends which implies a plan of salvation and the indication of the evil from which mankind, or a chosen section of mankind, is to be saved."[55]

This question of Marxism *as a religion* is of critical importance, especially when superimposed over the Christian background of modernity. We see in Marxism certain Christian reflexes still unexorcized. We see, for example, the desire for a kind of afterworld, for a climactic battle which brings an end to history and a return to Eden (the withering away of the state). The basic difference, of course, was Marxism's rejection of God and spiritual life. Marxism was positivistic, as Marx wanted to appeal to the prejudices of his time. I must cite Schumpeter again, who said that the Marxist message "was framed and conveyed in such a way as to be acceptable to the positivistic mind of its time — which was essentially bourgeois no doubt, but there is no paradox in saying that Marxism is essentially a product of the bourgeois mind."[56]

49. The most transparent of the bourgeois philosophers, who quite properly described himself as an economist, was Ludwig von Mises. He, too, realized that rationalism and liberalism had failed. And he was quite sad about it. Mises did not blame the bourgeoisie, but the masses. "The masses lack the capacity to think logically," he said. "A momentary, special advantage that may be enjoyed immediately appears more important than a lasting greater gain that must be deferred." Of course, he was right. This was also a part of the truth, and a part of the political failure of economic rationalism. But Mises never realized that all of this was sociologically intrinsic; that leftism (even in today's neo-conservative garb) is the firstborn of liberal democracy and cannot be made to go away.

[55] Ibid., p. 5.
[56] Ibid., p. 6.

----

50. I am afraid that the Communist Party Soviet Union (even though it officially no longer exists) is still fully committed to its own divinity. We in the West are only fooling ourselves that recent changes represent an internal conversion away from the old view.

It should be understood that beneath the rhetoric of the KGB ventriloquists and their dummy, Boris Yeltsin, there is not the slightest commitment to the sovereignty of the people. The fact is: Western-style democracy has no chance in Russia.

51. Americans believe in communism's doom because they believe that democracy is "the only way to go." America has faith in the hackneyed slogans of its demagogues. Democracy, Americans say, will triumph everywhere. It is only a matter of time. But this is a pathetic faith, which cannot possibly survive the shock of what is coming. For we will not find wisdom or virtue in the masses. We will only find those sheep-like qualities that invariably call forth a leader.

52. By investigating the two versions of secular civilization (consumerism and totalitarianism) we begin to suspect that one is Slow Suicide and the other is Mass Murder. The formula suggested by this odd conjunction is: Slow Suicide will one day ask Mass Murder for assistance.

53. And what about civil religion—which permeated the life of George Washington, for example?

With the true democratic system, which has reached an absurd degree of refinement today, the people aren't really capable of demanding obedience from themselves. Civil religion is therefore unlikely, as we are not sufficiently disciplined.

Also, we must agree that democracy corrupts people, as the politicians invariably attempt to buy votes. Here we have a disgusting formula for the downward spiraling of the soul as well as the state.

In this context one begins to notice that "democratic morality" is a self-defeating proposition. For under democracy the democratic authorities are hardly authoritative in the classical sense. They are impressionistic and subjective. In other words, democratic authority is an oxymoron. When the desires of the many are consulted, it is the desire to be free of responsibility which slowly, over decades, gets the upper hand. Here genuine authority is held to be odious. Here punishment itself is bounced out of court, replaced by notions of rehabilitation. The authority figure is automatically maligned as rigid, reactionary, backward, poorly adjusted, or even sadistic.

As a corollary to this collapse of authority, there is a collapse of morality. Democracy teaches the right of numbers, of sheer flesh, of the gross weight of meat. This is not a moral concept, but an expedient device for arbitrating conflicts. Aside from this, our extreme democratic morality is only a confused mix of pity, envy, sentimentalism, and libertinism.

54. I ought to interject that the top Bolsheviks did not talk about "justice" as their goal. Most of them were more honest. In many respects, this honesty has been underrated.

The founder of the Soviet secret police, Felix Dzerzhinsky, with that frankness only possible to a true aristocrat, once said: "Do not believe that I seek revolutionary forms of justice. We don't need justice at this point. We are engaged today in hand-to-hand combat, to the death, to the end! I propose, I demand, the organization of revolutionary annihilation against all active counterrevolutionaries."

Even Lenin, the "wise" and "humane" founder of the Soviet state, asked: "Is it impossible to find among us a Fouquier-Tinville to tame our wild counterrevolutionaries?"

Trotsky wrote a book called *Communism and Terrorism*. In this book, he stated: "Without the Red Terror, the Russian bourgeoisie, together with the world bourgeoisie, would throttle us...."

Maxim Gorky's diary contains the following passage, which relates to the outcome of the Bolshevik Revolution: "I feel terrible, like a Christopher Columbus who has finally reached the shores of America but is disgusted by it."

Communist principles, chock-full of pride and conceit, are the raw material of tragedy. Camus wrote: "To abandon oneself to principles is really to die, and to die for an impossible love which is the contrary of life."[57]

Louis Saint-Just anticipated the Russian system when he predicted: "Ingenious crime will be exalted into a kind of religion and criminals will be in the sacred hierarchy."

55. Perhaps our inability to understand communism may be found in our ideological nearness to it. For we, too, are creatures of principle *above* decency, as today's rationalist principle has been transmuted into deity. Consider the danger of overestimating the intellect in politics: principles alone cannot keep the imagination transfixed or purify a man's motives. Principle is, in the end, a weak and sickly god. But, as the communists found out, a stronger god does exist: the god of Terror.

56. The scientism of the Left, and of that whole crowd of meddling

---

[57] Camus, *The Rebel*, p. 130.

social engineers, is one of the roots of modern mass destruction. The rationalism inherent in scientism gives the social engineer a sense of knowing the correct path, even if he doesn't know every crook in the road. Therefore he represents a misunderstanding—personified. And we can see in this personification the missing link between the liberal mind and the mind of Felix Dzerzhinsky.

Related to this, Camus wrote: "He who does not know everything cannot kill everything." What is meant here is: He who does not know everything shouldn't take it upon himself to destroy everything, to overturn and revolutionize everything. For one can only destroy wisely when one knows what one is destroying. It is precisely this lack of wisdom which characterizes the Left. Here is the essence of communist destructiveness: *that the communists have no idea what they are destroying*. It is almost as if they have embraced a cult of destruction for destruction's sake.

57. We ought to learn a lesson from the age of revolutions. We ought to realize that absolute or abstract freedom, as sought by revolutionaries, leads to terrorism, and abstract law leads to repression. Camus was right to emphasize decency over principle. But sadly, Camus could go little beyond this. What weapon, may I ask, did he fashion to combat the passions?—to combat the darker side of human nature? The communists found such a weapon in the Red Terror, which was itself an aspect of the dark side of human nature. One might say that the logic of the Red Terror was: Evil would drive out evil. And in a certain sense, when you consider Stalin's purges against the Old Bolsheviks, we might even applaud.

58. The human capacity for evil must be considered. All our great projects of reform and social perfection run aground upon this one rock. Immediately we see, in the context of the American welfare state, the ugly effects of social service careerism, contract padding, and outright larceny. We find that our efficient bureaucratic machines lack integrity.

Goodbye, oh ye principles! Fare thee well! The day finally dawns when we discover the hollowness of mere bureaucratic efficiency.

59. What depresses us is not that virtue cannot win, but that virtue doesn't seem to appear at all. Non-virtue, in a variety of forms, decides everything and appears everywhere.

Camus writes: "and the earth will be delivered to naked force, which will decide whether or not man is divine. Thus lies and violence are adopted in the same spirit in which religion is adopted."[58]

---

[58] Ibid., 135 - 6.

60. Pleasure in destruction is a real thing. It is a fact with which we must contend. Sometimes the lust to destroy is unconscious, subtle; that is, underground. But with certain rare reflective men it shows itself. It eats its way to the surface.

The Marquis de Sade wrote of an "aristocracy of crime." He spoke of desire as the universal political principle leading to a hell of desires, a bureaucracy of vice, organized into an efficient system. De Sade declared: "I abhor nature.... I should like to upset its plans, to thwart its progress, to halt the stars in their courses, to overturn the floating spheres of space, to destroy what serves nature and to succor all that harms it; in a word, to insult all its works."

This satanic longing to wreck creation was also shared by Karl Marx, who wrote:

"With disdain I will throw my gauntlet
Full in the face of the world,
And see the collapse of this pygmy giant
Whose fall will not stifle my ardour.
Then will I wander godlike and victorious
Through the ruins of the world
And, giving my words an active force,
I will feel equal to the Creator."[59]

Was Lenin also obsessed by a destructive idea?

In this context, it is one of those prescient remarks of Dostoyevsky, that Christ's return would happen in Russia. One is immediately led to suspect an error in his formulation; namely, that it isn't Christ who comes via Russia, but Antichrist.

"We will keep in mind," says Schumpeter, "that socialism aims at higher goals than full bellies, exactly as Christianity means more than the somewhat hedonistic values of heaven and hell."[60]

61. According to Lenin's wife, Krupskaya, what Lenin feared most of all was the softness of his own comrades. When a resolution for abolishing the death penalty appeared, Lenin was infuriated. Why? Because he knew that every state is founded on violence. This fact cannot be denied. Trotsky acknowledged and Max Weber confirmed it. But Weber added that a state, if it is to stabilize itself, must establish its use of force as legitimate. In other words, brute force alone is not sufficient. Some element of persuasion is also necessary. The problem in Bolshevism, which necessitated such notoriously bloody measures,

---

[59] Trans. D. McLellan, *Marx before Marxism*, MacMillan.

[60] Schumpeter, *Capitalism, Socialism and Democracy*, p. 170.

was the fact that its doctrine is so boring that it fails to persuade. Not many people have believed in it, then or now. This being the case we cannot be surprised to learn of Dzerzhinsky's statement that: "Hostages must be taken from among...people of high social position, large landowners, factory owners, prominent officials and academics, close relatives of people formerly in power, etc." And, therefore, various programs were also initiated: concentration camps for "suspicious elements," enemy agents, profiteers, marauders, hooligans, counterrevolutionary agitators, saboteurs, and other parasites. Pretty soon you've got a solid twenty percent of the population either in front of firing squads or on their way to the camps. The rest, I might add, are kept under surveillance.

Of course, we cannot deny the subtle power of intimidation as a form of persuasion. It is entirely possible that people who are terrorized will allow themselves to believe the words of their tormentors. And this may be how it actually happened. Trotsky said that "Intimidation is a powerful instrument of policy, both internationally and internally. War, like revolution, is founded upon intimidation." And Stalin seems to have proved Trotsky right. If the lackeys of the bourgeoisie and the agents of imperialism are afraid of you, they might just lose their nerve. They might just melt away out of fear.

Unlike the White Terror, which consisted of isolated atrocities, the Red Terror was state-sponsored and systematic. It remains so today, under the cover of Yeltsin's liberalism. And the wisest people of Russia, though they are perhaps told otherwise, know instinctively that the Terror is still looming over them, not far beneath the surface of a bogus "Commonwealth."

62. One ought to read the story of Lenin's regime at its inception. The communists thought of themselves as a new race of samurai. At that time one of these samurai wrote the following note to Lenin: "The death penalty...is utilized so often at the front, for all possible reasons and on all possible occasions, that the discipline of the Red Army could be called sanguinary in the full sense of the word."

One searches in vain the annals of the American Revolution and the American Civil War for anything remotely approaching this. Perhaps that's because our leaders of 1776 and 1863 weren't promising a utopia. And since they didn't promise a utopia they had no justification to commit so many homicides.

63. The communist "Peace Offensive" was a Lenin original. First Lenin signed a peace treaty with Germany, which he regarded as a tactic to get the upper hand. Then, when the Russian Civil War was going badly and Polish troops were converging on Minsk, Lenin proposed an

armistice with Poland. Through an envoy Lenin suggested that the Poles could get everything they wanted. In reality, Lenin was playing for time. But the Poles were tempted, they began licking their chops, and halted their advance (expecting to reap the rewards of a peace settlement). This gave Lenin a free hand against the White Army, so that the Whites suffered a severe blow on 14 December 1919. On that very day Lenin's Polish envoy returned to Moscow, having broken off the talks with Poland. The Poles had been swindled and were left without support from the defeated Whites. "Red armies forward! Onward, heroes. On to Warsaw!" The Poles almost lost their national sovereignty then and there.

This was the first example of a Soviet "Peace Offensive." It worked then and it still works. The technique is simply one of insincere negotiations to gain time or other advantages, with no intention to keep faith. Today we see this sort of thing in the START Treaty, and in the new non-aggression pact with Germany. Each party imagines that it is getting what it wants. In reality, the Western countries will never get what they want, because the only cure for Bolshevism is bullets, not diplomacy.

But now we believe that communism is dead! — *An even better, and much improved, form of the "Peace Offensive."*

64. In passing, as we examine the Soviet attempt to conquer Poland in the year 1920, it is of interest to recall that Trotsky and Tukhachevsky both blamed Stalin for the military disaster which the Reds suffered during the following July. What is amazing is the perfectness of Stalin's final revenge against all parties involved. Trotsky and Tukhachevsky were both murdered by Stalin's henchmen, and twenty-five years later Stalin would conquer Poland without them. The effect of this sort of historical "cleansing" almost tempts us to think that Stalin wasn't to blame for the Red Army disaster of 1920. And the prowess he later showed makes us suspect that in 1920 Trotsky and Tukhachevksy were overrated. This idea (or impression) is one of those curious tricks of Stalinism, which actively and subtly influences the historian by the sheer weight of its later successes.

65. There was much to do about the autonomy and independence of the outlying Soviet Republics in the early years of Bolshevism. For example, there was the People's Republic of Buhhara, of Khorezm, of Armenia, Georgia and Azerbaijan. "It was no secret to anyone," said the Georgian leader Makharadze, "that under the circumstances of the time [1920] the activities of the Communist Party consisted exclusively of preparing for armed insurrection against [us]."

In seventy years' time, little has changed.

66. The key to Soviet history does not really lie in the Stalin period. The Stalin period is mere algebra, a mere extension of necessity from the Russian Civil War. The key period is when the foundations were laid by Lenin, Trotsky, and Dzerzhinsky. During this initial phase of Soviet history we see the same blindness and foolishness in the West, the same abandonment of the White Army (later repeated in Vietnam, Cambodia, Angola, and now, with the merest sleight of hand, in South Africa), which always spells defeat for the anti-communist cause.

67.   Something should be said about Lenin's fascination for the Prussian general, Carl von Clausewitz, for it was Clausewitz who emphasized the "dominance of the destructive principle," denying the likelihood of bloodless victories.

Considered in this light, the ideal weapons, from the Leninist-Clausewitzian viewpoint, have now been fielded. These are the atomic weapons. This fact has not received the attention it deserves. It has neither given pause to our analysts nor shivers to our politicians. We glide along with our anti-Clausewitzian concepts of "bloodless victory" and "balance of terror," but twenty or thirty thousand Soviet-built hydrogen bombs will not go away.

68.   Clausewitz wrote that "one must keep the dominant characteristics of both belligerents in mind. Out of those characteristics a certain centre of gravity develops, the hub of all power and movement, on which everything depends."

In the present crisis, we have forgotten that a hub exists. We have neglected the dominant characteristics. Specifically, the superiority of the totalitarian, in his struggle for dominion, comes from his classic warrior stance, while the Westerner is, at best, a business man. Western strategy has dropped war as its central concern. The writings of Thomas Schelling and Edward Luttwak, as two examples of this, deal with the problems of war *and* peace, with the emphasis on peace. The bourgeois mind is repulsed by the absoluteness and the harshness of war. And the intellectual background of the bourgeois strategist, which is full of mathematics and "game theory," leads him into a curious kind of naivete. Instead of confronting problems realistically, he rationalizes his wishful thinking (*i.e.*, that war can be avoided).

Contrariwise, the Clausewitzian mind, as Lenin adapted it to communism, sees reality as a process rather than something frozen in a web of principles. Thus, recent Western concepts — deterrence, balance of power, containment, etc. — fly in the face of Clausewitz's basic teaching. Since each of these contain a formula, each represents a crude reductionism. It must be pointed out that Clausewitz was suspicious of principles. He saw war as a flux, and refused to make superficial generalizations about it. Generalizations were traps to ensnare the lazy and the stupid. War, said Clausewitz, is very complicated. *This* is the wisdom of Clausewitz, whose thinking shied away from too much abstraction, and who abhorred dogmatical pronouncements. Thus, the ideas of our American strategists and "game theorists" would probably have appalled him.

69. Camus writes: "Does the end justify the means? That is possible. But what will justify the end? To that question, which historical thought leaves pending, rebellion replies: the means."[61]

We look into Soviet history and find the most brutal instruments of power in the service of a future utopia. Underneath this outward appearance, however, we find the communist infatuation with various instruments of power. The goal of a future communist world, of course, remains; but the passion and allegiance of the top people has been subtly transferred from Utopia to Power. The obsession ceases to be ideological at the deepest and highest level. This is why communism is so strong. Mere ideology is quite feeble, as it is usually only the idiots and clowns who long remain infatuated by it. Power, on the other hand, can obsess an intelligent man. And it can obsess him for a long time. Therefore, Camus is right when he suggests that the real code of "the rebel" is actually satanic: to rule in Hell rather than serve in Heaven.

70. The Soviet Union is satanic, not only in its methods, but in its purposes. It is satanic in the sense of shaking one's fist at the heavens, of defying Nature and "Nature's God." The formula for Soviet communism has been, from the beginning, a rebellion not only against nature, but also against human nature. Here the idea is to remake man in the rebel's image. To mold a new kind of human being called *Homo sovieticus.* This formula is, in a strange way, moralistic. It purports to be a new moral foundation. But in reality it is nothing but arrogance. You cannot make a mockery out of that which is inherent. You cannot wipe away the heavens. It is no wonder that, in this effort to tyrannize over reality, the communist comes to practice an inverted morality which says: "Thou *shalt* kill." This strange inversion, this ultimate pathway leading down from the Enlightenment, also leads us inexorably to the war of mass destruction itself, or the negation of the negation (*i.e.*, nihilism annihilating itself).

71. Albert Schweitzer, writing in the early 1920s, noted: "The

---

[61] Camus, *The Rebel*, p. 292.

----

future of civilization depends on our overcoming the meaninglessness and hopelessness which characterize the thoughts and convictions of men to-day."[62]

Indeed, this is the problem. "It is clear to everyone," wrote Schweitzer, "that the suicide of civilization is in progress. What yet remains of it is no longer safe. It is still standing, indeed, because it was not exposed to the destructive pressure which overwhelmed the rest, but, like the rest, is built upon rubble, and the next landslide will very likely carry it away."[63]

Schweitzer tells us that ethical ideals, based on reason, began to alter the general environment; the environment, in turn, gave rise to new ethical ideals. After four generations "this mutual understanding and co-operation between ethical ideals and reality began to break down."

Schweitzer adds that "Without resistance, without complaint, civilization abdicated."[64] He further says that philosophy renounced her duty, rationalism failed, and nothing came in its place except nihilism. Why rationalism failed is, of course, a problem unto itself. But why humanity failed is more to the point, perhaps having to do with humanity's neurotic optimism and sensualism.

I know that my analysis, in this regard, is a bitter pill. Every sensualist is bound to be galvanized against this kind of prognosis. It is unpopular to attack a good time. To avoid this unpopularity, and to appeal to other emotions, the usual way of attacking sensualism has been to attack money. Therefore, when Oswald Spengler says that money is bound to succumb to blood, he is merely saying that sensualism will eventually be brushed aside by martial discipline. That's really what it boils down to.

72.   Aristotle taught that man belongs to a certain level of moderation. Leftist rationalism has taught us how to idolize the extremes. In doing this it has promised us too much reason, too much freedom, and too much democracy. It never occurs to us that too much of anything can be fatal. You might have noticed, in this context, that the world isn't rational or democratic enough for the leftist. The everyday world doesn't fit nicely into all those enlightened categories and "ought-to-have-beens." The manic humanitarianism of the Left, with its boiling indignation against the stupidities of the past, prepares the way for a boiling indignation against the stupidities of the present. In relation to this Camus explains that "the secret to Europe is that it no longer loves life. Its blind men entertain the puerile belief that to love one single day of life amounts to justifying whole centuries of oppression."[65]

---

[62] Albert Schweitzer, *The Decay and Restoration of Civilization* (London, 1950), p. xi.

[63] Ibid., p. 3.

[64] Ibid., p. 4.

The Left's rejection of the world, in fact, compliments the other dangerous aspects of its creed. It refuses to accept reality gracefully, and it refuses to acknowledge its own foolishness in seeking impossible and unearthly extremes.

73. If we dare to think about nuclear world war, then let us do so in the context of the sixth to seventh of November 1917. This is when Bolshevism seized power in Russia. What is interesting about this first episode is the character of the power that was being overthrown. I mean the Kerensky government—that epitome of flabby moderation. It was a government in the *coming* style: impotent in the face of Bolshevism. It exemplified the incomprehension of the propertied classes in the face of the Red samurai; that is, incomprehension in the face of infiltration, propaganda, deception, and demagoguery. It seems to have been of no importance whatsoever that the Bolsheviks were unpopular and out-numbered. What counted was their ruthless energy pitted against the slipshod complacency of the Kerensky liberals.

74. The Bolsheviks strove, through various means, to bring about unrest and confusion. This type of environment was, and is, more suitable to them. In the international sphere, on the eve of a thermonuclear missile war, a similar confusion in international affairs will also prove "helpful." In this sense the great thermonuclear coup will probably resemble the coup against Aleksandr Kerensky. For the pattern of revolutionary tactics has been seared into communist thinking. And as all other thinkers, the communist thinker acts from what he knows and from what he studies.

It is interesting, even darkly humorous, to learn that the Menshevik Dan said the Bolsheviks couldn't succeed for economic reasons: that the grain supply would be cut off by the peasants, who would starve the Bolsheviks into submission. I wonder if Dan ever lived to see the Ukraine famine a decade later? Certainly his "economic" critique of Bolshevik plans was a very self-satisfied and "bourgeois" critique. We've heard this sort of thing again and again. "The Soviet Union cannot economically survive the consequences of its own policies. Ergo, it cannot survive a Third World War."

Humbug!

History shows us a string of communist victories, in country after country, as socialism slowly creeps across the globe. If nothing more formidable than bourgeois economic theory stands to prevent a Bolshevik takeover of the world, then the world shall be taken. Bad theories are no match for bullets.

---

[65] Camus, *The Rebel*, p. 305.

75. Hitler, as a visionary, appears to have seen that the bourgeoisie was totally weak and helpless. He saw that Leninism threatened to take over the world. He therefore adapted some ideas from Lenin, mixing them with Nietzsche and racism, into a new conception, which was the Nazi state. But Hitler's sociology, which was domestically superior to Lenin's, proved internationally inferior. Hitler was a treaty-breaker, but he had a bad habit of telling the truth, of wearing his intentions on his sleeve. Hitler never understood how to milk the Great Western Cow. Stalin, however, milked the cow and won.

76. I think it should be obvious, at least by now, that Nietzsche vaguely anticipated Lenin. For Nietzsche asks: "Where are the barbarians of the twentieth century?" He fully recognizes that Western civilization is about to be swept away. His only question is: Who will wield the broom?

It may be argued, as well, that Nietzsche's spirit awaited the inevitable destruction of the old order. His writings were meant for the period "after" the holocaust. Therefore, Hitler was premature. A premature birth. From this I derive the notion that more Hitlers are coming: an age of Hitlers. *The twenty-first century.*

77. Kerenksy's Provisional Government defended its key stronghold with a women's battalion. That was the type of military unit Kerensky used to prop himself up. In keeping with Kerensky's style, on the night of the Bolshevik coup, this battalion of women launched a "vigorous" counter-attack. When the smoke cleared, Kerensky's women were captured and raped.

In the midst of this a Cadet minister asks a Cadet minister: "What kind of a party is it that cannot send us three hundred armed men?"

But nevertheless, they had—at least—three hundred women!

And isn't America governed by this same Kerensky government? And won't our own Cadet ministers ask the same perplexed question?

78. It almost seems as if God has suffered communism to come into existence *expressly* for the purpose of carrying out His will. In this context we shouldn't deny the historical pattern of Babylonian captivities linked to a notion of divine chastisement. It is much more useful for us to say that God has arranged a sort of cleanup, so that when the power suddenly drains out of our television sets and the spell of video nirvana is broken, we can sing "glory hallelujah" as we are butchered and terrorized back into the heavenly fold.

79. Politics, of course, is a jumble. It is a game of great complexity.

But when the enemy is so absolutely fixed in his objectives and so long-standing in his methods, how could we miss the boat, as we apparently are missing it? The contradictions and obfuscations, intentional and incidental, which are now clouding up our skies, defy cognitive dissidence. I refer to the fake revolutions, the proxies, the false fronts, the bogus analyses; where Left is called Right; where revolutionaries are called reactionaries and dictatorship, democracy; where peace is war and arming is disarming. Who is not confused? It is perfectly understandable that in the Age of Casualness, at a time when the experts are casual to the point of idiocy, we have failed to detect the bad smells, the carnivorous smiles, and the hidden daggers that are prepared for us.

80. Those who have never interacted with communists, who do not realize what rationality and science have done to our faith in God, will never accept my conclusions. Those on the right who only know economic theories, who only understand the economic and technical strengths of capitalism, will fail to see that hedonism is inherent in the capitalist ideal, and that hedonism is more destructive of the soul than communism's Spartan cruelty. In this context, was it not Adam Smith who proposed the moral superiority of an Epicurean social system in his *Theory of Moral Sentiments*? In our own time, I believe that Adam Smith's experiment has been accomplished, but I am afraid the results are not what he hoped for. Cicero warned in his *de Finibus Bonorum et Malorum* that Epicureanism is a watered-down hedonism and, as such, highly destructive of the state and its interests; especially destructive of the national security, where the ability to attack and defend is paramount. In America, despite our religious background, a subtle sensualism has eaten away our spiritual armor. We are no longer as morally strong as before. We are no longer as intellectually honest. Surely, corruption and weakness have always been part of the human condition. Even so, there are degrees of corruption. And in our Cold War history, in the very term "Cold War," there lies a hedonistic rottenness, an unwillingness to make the necessary sacrifices for the sake of our children. We hoped, throughout all of this, to entice our foe with prosperity. All the while, we were the ones enticed, by dreams of peace and plenty.

81. Either kill the tiger or be eaten by him—one or the other.

4

Fiendish Logic

Now, philanthropists may easily imagine there is a skillful method of disarming and overcoming an enemy without causing great bloodshed, and that this is the proper tendency of the Art of War. However plausible this may appear, still it is an error which must be extirpated; for in such dangerous things as War, the errors which proceed from a spirit of benevolence are the worst.

— CLAUSEWITZ[1]

...war, which is simply the subjection of all life and property to *one* momentary aim, is morally vastly superior to the mere violent egoism of the individual; it develops power in the service of a supreme general idea and under a discipline which nevertheless permits supreme heroic virtue to unfold. Indeed, war alone grants to mankind the magnificent spectacle of a general submission to a general aim.

And since, further, only real power can guarantee a peace and security of any duration, while war reveals where real power lies, the peace of the future lies in such a war.

Yet it should, if possible, be a just and honorable war —

— JACOB BURCKARDT[2]

What will become of the man who no longer has any reasons for defending himself or for attacking? What affects does he have left if he has lost those in which lie his weapons of defense and attack?

— NIETZSCHE, *Will to Power* , #924

1. Mine is a question mark against optimism, against the Soviet collapse, against the so-called end of history and the liberal rationalist millennium—a question mark whose father is a black-souled ideologist and whose mother is a weapon of mass destruction.

2. *A thought experiment:* — To believe in the Bomb and ask

---

[1] Karl von Clausewitz, *On War*, ed. Anatol Rapoport (Great Britain: Penguin Books, 1982), p. 102.

[2] Burckhardt, *Reflections On History* (Indianapolis: Liberty*Classics*, 1979), p. 218.

whether the weapons and ideologies of mass destruction have received our just appreciation.

3. I notice during the course of this experiment: (A) the modern imagination in a state of atrophy; (B) pacifism and a moral prudishness surrounding the issue of war; (C) the notion that economics is primary over politics; (D) the weakness and sickliness of a ruling elite that thrives by good economic news, or else by closing its eyes.

4. For us *war*, as the most terrible thing of all, becomes the most fascinating thing of all and serves as the key to yet another fascination, namely, the future. These two fascinations belong together; and now, as at no other time, imply one another. Even so, there is a soft, bloated, complacency; an unrealistic expectation that history collapses into the flatland of universal bourgeoisification, with all wars coming to an end.

5. The perspective of military strategy, with its new instrumentalities of mass destruction, now denies the sociological primacy of economics. It denies that the nation with the strongest economy is destined to win its wars. Military-technical progress has brought about an inversion. At last the forces of destruction turn the tables on the forces of production, and weapons of war now promise transformations more sudden and dramatic than ever did the implements of peace. The day is coming when the finance capitalist and the factory owner will be blasted into dust by the atomic Napoleons.

6. Until recently American superiority and arrogance, together with tremendous economic successes, depended on our geographical isolation. Today that isolation is no longer possible. Thanks to the intercontinental rocket, external danger makes its glorious debut.

7. America refuses to understand the intercontinental rocket, the H-bomb, poison gas, and bioweapons. Harking back to the Pentagon Papers, to Vietnam and before Vietnam, the pattern is psychological unreadiness for impending wars. We are without bomb shelters. We refuse to make adequate preparations, to accept a military draft, to require greater economic sacrifices from our citizens.

In addition, Americans believe that economic power *is* military power. For us it is not a question of diminishing the one for the sake of the other. The economy is viewed as the basis of national security. We expect Mammon, at whose temple we worship, to marshal our military forces. But Mammon is not a god of war. He is a corrupter who confiscates the concrete of the nation and diverts it from fallout shelters to freeways. At every turn he cries butter and not guns. He makes us eager to accept the friendship of Mr. Yeltsin or Mr. Gorbachev who talk smoothly and flatter; communists who say, "We represent the primacy of economics in Russia." And so we rush headlong to embrace these play-actors, even while the strategic rockets stand ready, hundreds upon hundreds of them, capped with fire, poison, and pestilence. Behind these rockets, the atomic Napoleons are waiting. "You cannot escape us," they whisper. "Our day is coming."

8. The primacy of economics means an unswerving faith in the power of money. To put this in the simplest of terms: *We believe that the dollar is mightier than the gun*; that the dollar is the source of all guns. This perspective fails to appreciate that guns can be a source of dollars; that sociology, on this point, is a two-way street; and that guns capable of getting hold of dollars can make more guns and achieve, thereby, more dollars.

9. The liberal capitalist state, though it can build the greater war machine, is disinclined to do so during its last and most decadent phase of existence, and often fails to produce great military leaders because of its conformism and bureaucratism, its clerkish effeminacy and democratic pretensions. Latter-day bourgeois society is a society which prefers the joys of consumption to the thrill of battle. It is a society made up of economic men, all other types being excluded from respectability. Military man has now shrunk to a thin idiot shadow of his former self. Classical economic theory, failing to learn from Marx, does not stop to think how capitalism, as an evolving process, has altered human nature; how it has strengthened the "economic soul" of man. We forget human variability. We forget that efficiency is only the most recent of our fads: supplanting custom, undermining religion, while replacing the cult of strategy and war with the cult of products X, Y, and Z. Consider the cold, hard, efficient facts: Military power is economically wasteful. It brings no return on its investments, especially with the appearance of weapons of mass destruction. War means absolute loss from the general economic viewpoint. It means the suspension of trade, the obliteration of industry, the waste of manpower, the collapse of consumption, and a life not worth living (that is, from a hedonistic perspective). Therefore, in practice, a non-bourgeois society, laboring under every kind of economic difficulty and theoretical misapprehension, will alone have the wherewithal to build the mightiest of military machines because it is not inhibited by the logic of economics; because it views war as inevitable and victory as the highest prize. Thus what follows, in practice, is that socialist states, which are deeply confused on the subject of economics, shall alone strive for victorious means. For they have no faith whatever

---

in peace and free trade, but all their faith is in armaments. Therefore, the socialist republics (which have allegedly collapsed) represent a new Caesarism. And as Oswald Spengler said: "The coming of Caesarism breaks the dictature of money and its political weapon democracy."[3]

The new formula is: Blood over money.

10. Let us consider the problem like this: Modern economics assumes order and the armed man is the creature of order. An economist might show that the armed man requires logistical support and an economic system to fight effectively. Therefore, the armed man is seen as the child of economic forces. On the other hand, economic forces depend on the establishment of a stable order, and a stable order depends on armed men. Therefore, a sociologist might argue that the armed man is the foundation of the economic system.

It ought to be asked, at this point, which argument contains the largest grain of truth?

At the very least we've got a neat little circle, a paradox, a chicken-or-egg problem. The ideologists of capitalism are quick to proclaim the virtues of the chicken. Medieval bandits, called aristocrats, posthumously exemplify the side of the egg. What made the ideologists of capitalism seem correct was our bad memory, our ahistorical vantage point. The fact is, as chronology shows, the bandits came first and the modern economists came after. If not for the artistry of the men with weapons, there would be no order, no foundation on which liberalism and capitalism could build.

11. Among other conceits, Westerners tend to believe that "the people" always win and that right conquers might; i.e., that right *is* might. Under this view, if we suffer a military setback it is assumed that we are morally off course; that is, we are at war with those exemplary and beneficent gods, the Forces of History. The paltriest combat losses indicate guilt. To prove the immorality of a cause one merely has to show that its chances are poor. This instinct, growing more and more pronounced since the advent of television, supplants the sensible morality which once emphasized an unconnectedness between victory and moral goodness.

12. The doctrine of Mutual Assured Destruction is meant to assuage fears. Here we imagine invulnerability because destruction is mutual. But this is a non sequitur because the power to destroy and be destroyed, on both sides, implies vulnerability and not invulnerability. And let us examine this word—*destruction.* Since when is destruction the same thing for Russia as America? In what sense is there mutuality between

---

[3] Spengler, *The Decline of the West*, p. 414.

----

the bombing of a soft, consumer society and a militarized society, dug in and trained for war? And what can we say about the idea that destruction is *assured*? Here again, a fable for children. Mutual Assured Destruction is merely a way to convince ourselves that our institutions are still practicable; still compatible with the strategic rocket and with the biological, nuclear, and chemical weapons of mass destruction.

13. Through these thoughts we might divine the future, but who will credit such divination? Instead of facing facts, modernity is infected with utopianism and hope. There are people who today believe that science will soon cure aging, death, and stupidity. This fact bears witness to the impregnability of modern optimism. *Optimism as a disease.* The symptoms are all around us. But we don't want a cure. We want to feel good. That is why we are optimists — because we are hedonists.

14. *Means condition ends.* When are we going to learn this? Our whole political system has failed to adjust its ends to the means available. We continually overreach ourselves in our wars against poverty, crime, and drugs. Yet we ignore the new instruments of mass destruction. We regard these instruments as self-negating and ignore the horrifying possibility that weapons of mass destruction may suddenly imply new ends: *ends of mass destruction.*

15. The weapons of mass destruction open up new horizons to the military planner. Those who take advantage of this situation, and adapt themselves, have a future; a chance to survive into the nuclear hereafter. Those who place world peace, compassion, and goodness far above these weapons of mass destruction, subvert themselves with their own idealism and put murderers in the forefront.

This brings us to the question: *what could be more evil than this absolute morality of the good?*

16. The Bomb has never been realistically integrated into our consciousness. This is because the Bomb heralds, in fact, the end of our utopian dreams. These utopian dreams are based on modernity's rejection of the traditional family. This rejection of the family is based on a rejection of motherhood, and the rejection of motherhood is grounded on a rejection of manliness and fatherhood. No fathers for the country, no patriots. Instead, we are progressively becoming careerists, bureaucrats, and opportunists. A country made of *these* is not a country. Statecraft grows hollow without the proprietary interest of the father. Today, every sort of cheapness and treachery, every sort of circus act and

every sort of bizarre nonsense gains access to leadership and the public ear. The people are children and always shall be children. Now, under democracy—*orphans*.

17. Disarmament is not the ultimate solution because the Bomb can be reintroduced at any time. Potential rearmament precludes the possibility of true disarmament. In the end we cannot get rid of the Bomb because we cannot get rid of the idea of the Bomb. True disarmament would mean lobotomizing the whole human race. Let us be men and prefer the Bomb.

18. Lower living standards would be the price if serious civil defense were attempted, but the voters would never accept this. They would always vote for the man who tells them of "another way." The technical ignorance of the masses guarantees an uncritical acceptance of "other ways" (e.g., the arms control process).

19. A society determined to survive modern war cannot be democratic after the latest American fashion. Military preparations need to emanate from an efficient executive. Domestic politics and the luxurious regime of "total rights" must give way to emergency measures: the merciless protection of state secrets, the uprooting of subversive elements, and the reestablishment of moral standards. This grotesque imperative, so inconsistent with our liberal ideals, must one day transform our Republic; but not in time to prevent the death of two hundred million Americans.

20. A generous inclination to liberate Soviet and Chinese peoples from oppression is no longer practical in the context of world nuclear rocket war. Now all civilians are iron-bound to their governments; not only as hostages, but as tools of war. One cannot hesitate to destroy all the adversary's tools of war. If we are depopulated then the enemy, too, *must* be depopulated. The logic of the weapons speaks irrefutably. The Russian population, in the event of war, would necessarily find itself inextricably bound up with Kremlin gangsters. A sense of self-preservation therefore dictates solidarity with the regime. Even the White Guardist gives his blessing to the Great Patriotic War. Make no mistake about the logic of thermonuclear noontide: the Russian people will support their government precisely because they will fear and expect total annihilation unleashed by other peoples' governments. The more widespread the destruction the more desperately they will believe in the necessity of further destructive acts. And every drop of spilled Russian blood shall justify the initial preemptive strike; strengthen it, hallow it, and make it pregnant with moral force.

21. The idea of killing millions of people to achieve a relative positional advantage is absurd from the point of view of liberal democracy. From the point of view of positional advantage, it is liberal democracy that proves absurd.

22. In the final analysis: it is the nature of the weapons and the nature of their creators which render nuclear rocket war inevitable. From this highest ground we might survey the whole of history, without condescending to debate small points and niceties. One should, instead, stand above the optimists and the pessimists of the moment, transcending fate by recognizing fatality.

23. Unleashing the weapons of mass destruction would mean a break in the historical continuum unlike anything experienced before. This truth becomes an obstacle to the atrophied imagination of modern man, waterlogged as it is, floating in the thin gruel of tepid optimism. We cannot picture such a break, in light of which our old ideas—the ideas of modernity—will appear useless, perhaps dangerous. History, like never before, will lay down the law to philosophy, and will present to us a new set of ideas based upon an entirely new and unanticipated set of experiences. It will seem as though we have been hit over the head; our consciousness will be altered by the sheer force of the blow.

24. *Contradiction by infinite regress.* — Any social theory, when widely accepted, negates or distorts itself. Imagine that society can be represented adequately by Theory X. But Theory X, if widely accepted, alters society and then, subsequently, the "correct" theory of society becomes Theory X plus the *acceptance* of Theory X. But then if X + AX is accepted, then X + AX + AAX, on into the depths. Whatever sociological theory you postulate, if accepted, negates itself. To remain true to himself the theorist must prevent the acceptance of his theories.

25. *The cycle of the ages.* — Chaos molds the conqueror, the conqueror molds the chaos, and a new civilization appears. But civilization wants to do away with conquerors. This results in a new kind of spirit: refined, soft, romantic, pacific, abstract. This type of spirit develops a Buddhist-like, scholarly and escapist mentality. Then comes the idea of a gentle "liberal-philanthropic" world, managed and micro-managed by soft people, which gradually sinks back toward chaos because it lacks an element—but no more than an element—of the hardness and bloodiness which is needed for the preservation of order. With the return of chaos there appears new conquerors, and the world

begins again.

26. When presented with a well-reasoned proof for the inevitability
of world nuclear war, our composure disappears and emotion creeps into
our counterargument. Rationalizations, dishonest dismissals, hunch-
backed and limping bits of fact appear throughout. A willful ignorance
of syllogism and a lack of playfulness, good sportsmanship, and
coolness, peep at us from behind the shabby structures of denial. One
finds, as standard quip, that nobody is stupid enough to start a nuclear
war, that nobody wants to die, that it is unhealthy to think about such
things, that only fools study the subject and only fearful neurotics
predicate themselves upon it.

Each of these responses refuses to say anything sensible about the
reality of nuclear rockets: their purpose, their irrevocable existence,
their seductive power over the minds of would-be atomic Napoleons.
Nobody seems to notice that all the arguments against the inevitability of
such a war are patently false and ridiculous: that many men are quite
stupid enough to start such a war, or intelligent enough, as the case may
be. So feeble is our age of doubt that we no longer think it conceivable
that some men are willing to die for their beliefs, and are willing to
murder for them; that people can live quite happily while giving thought
to such things; and that neurosis is hardly evidenced by a willingness to
face these grim facts. On the contrary, all the neurotic fearfulness is on
the side of the optimists and the thermonuclear naysayers, who constantly
chant to themselves that "nuclear war will never happen." Theirs is the
standard view. World nuclear rocket war, as a subject for discussion, has
been declared by them taboo. Who will deny, in this case, the existence
of an informal censorship? The topic, therefore, is undeveloped.
Intelligent public discussion cannot take place.

Why is this? Because the topic strikes at a raw nerve. It is too real,
too possible, and too inevitable for us to acknowledge its reality,
possibility, and inevitability. Naked fear, which we've managed to push
out of our minds, must not be invited back. We despise fear. It makes us
uncomfortable. Away with it!

All of this only points to our instinctual grasp of the situation. The
fact is, we understand nuclear war very well, and we know that there isn't
a satisfactory solution to the problem. For if there were such a solution,
then constructive discussion would exist. Since it does not exist we
instead embark on a program of illusion, or perhaps a campaign of
silence. We must put the whole problem out of our heads. Notice our
reaction when a child reveals to his playmates that the Easter Bunny is a
lie. We have no counterargument against this child. Our instinctive
reaction is to call him a spoilsport. Likewise with our nuclear illusions.
When somebody dares to challenge them with facts, only one possible

----

weapon is left: the *ad hominem* weapon.

27. The hard man detests utopian ideas; he opposes the notion of solving all difficulties, of creating heaven on earth. The hard man distrusts utopia, especially for what it would make of mankind. But this is an irrational attitude because utopia is impossible. Therefore, it is the worst of catastrophes, the darkest storm cloud, the most terrifying page out of history's book. By all means, say *yes* to utopia.

28. For those Americans who think our nation was the result of utopian dreams, I say *think again*. The authors of the American Constitution were pessimists about human nature—the opposite of utopians.

29. This incomprehensible change of climate, this bloodsoaked storm cloud, this Bomb of Damocles—it alters us. But what if we whistle a happy tune? What if we refuse to take notice? Then how could we be changed?
Answer: As Nature changed the dinosaurs.

30. Our experts say that security now depends upon the self-restraint of one's adversaries; that is, self-restraint from those who have every intention of wiping us out. But what if, in fact, restraint is murderous patience and predatory cunning; an ability to move closer and closer without spooking the intended victim? What does the so-called self-restraint of one's adversaries signify then?

31. David Riesman, a Harvard sociologist, wrote a book called *The Lonely Crowd: a Study of the Changing American Character*, in which he argued that Americans were becoming progressively "other-directed," i.e., governed by cues from the peer group. More recently, Christopher Lasch authored a book entitled *The Culture of Narcissism*, wherein he expressed growing concern with what he called "paternalism without father", "the flight from feeling", "schooling and the new illiteracy." In the work of these two authors, we find evidence of deep changes in America's human material.
Herman Kahn, author of *On Thermonuclear War*, gives us another problem to look at. He says that a thermonuclear war is far from unlikely, that such a war would not be the end of the world, that civil defense is necessary, that deterrence is a questionable long-term proposition, and that for some strange reason we are failing to adjust ourselves to these horrible new realities. I believe that the reason for this failure to adjust can be found in the works of Lasch and Riesman.

32. It is difficult to explain why we cannot be good judges of ourselves in the military sense. Let us merely say that the Western soul is too far removed from the military spirit of barbarian times. Clausewitz talked about this. But he also talked about the lack of science on the part of the barbarian. He noted that barbarians, despite possessing the correct spirit, lack the intellectual sophistication to carry it into genius. What is needed, he claimed, is a rare combination: a warlike spirit with cultivated judgment. When the frontier was still a fresh historical backdrop, and when "characters" like Douglas MacArthur and George Patton could still rise to the rank of general, we achieved this admixture. But there is reason to doubt that these rare birds are still being hatched.

33. Josef Stalin said: "Atomic bombs are meant to frighten those with weak nerves." In this we find insanity confounded with reason. For the Bomb entangles the two, and nothing can untangle them. The Bomb is like the Philosophers' stone, only that it works in reverse. And with its appearance lunacy becomes reason and common sense becomes absurdity.

34. A thought for the chess player: America—as an open society—cannot castle her king.

35. The problem is not that our civilization willfully destroys itself. Civilization cannot willfully do anything, for its consciousness is polymorphous and has no center of will. It comes into existence quite by accident, not giving birth to itself, not intending itself, and never really knowing its own springs and levers. Civilization, so explained, remains a limited entity which hardly knows anything at all. Actually, in many cases, knowledge endangers it. Furthermore, civilization can only jump so high and live so long. It is not a person. It has no freedom. Therefore, fate is much stronger in history than anyone dares admit. But *that* has now changed. What is new today, appearing for the first time with the weapons of mass destruction, is that a civilization can now be consciously destroyed by the act of a single cunning individual or small group of individuals. A global civilization built up over the course of many centuries can be pulverized and burnt to cinders by a pack of medal-bedecked ideologues. And since civilization is not a person and has no sense or mind, no brain, no unified consciousness, but is only a set of relationships, a tangle of process, a jungle of decay and growth; then it cannot defend itself from the medal-bedecked. It must, in the final analysis, fall prey. It lives, as all natural growths, an unthinking life; and it faces death like every weed in the garden, without realizing the advent of the rake.

----

36. The deeper minds of military science recognize that the horrors of war are not at all objectionable. Such minds would like to learn how these horrors can be intensified, sustained, and turned into victory. Victory is the object of war. Victory sometimes demands that we employ horrible means.

37. Nuclear-biological war will impoverish the world. A certain kind of politics seeks out impoverished people. Impoverished people are easy to rule. Dictators meditate on these things.

38. *Devolution: Man to ape.* —
Eisenhower: "Massive Retaliation," meaning we will destroy our enemy if he gives us cause.

Kennedy: "Flexible Response," meaning we are unsure what we will do.

Nixon: "Strategic Parity," meaning it is perfectly okay if the Russians outnumber us in strategic weaponry because that will make them feel safer and prevent a war.

Today: "Intra-war deterrence," meaning we do not intend to crush our opponent in a nuclear war. We intend to wait for a miracle.

39. We utilitarians, we objectivists, capitalists and economists, cannot help but curl our lips in disgust and snicker at war and sacrifice as stupid, irrational, even insane. Why risk life and limb, which is everything, for a cause or an abstraction or what is practically the same thing: namely, for people yet unborn, people who will go on living when we are in our graves? We cannot abide the illogical aura of the military uniform. It is immoral. Only logic is moral: that is, only *our* logic. The dead cannot benefit from the living, even if the living worship them as heroes and saviors. The relationship between the dead patriot and his beneficiary is totally one-sided—or so it seems to us. Gone is the idea that there ought to be affection between generations as well as between people of similar background. The keeping of faith between fathers and forefathers is utterly lost to us. The dead are in their graves and know nothing. The past is gone and insignificant.
—Out of sight, out of mind.

40. The best way to guarantee that nuclear war never happens is to surrender. It is not the aggressor who starts wars. The aggressor hopes to win without having to fight, by parading through surrendered territory. It is the victims of aggression who start wars by firing on the parade. Therefore, appeasement is the surest way to protect the peace while self-defense is the surest way to trigger a holocaust.

41. Our own thoughts terrify us, and we cling to illusions. In this grand manner, with these paltry towels in our hands, we march to the showers of a new Auschwitz.

42. When we are first confronted by the weapons of mass destruction, we think nothing of them. Perhaps we feel vaguely depressed. I call this the "first stage": the stage of marginal awareness during which we say to ourselves that nothing can be done; that in such matters we are Lilliputians and that worrying about nuclear war is ridiculous. Why waste the time?

Then, late one night, tossing and turning, there comes a flash of insight and all the rationalizations fall away. I call this the "second stage," which hardly anyone ever reaches. It is nuclear age man's "dark night of the soul." At this point a vision of the necessities of mass destruction force themselves upon the mind. I emphasize again that this is a rare experience with everything set against it; a near impossible birth which requires, at the very least, a willingness to suffer on behalf of someone or something else; and in an age of decided squeamishness, this is almost too much to ask. Even the most famous thermonuclear war analyst, Herman Kahn, never reached this phase. For Kahn's investigations of thermonuclear war were not born of genuine insight, but came from professional interest, as well as from a lifetime of habitual intellectualization; and also, from a certain curiosity which defied his silly optimism, and which taunted him, but never forced him to drink the dregs. He was a strategist who said "what if." *That is all.* And as far as he went, Kahn is invaluable. But the logic of nuclear war, for him, was mere logic. For he didn't understand the larger significance of mass destruction weapons. With other writers one recognizes some twinklings of insight, here and there, especially on the part of Albert Camus and Hannah Arendt—thinkers who penetrated into the psychology of mass movements. But these are merely passing chills, philosophical intuitions, and nothing that readers seriously remember. For the reader cannot long retain these profundities, and thinks to himself: "Interesting! But now I shall go back to the *real* world." We can only imagine the great shaft of lightning that would come crashing down upon his head, if this selfsame reader were to put Camus side by side with someone like General Rothschild, a former top leader in America's biological weapons program, and a man who explains the weapons of mass destruction with elegance and simplicity. Then our reader would have the elements, in all their immediate terribleness, lined up before him. True understanding would then be his. And what are these elements which lead to true understanding? Military fact combined with the feeling that history is not the story of progress, but an eternally recurring tragedy.

The "third stage," what I call "the phase of bitterness," comes quite naturally, following from the second stage. One realizes that the facts are darker than anyone has dared to say. One becomes enraged at the stupidity of man; indignant at the universal complacency of liberalism. All that one previously shrugged off, now embitters. Blame makes its appearance; for one's finger now has the urge to point, to excoriate, and to inflict itself on others. All the world drips with the blood of an imminent thermonuclear crime. I should say that this third stage is a place where one can become stuck.

Here it becomes necessary to keep in mind one's size in relation to this thing that moves, that rotates, that orbits the sun. If one avoids bitterness, if one refuses to become a living sneer, then one ascends to the "fourth stage": to realize that the world cannot always be changed; that perhaps the world is a process, an accident, or rather—a fatality. It is not merely that most people do not know what they are doing, but cannot know it. *This defines them.* This is their character, and a fundamental law of the universe. Such a hard truth, which puts people in their place without making off with their innocence, may seem at first to imply resignation. But no, it is merely a kind of wisdom which finally discerns what cannot be changed from what can. It is not that one should resign, give up, or quit; but only that one must avoid beating one's head against an impregnable wall.

And the "fifth stage"? It is a stage for those who have discovered a positive program; who know what is mutable and what is immutable; who await the historical window, the vortex, the passage through which some lesser evil is consolidated and conserved at the expense of some greater evil. This is the moral perspective of high politics and of true statesmanship. Only those who reach this fifth stage can transform world calamity into world regeneration.

43. As the new Columbus, as the navigator of uncharted seas, I can hear people saying: "Columbus! You're going to fall off the edge of the world! because there isn't a land beyond nuclear war. There's only an abyss which marks the end of all life on earth."

—Nonsense! I, Christopher Columbus, know that the world is continuous. And I hope to discover new and future continents.

5

The Madness of Columbus

> In individuals, insanity is rare, but in groups, parties, nations and epochs it is the rule.
>
> — NIETZSCHE, *Beyond Good and Evil*

> Men are mad so unavoidably that not to be mad would constitute one a madman of another order of madness.
>
> — PASCAL, *Pensées*, iv

1. I was in an academic seminar in 1988 where the question of the Soviet threat came up. I said that the Soviet Union was a dangerous enemy of the United States. The graduate student seated next to me leaned forward, his face contorted with rage. He then exploded, shouting at the top of his lungs: "YOU'RE INSANE!"

2. A friend of mine read an earlier draft of this book and asked: "Why do you—and you alone—believe in a Soviet conspiracy?"

3. A close relative advised me to do some soul-searching because I had placed myself "outside the mainstream."

4. Another relative thinks that I am small-souled and mean. He says this book is filled with indignation, hatred, bitterness, and bad manners. Other adjectives he uses include self-conscious, deficient, tedious, dogmatical, one-sided, loud, monochromatic, insincere, non-philosophical, and he says I lack "historical sense."

5. When all is said and done, I could be wrong. My critics may have the better case. Columbus did not know he was right, either; in fact, he was only guessing. As it happened, Columbus guessed right, and we

honor him. But that is hindsight. Consider how Columbus was judged at Salamanca in 1486 when an assembly of wise ones met to review his intuitions about undiscovered lands in the west. Some criticized him for believing the earth was a sphere. To refute him they quoted Lactantius, St. Augustine, and the Bible. There were those who said the Atlantic was too big for anyone to cross. There were those who predicted that his expedition would perish in the heat of the torrid zone. And after so many navigators, philosophers, and cosmographers had studied the form of the world, after thousands of years of investigation, it was sheer presumption for an ordinary man to think that such a stupendous discovery remained for him and him alone. In this context even I might have thought Columbus's statements were arrogant. To challenge centuries of learning and seamanship has something ill-mannered in it. Certainly, Columbus was not trying to be rude; but new ideas, by their very nature, contain rudeness in them—intrinsically, inescapably. For myself, I feel impatience at the slowness of other observers to face the most disturbing facts. Truly, it is difficult to avoid an impolite outburst. If such outbursts slip out of me, they represent nothing more than the frustration of someone whose ideas are dismissed out of hand without real consideration. I do not mean to insult anyone. It is the urgency of the situation which animates my critique. There is no happiness for me in these predictions—in discovering a land beyond nuclear war. To paraphrase what Gorky said about the Revolution in Russia: He felt like Columbus, only the New World disgusted and revolted him. Indeed, I sympathize with Gorky's remark.

In this context, I have many thoughts on what the future might look like. I have distilled, in these pages, ideas from sociologists and certain notions borrowed from Burckhardt and Nietzsche, who share a queer similarity of vision in matters historical. Also, note that Schumpeter, Pareto, and Weber also have an apocalyptic side which I have drawn from; not to mention Spengler, Christopher Lasch, and Ortega y Gasset.

It is, I admit, arrogant in a lowly student of affairs to presume any foreknowledge. But there are many facts suggestive of looming catastrophe, and no one is discussing them. There is, without doubt, something deeply wrong with our present-day optimism.

6. One notices that many significant United States officials are dying unnatural deaths, one after another, and nobody is getting to the bottom of it. Deputy White House Counsel Vincent Foster allegedly commits suicide under suspicious circumstances; Commerce Secretary Ron Brown's plane goes down; the top admiral of the Navy, Jeremy Boorda, shoots himself; and a former Director of Central Intelligence, William Colby, dies in a mysterious accident, his body later found at the bottom of a lake (while a close friend remains puzzled because Colby

----

never went out on the water without a life jacket).

And then we read Deroy Murdock's column, where he writes:

> As I reported in March, either through concerted action or a series of
> coincidences that expand that word's definition to the breaking point, an
> apparent pattern of violence and intimidation has befallen a number of men and
> women with ties to Bill and Hillary Clinton, their partners in business, law, and
> politics, and people investigating their affairs.[1]

Again, some element of bad manners or presumption enters into the
equation. Truly, this is lamentable, and I wish it could be avoided, but
there it is. Alarm bells are ringing.

7. Notice, too, Lev Timofeyev's book, *Russia's Secret Rulers*. It
was the one book, of all books, that disagrees with the Golitsyn thesis,
yet confirms the thesis despite itself. But even there, in the midst of
Timofyev's honest yet trusting confusion, one reads his interview with
the former communist official, Gavril Popov, which is more than curious.
In fact, Popov said something that kicked to life every suspicion I had
ever harbored concerning the internal Russian reality. Timofeyev asks
Popov if the Russian mafia might be the tool of "the old political
structures." Popov gives a most interesting answer:

> Theoretically that would be possible, if in those political structures one
> competent person could be found. There is complete degradation there. It's
> hard for me to imagine that a person could be discovered who is capable of
> designing a major strategic plan. If there were people like that, they would have
> long ago found a more effective option.[2]

This is quite extraordinary, and now we have reason to worry. Why?
Because these so-called incompetents oversaw the building of the first
hydrogen bomb, they launched Sputnik and put the first man in space,
they built the largest nuclear strike force and the most awesome civil
defense system on earth while governing an empire so vast and
militaristic that many serious persons in the West were understandably
frightened. Not only this, with the recent revelations about major
Russian penetrations of the CIA (e.g., in the cases of Ames and
Nicholson), there is a striking lack of incompetence in all essentials. And
is not the KGB a police organization? What chance then for the
criminals to get hold of the system? I fear the degradation Popov speaks

---

[1] Murdock, "Arkansas Trail of Tears," *Orange County Register*, 8 June 1994, METRO, p. 7.

[2] Lev Timofeyev, *Russia's Secret Rulers: How the Government and Criminal Mafia Exercise Their Power*
(New York: Alfred A. Knopf, 1992), p. 23.

of is more likely to afflict the West. Therefore, his suggestion is something more readily accepted by Westerners because it makes sense from our standpoint, but not from the standpoint of an efficient police state. In a police state the largest criminal organization is the state itself. That is the real mafia in Russia. Let us not fool ourselves.

Some facts are so obvious that we can miss their significance. In this context, Popov's tune could not be more of a piece with other official lies; in fact, a vast disinformation effort is now discernible to anyone who studies Russian politics with an open mind. For example, I could easily quote a top Russian intelligence leader who publicly claimed, at the end of the Cold War, that the KGB was packed with incompetent timeservers, and that it failed to recruit any significant agents in Western intelligence organizations.[3]   Was KGB General Leonid Shebarshin embarrassed by his remarks when months later the Ames case broke and a top CIA official proved to be a longtime Soviet mole?   And think of how extraordinary the KGB's self assertion is: Do retired or active officials publicly admit the incompetence of their own organizations? Do they like to recall the failures of their own work?

8. If somebody asked me: How do you know you are right? Well, I do not know. I am not sure on every point. And if the same question had been put to Columbus he probably would have answered: "Are you sure I'm wrong?" Well, let us find out. Let us explore it. Will you give the truth a chance, whatever the answer may be?

9. I am driven by an insight into the future. And because of this I must apologize for the irregular manner in which I advance my case. Literary excellence and scientific exactness do not concern me.   My concern is with another type of excellence, which is strength against enemies. This forces me to take a tough stand, to speak of brutal realities.

10. The problem with having a vision or intuition about the future, and of abiding in a colossal hunch, is that people whose instincts and intuitions have been lost in the general opinion, tend to reject new and unusual ideas without due consideration. They do not give such ideas a chance, though if they did, they might find themselves wondering what the truth actually is. Of course, time changes people, and in a crisis they look for new perspectives. That is the time when writings such as these will become more useful.

11. These pages are full of probings, questionings, dragons painted

---

[3] "Soviets Lost 'Secret War,' Ex-Spy Says," *Los Angeles Times*, 11 August 1992, A-11.

----

on the unmapped and uncharted edges of the present. Perhaps it is a self-grandiose error, but I claim to have entered nether-regions, to have espied them; and now I return, dropping hints about things to come. I am convinced that the ideologies of mass destruction have entered into matrimony with the weapons of mass destruction, and their progeny will be a nuclear world war. Perhaps this book is one of the last paranoid gasps before the greatest age of peace the world has yet known. Perhaps I am crazy. But again, what if I am right? After all, ours is a world with fifty or sixty thousand hydrogen bombs kept in constant readiness. Could it be that I am on to something? And in the final analysis, isn't a flat and peaceful future more dubious than a round thermonuclear one?

12. Jacques Barzun, the cultural historian, once pointed out that the modern ego is strikingly self-conscious; that the modern ego is more concerned with how it appears to others and less concerned with the fearless pursuit of truth. Partly because of this, I think we have lost our playfulness, our intellectual bounce, and our good-sportsmanship. Perhaps this will surprise some readers, but I sincerely hope I am wrong. Such is my good-sportsmanship. And what a jolly time I will have laughing at myself when I reach old age in the peaceful liberal world of tomorrow! On the other hand, the liberal is so humorless about his happy endings, so earnest, so missionary, so dull, that I cannot help but yawn a little. If only he had the courage to poke fun at himself, how rapidly I would shrink away, my ideas slowly drained of their fluid.

13. But how? How can the majority, since they have the advantage of numbers, be mistaken?
Because the simplest facts are much more treacherous than we have heretofore realized. For facts must be placed in proper context, or else they will most certainly deceive us. And to arrange facts into their proper context requires a sensitivity and a skill which Americans seem to have lost. Perhaps our taste for facts has been spoiled by the manner in which we have been schooled; a manner which teaches that facts are boring and contexts should be dropped. We memorize many facts, cramming them into our heads in order to pass some silly test; and then, as quickly, we forget them. Facts are a game. Also, our wariness with regard to the meaning of facts has been undermined by television and newspapers. The essential lesson of the mass media has been that facts are discreet things: simple, unidimensional, and easy.

14. Philosophers and historians cannot help blundering. Man's intellect and memory are powerful, but wide areas of incompetence remain in every human being. Therefore we writers and thinkers have learned to cultivate more modest assumptions. Yet even here dangers

abound; for today's situation damns the modest man because the modest man, though he escapes ridiculousness, makes himself an insect— powerless to say or do anything of significance.

Once we might have been in danger of jumping too far or too high, but today we are in no such danger. Today we are in danger of not moving at all.

Today we are in danger of rigor mortis.

15. The Cold War has attracted, as pollen attracts bees, a great many scholars and researchers. And these have written many billions of words which conform to the rules of decorum and modesty, but are nonetheless arid, empty, and pointless. It turns out that our Cold War scholars have failed to attain true grandeur of conception. Though this would not normally be fatal to the work of history, it is absolutely fatal for today's historians. For here history reaches its pinnacle. Here, the object of contemplation is grand in itself. From this summit we can survey all that has gone before and all that lies ahead. But this wondrous vista is lost on those whose modesty represents a denial of what lies before us.

16. In addition to poor eyesight there are mirages. In the case of America's future, the great mirage, called "green-pasture happiness," is everywhere reflected in the landscape. It encourages, quite naturally, the expectation that things will continue somewhat as they are. There is a general failure on the part of most educated men—liberal and conservative—to penetrate the falseness of this mirage and recognize the possibility that a very unpleasant future awaits us. We have hardly yet realized that none of our solutions to the current crisis have any plausibility except for the thermonuclear solution, dictated by Nature's Iron Law of Equilibrium, which says that every unbalanced thing must eventually face its day of correction.

17. What is grandeur of vision? It is an ability to integrate the whole situation. It is knowing the important from the unimportant. It is good judgment carried into larger questions. It is empirical without being concrete-bound. It is rational without being rationalistic. It is modest and, when necessary, immodest.

Grandeur of vision is difficult to attain in any age. In our age, it is practically impossible because ridicule plays such a large part in our culture. Symptomatic of this is the modern mind's inability to ask the right questions; for the modern mind is a small mind, an objective mind, grown nearsighted from peering into too many microscopes. And when we manage to discern the crux of the matter we are sure to misunderstand either the context, the crux, or the matter itself. We are either modest to the point of mental disintegration, or immodest to the point of concentration camps.[4] We have for some time scolded ourselves for carrying generalizations too far. But now we make for the opposite extreme. A profound timidity has filled our thoughts with so many qualifying phrases, caveats, and reservations that our simplest ideas are mangled beyond help. In short, ours is an unfortunate mind which adds its own special stupidity to a tragic moment in history.

18. That facts are treacherous leads us to uncover two extremes. Each can be fatal. These two extremes are: exaggeration and barrenness. The two faculties which lend themselves to these two extremes are reason and imagination, which ought to be partners but are more often adversaries. Consider, for the moment, that reason is a form of discipline while imagination provides the stimulus. Together, these two fundamental aspects of the human mind might achieve almost anything. Split asunder, they can achieve almost nothing.

19. We desperately need a better interpretive methodology for international affairs. We need to rehabilitate paranoia, give it brains and elevation, cool it off and force it to work with facts. This would be, in my view, a "golden paranoia," and should by no means be regarded as a mental aberration, but as a gift. We need this gift because our warrior instincts have atrophied, and our capacity for enmity has shriveled. Yet there remains the objection that such a golden paranoia might take us into eccentricities of the most fanciful and disturbing kind. Here our politics would break down into madness. Certainly, that is a danger, one which we must guard against.

20. The cult of suspicion, far from being lily-white, has often been contaminated by a multitude of garden-variety cranks. It is for us to avoid these dead ends and missing links. Let us develop some nuance and honesty. Let us begin to notice ambiguities and complexities beyond those which can be appreciated by the paranoia of the barn yard.

21. We insignificant ones are sometimes at an advantage in discussing great themes. For we have nothing to lose by speaking out. The Marxists call this "the sociology of knowledge." Unfortunately the fact of insignificancy is no guarantee that one is speaking the truth. For even if we have nothing to lose there is always the chance that we have something to gain. This, too, is "the sociology of knowledge." But the Marxists do not want to give themselves away.

22. That which holds fast has royal rights over that which is weak

---

[4] A modest man, by his very nature, could never build a state on the basis of concentration camps.

and uncertain. A thing cannot persuade unless it stands forth boldly, even arrogantly. But, in response to this arrogance, I hear people ask: Why should we believe you? What's so special about you?

My answer is: There are public libraries. And in those libraries there are books about Soviet concentration camps by men like Aleksandr Solzhenitsyn and Avraham Shifrin. There are books on Soviet strategy by former Eastern bloc insiders like Jan Sejna, Anatoliy Golitsyn, and Viktor Suvorov; by CIA analysts like Peter Vincent Pry; and by political scientists like Edward Jay Epstein and Joseph D. Douglass, Jr. All you have to do is read them. All you have to do is a little homework. I am not asking that you believe me. I am challenging you to check out the facts and discover for yourself.

This is called exploring the world.

6

Treaties

If you only knew how the youngest of the officials in Moscow's Old Square roar with laughter at your political wizards!
— ALEKSANDR I. SOLZHENITSYN

The struggle for total domination of the total population of the earth, the elimination of every nontotalitarian reality, is inherent in the totalitarian regimes themselves; if they do not pursue global rule as their ultimate goal, they are only too likely to lose whatever power they have already seized.
— HANNAH ARENDT[1]

A diplomat's words must contradict his deeds — otherwise, what sort of a diplomat is he? Words are one thing — deeds something entirely different. Fine words are a mask to cover shady deeds. A sincere diplomat is like dry water or wooden iron.
— STALIN, 1913

Leave, leave Geneva everyone, Saturn will change from gold into iron. Those against RAYPOZ will all be exterminated. Before the rush the sky will show signs.
— NOSTRADAMUS, 9:44

Thus in a pageant show a plot is made
And peace itself is war in masquerade.
— DRYDEN

1.   Of all delusions, one delusion, above others, worms its invertebrate way into the American consciousness. It is the misbegotten fancy of every full-blown peacemonger and treaty-maniac. Its name? Disarmament — which means: a predilection for walking naked into the jaws of destruction.

State Department Publication No. 7277 of the Disarmament Series 5, released in September of 1961 by the Office of Public Services, is *must*

---

[1] Arendt, *Totalitarianism*, p. 90.

reading for every American, and proves that soft brains exist; that soft brains make government policies. The aforementioned publication begins by claiming that revolutionary developments in weaponry and ideology have "produced a crisis in human history." And this so-called crisis in human history has led the United States to submit a petition to the Sixteenth General Assembly of the United Nations called a "Program for General and Complete Disarmament in a Peaceful World." This program calls for the eventual elimination of national arsenals and national war-making capabilities along with the simultaneous strengthening of the war-making power of the United Nations.

2. It is worthwhile to remember that treaties are only as good as the intentions of the signatories. If the signatories become active enemies (or are active enemies already) then an agreement becomes meaningless. Also, let it be noted that bad men break treaties, stupid men break treaties; even — dare we say? — well-intentioned men break treaties; because keeping treaties with bad men or stupid men can be dangerous for well-intentioned men. Even so, America is anxious to sign as many treaties as it can before the onset of writer's cramp. We believe in peace and good intentions; in brotherhood, progress, and a full stomach for the Third World. Therefore, it is only natural that we also believe in pieces of paper (i.e., treaties).

3. *A brief history of arms control agreements. —*
Advocates of arms control point to the Rush-Bagot Agreement of 1817 as proof of the efficacy of treaties. Rush-Bagot limited British and American naval forces on the Great Lakes and Lake Champlain. While considering the success of Rush-Bagot, we should remember that prosperous bourgeois countries are unique. As long as they remain prosperous there is no motive for sack and pillage. Aggressive war between such countries has become increasingly infrequent (for economic reasons). Disarmament treaties are less successful when non-bourgeois countries are involved. A disarmament treaty is especially suspect when one side subscribes to an ideology which favors treaty-breaking, subversion, murder, blackmail, and the mass extermination of whole classes and races of people. In this context it is useful to recall Lenin's statement that treaties are like pie crusts—*meant to be broken.*
We should not, therefore, be surprised if the history of international disarmament generally proves a history of successive failures. We should not be surprised to find that such agreements have weakened the West while strengthening the totalitarian powers. For this reason alone disarmament should not be the policy of Western governments, and should only be considered under circumstances similar to Rush-Bagot.

---

*   *   *   *   *

In 1899 and 1907 Czar Nicholas II put together conferences at The Hague to prohibit dum-dum bullets, asphyxiating gases, and the launching of projectiles or explosives from the air. Within two decades these agreements proved their worthlessness, especially during World War One. In the course of this war, Czar Nicholas and his entire family were murdered.

Make a note of this. Drum it into your skull: *Arms control agreements can be hazardous to your health.* If the czar had realized that wars are entered upon in desperation, and desperation relies upon the most terrifying methods, then the czar would probably have survived. The simple political fact is: that terrifying methods *ought* to exist; and decent men, like the czar, ought to brace themselves and use such methods in order to avoid falling victim to men who are *not* decent.

*   *   *   *   *

After the First World War the lessons of failed arms control were not learned. Enthusiasm for international arms limitation continued. The Covenant of the League of Nations leapt out of the world's rubble, and again a whirlwind was reaped. The Treaty of Versailles, which imposed near-pacifist limits of disarmament on Germany, ended with the German conquest of Europe. *Make a note of that!* Versailles proposed to disarm Germany, but instead disarmed France and Britain. The English and French sought comfort in the signatures of the so-called November criminals. Here is an ominous example of the stupidity of liberal democratic leaders. Consider also the silly phrase of an even sillier League of Nations, calling for "enforcement by common action"; which translated, in reality, to Britain standing alone against Hitler. In the final analysis, Britain's survival was only due to the fact that the aggressors fell into quarreling with one another. And so we ask: What good was this League of Nations? What good was this "enforcement by common action"?

All of it—no good.

In 1928 there came yet another escapade in the history of treaty mania. Sixty-three nations renounced war as an instrument of national policy by ratifying the Kellogg-Briand Pact. They should have abolished the sun, the moon, and the stars while they were at it. For within fifteen years nearly all of these countries were at war or under wartime occupation.

What? Entire governments turning moron? Let us say, instead, that the well-intentioned signatories were merely self-dishonest, silly, frivolous, and dreamy; especially since this Kellogg-Briand Pact had no provision for the enforcement of its own articles. Think of it this way: The treaty asks the signatories to renounce war and so the treaty *itself* must renounce war—on its own behalf. Thus the treaty is, at the very least, self-consistent; and an example of a liberal ideal without any illiberal supports. For treaties, as serious things, must be guaranteed by blood. If not, then who will respect them? Ironically, disarmament treaties cannot work if men refuse to kill and die for them; which is one of the absurd aspects of the disarmament treaty *as a type.*

Poor, unserious, weak-willed, anemic Kellogg-Briand Pact! Thou art an oxymoron compounded and composed by well-intentioned political morons. Thou art an unenforceable treaty; therefore, thou art a nullity, a gaseous vapor, a dream!

Despite the League of Nations and the various arms limitations, World War Two gushed bloodier, and was less limited, than any war ever. And given the current trend in favor of treaties, we can expect grislier results from World War Three, especially since far-reaching arms control measures have already been signed.

Is it possible that the 55 million corpses left by World War Two were the result, in part, of the naiveté of certain leaders combined with the cynicism of certain other leaders? What is it when free and liberal countries place their faith in scraps of paper rather than vigilance, strength, and prompt unilateral preemption? Perhaps it is fate. Perhaps human stupidity cannot be gotten around.

And so we should not be surprised that there arose from the smoldering wreckage of the Second World War a thing made in the likeness of the First Beast, but calling itself the United Nations Charter. This has an Article Eleven, which is intended "to consider the general principles of cooperation in the maintenance of international peace and security, including the principles governing disarmament and the regulation of armaments."

President Harry S. Truman signed this charter at San Francisco on 26 June 1945. Incredibly, in the following year, a so-called United States representative to the U.N. Atomic Energy Commission proposed that all American atomic weapons be placed under U.N. control.

In 1952 treaty-idiocy condensed and transmogrified into a full-blown U.N. Disarmament Commission whose members were the United States, Great Britain, France, Canada, and the Soviet Union. Soon thereafter efforts were made to "blunt the sharpness" of East-West rivalry by expanding the commission to include various nonaligned countries which, until recently, worshipped trees, wore rings in their noses, danced naked through the forest and ate their neighbors.

4. Did you ever hear of the Outer Space Treaty? Or perhaps the

----

limited Test Ban? Or how about the Treaty for the Prohibition of Nuclear Weapons in Latin America? Oracles whispering apocalyptically in *this*, our Tarot pack of treaties, sprouting staves and swords and Blasted Towers. In astrological lingo: the world's horoscope has never been so dominated by Saturnine influences. Such are these treaties, these omens, these retrograde stars in diplomatic heavens: ratified scraps and derelict promises.

5. *The way a treaty talks.* —
"Convinced:
"That the incalculable destructive power of nuclear weapons has made it imperative that the legal prohibition of war should be strictly observed in practice if the survival of civilization and of mankind itself is to be assured,
"That nuclear weapons, whose terrible effects are suffered, indiscriminately and inexorably, by military forces and civilian population alike, constitute, through the persistence of the radioactivity they release, an attack on the integrity of the human species and ultimately may even render the whole earth uninhabitable,
"That general and complete disarmament under effective international control is a vital matter which all the peoples of the world equally demand."

              *   *   *   *   *

Pay attention. Here is the essence of the modern Western diplomat, mouthing his fear-ridden proclamations. It is, in essence, the language of the final treaty; of the treaty that is coming, that is being hatched; the treaty that removes many thousands of nuclear weapons from the United States and paves the way for the extermination of the English-speaking peoples. It is coming in the form of a Strategic Arms Reduction Treaty. Alas, it is already *here*! It is already too late.

6. And then, of course, there is the *Convention on the Prohibition of the Development, Production and Stockpiling of Bacteriological (Biological) and Toxin Weapons and on Their Destruction*—a crucial piece of our pie crust destiny; an artifact which eats up all biological weapons and excretes, out its tail end, peace and harmony.
And who played Dr. Frankenstein to this hodgepodge from an idiot's bone-pile?
It all began in the late 1960s, when a British draft convention suggested the separation of biological arms control questions from chemical arms control questions. Soon after this, in November 1969, and

on the basis of information provided by a Soviet triple-agent, President Richard Nixon broke out into ecstasies and ordered the destruction of all United States stockpiles of bioweapons, drawing international applause as he went. Vanity took its bow, bloated up, head swollen; then the band played *Hail to the Chief.*

After this bold Nixonian Quakerism, on 30 March 1971, the Soviet bloc introduced a revised version of the British draft convention. Then it became possible to work out a treaty to uninvent the biological weapon. On 16 December the General Assembly of the U.N. approved a resolution, 110 to 0, recommending adoption of the convention, and expressing adherence to it.

And the angels sang and the press buzzed, while mass killers clinked glasses with their milksop counterparts.

Nixon pressed for ratification of the convention in 1972, but Watergate cut him short. In late 1974 President Ford undertook the effort anew. It was then that the Senate Foreign Relations Committee voted unanimously to send the treaty to the Senate floor where the full Senate approved it without a single opposing vote. Thus, the most significant disarmament measure in the history of the United States came into being. It was signed into law by President Ford on 22 January 1975. The terms were simple: No development, production, or stockpiling of biological agents or toxins "of types and in quantities that have no justification for prophylactic, protective, and other peaceful purposes."

And what is the penalty, among lawless persons in lawless nations for violating, for bypassing, for circumventing this marvelous convention?

Complaints to be lodged with the Security Council of our glorious United Nations.

7. The Biological Weapons Convention of 1972 was the world's greatest disarmament agreement, dealing with the most destructive class of weapons. One single *Coxiella burnetti* organism, inhaled into the lungs, can initiate Q Fever. And even though such an inhalation is readily done, Fred C. Ikle, then-director of the U.S. Arms Control and Disarmament Agency, in 1974 declared that the "military utility of these weapons is dubious at best."

Q Fever insulted? What audacity!

It is hard to understand how a Fred C. Ikle comes into existence, thrives, advances, preaches, makes policies, and condescends to microorganisms. He is a phenomenon peculiar and important: improbable in and of himself but nevertheless, in our era, commonplace. Today it seems there is a proliferation of these improbable types; elected, appointed, bememoired. The Soviets have considered the phenomenon too, and have based an entire system of conquest upon it.

8. *Meanwhile, in the Infantry.* — Field Manual 100-5 says: "U.S. policy prohibits first use of lethal or incapacitating chemical munitions. It also prohibits any use of biological weapons." Imagine what this means: The manual comes down the policy-making chain and the soldier reads his doom. For he cannot enjoy the same advantages as his enemy. Imagine George Washington telling his troops: "You are prohibited from thrusting with your bayonet until you are stabbed, or from using your bullets until you are shot."

First there was Korea, where men were commanded to bomb but half a bridge; then Vietnam—restrictions getting ever tighter and more ridiculous—and now, by means of legislation, our soldiers are systematically prohibited from all chances of winning the next world war.

9. *The ABM Treaty.* —

Between November 1969 and May 1972 hot air of almost hurricane force stirred Switzerland. Competition in rocket construction had to be restricted because the United States Congress was balking at further expenditures. Also, the Soviets did not like the looming American anti-ballistic missile program. The Kremlin bosses were saying to their underlings: "Nip this in the bud."

And off to Switzerland went a pair of Foreign Ministry nippers!

The Soviets had long been looking for a technological solution to anti-rocket defense, and had begun to deploy their own ABM system in 1966. United States developments were proceeding as well. On 18 September 1967 the United States announced the initial deployment of a "thin" ABM system. The Johnson administration explained that this system was meant to meet "limited" Chinese threats and "accidental" Soviet launchings.

Johnson's ABM program inspired controversy. Some thought an ABM system was useless if it didn't offer 100 percent protection. Others believed that ABMs would destroy the peace process. Defense Secretary Robert Strange McNamara tried to reassure the American people by saying: "Let me emphasize—and I cannot do so too strongly—that our decision to go ahead with a limited ABM deployment in no way indicates that we feel an agreement...is in any way less urgent or desirable." In other words, McNamara reassured the nation that this was not a serious attempt to defend the United states. For McNamara believed that limiting America's defense would increase America's security; and he fully intended to increase America's security. Therefore he made it perfectly clear that Johnson's ABMs were not serious ABMs, because serious ABMs would make Mutual Assured Destruction impossible.

—Cut to Leonid Brezhnev laughing until tears are streaming down his face.

10. *On the Question of national technical means.* — As mentioned previously, none of the treaties on bacteriological warfare contain solid provisions for verification. Nonetheless, we have a "semblance of verification" called "national technical means"—which is a good thing, as we all know. It allows the turkey to sleep soundly till Thanksgiving. Consider how rich we are in these advocates of "verification," and how poor they are in verifiables. United States Ambassador L. G. Fields called for "a combination of nation and internation [*sic*] measures." Imagine how absolute this faith is in the science of snooping. We will have United Nations cops rampaging throughout the "former" Soviet Union, peeping into everything; and the world will remain at peace until the snoopers lose their sniff; and, growing tired of chasing shadows, sink into bureaucratic slumbers. And what of our spy satellites? Nothing but electronic crutches for our crippled CIA.

U.S. Congressman Les Aspin, later to become top Pentagon boob, said that "The keystone of an international arms-control agreement is the ability of each side to make sure the other side abides by it." Sounds sensible, except Mr. Aspin will tell you that verification is possible without actual on-site inspection by way of — what else?! — "national technical means." This is funny. This is fantastic. For even on-site inspection must prove fruitless when considering the problems of off-site inspection. Who has sense enough to mention *that*? Notice how the very terminology of arms verification is laden with booby-traps for the credulous and the unwary. For such are Les Aspin and his ilk in these days prior to the rockets and the bioclouds.

11. On 26 May 1972 Nixon and Brezhnev signed the ABM treaty, and with it, an interim agreement on strategic offensive arms — both of which stipulated that compliance is to be assured by "national technical means." Of course, due to the insistence of the Americans the Soviets promised not to undertake any cheating, or any concealment of activities. Imagine: you make a treaty but ask that additional promises be made; specifically, that the other party will keep their word. Why not make them promise to keep their promise to keep their promise ad infinitum? Is the treaty-maniac, at long last, found wanting in his mania?

*   *   *   *   *

The actual ABM Treaty is formally called—mark this!—*The Treaty on the Limitation of Anti-Ballistic Missile Systems.* Nationwide ABM defense is therein prohibited. From now on each superpower agrees to have only two ABM deployment areas.

The treaty says that each ABM site can have no more than 100 interceptor missiles and 100 launchers. The Soviets have been clever about violating this one. The Soviet launchers have reloads. And the Soviets have salted away *thousands* of these reloads where "national technical means" cannot find them. The ABM Treaty was ratified on 30 September 1972. An Agreed Mutual Statement of the USA-USSR follows: "The Parties understand that, in addition to the ABM radars which may be deployed in accordance with subparagraph (a) of Article III of the Treaty, those non-phased-array ABM radars operational on the date of signature of the Treaty within the ABM system deployment area for defense of the national capital may be retained."

It continues: "The Parties agree not to deploy phased-array radars having a potential exceeding three million...except for the purposes of tracking objects in outer space or for use as national technical means of verification."

We can see that these qualifications are *not* loopholes. For a hole has material substance around it.

12. *And Soviet views on verification?* —

Andrei Gromyko, that wonderful humanitarian and all-around nice guy, counsels the use of "national technical means" because his people have such means, available at newsstands everywhere.

13. Trust looms up. It gapes and swallows our critical faculty, then burps: *the beginnings of indigestion.* On 24 June 1975 the Soviet representative to the Committee on Disarmament says that the USSR has no biological weapons. He also adds that the USSR doesn't even possess the means of delivering them. Ergo: nothing for our inspectors to inspect. *No reason for any inspections whatsoever.*

But sub-snooped Sweden is dissatisfied. Poor, frozen, anti-Soviet Sweden. She smells something rotten in Leningrad. She demands strengthened compliance, and mumbles about genetic engineers in Forced Cogitation Camps. The Soviets respond: "The proposals made especially by Sweden to strengthen compliance...are totally unjustified and cannot serve a useful purpose..." —to wit, cannot serve the Soviet purpose. And thus goodbye to Swedish mumblings.

14. Paranoia is a psychological disorder. And anyone suspicious of the "former" Soviet Union is certifiable in this regard. Nevertheless, persons unafraid of certifiability continue to write and talk about the Sverdlovsk anthrax epidemic of 1979; an epidemic only possible in the wake of large-scale Soviet preparations for a biological attack on the United States. And then there is the precipitation of "yellow rain"—a

biologically derived toxin—in Southeast Asia and Afghanistan. Treaty-maniacs dismiss such incidents as due to freakish swarms of bees. We find, quite to our surprise, that such bees like to amass themselves wherever Soviet advisors or troops appear. Andrei Gromyko, the Soviet spokesman on such matters, has denied any Soviet involvement. He says to us: "If these weapons were used I'd know about it." And whenever anyone wants to check things out independently, Mr. Gromyko is quick to stress the notion of "self-policing."

At this point we cannot avoid a salute to the KGB.

Mr. Gromyko has also explained that on-site inspection can only occur if the nation to be inspected determines when, how, and if. We can see he's anxious to keep his country's obligations, and is sedulously concerned with the safety of American inspectors. He would not want them to needlessly contract pulmonary anthrax while inspecting a place like Sverdlovsk, even though our politicians feel that anthrax is, after all, a weapon of "dubious" utility.

Yeltsin's regime continues the old policy. The violations continue as Russia moves ahead in creating a superplague weapon. The ghost of Gromyko yet walks the Kremlin.

15. *SALT I.* — And then came a treaty which allowed the Soviets to surpass us in ballistic missile firepower. I refer to the Strategic Arms Limitation Treaty, which restricts the number of ballistic missiles on both sides. Sounds fair, right? Not really. Soviet ballistic missiles are much bigger than American ballistic missiles. At first we thought this was due to Soviet clumsiness. But today, according to Angelo Codevilla, a single Soviet missile can probably deliver up to twenty-eight warheads while the best American missiles can only deliver approximately ten.[2] Therefore equality in missiles doesn't mean equality in firepower.

16. *Incredible Agreements, continued.* — An agreement Between the United States of America and the Union of the Soviet Socialist Republics on the Prevention of Nuclear War was signed at Washington on 22 June (!) 1973 and entered into force on that same day. Notice the odd date upon which the treaty was signed; in other words, on the anniversary of Hitler's surprise attack on Russia.

But let us read the text:

"...the Parties agree that they will act in such a manner as to prevent the development of situations capable of causing a dangerous exacerbation of their relations, as to avoid military confrontations, and as to exclude the outbreak of nuclear war between them and between...other countries."

---

[2] Angelo Codevilla, "The Abuse of Arms Control," *Global Affairs* (SUMMER/FALL 1990), p. 36.

It continues: "The Parties agree, in accordance with Article 1 and do realize the objective stated...that each Party will refrain from the threat or use of force against the other party, against the allies of the other Party and against other countries, in circumstances which may endanger international peace and security."

What purpose is served by such an idiotic waste of ink and paper, signed on 22 June!?

17. Have you ever heard of the *Treaty on the Prohibition of Military or Any Other Hostile Use of Environmental Modification Techniques*?

One gasps at the thing. What could it mean? The implication is that environmental warfare is possible, and not only possible but the cause of negotiations leading to a treaty, which entered into force on 5 October 1978 when the twentieth state to sign the convention deposited its instrument of ratification. The United States Senate ratified this treaty with a vote of 98 to 0.

The text of the treaty reads:

"1. Each State Party to this Convention undertakes not to engage in military or any other hostile use of environmental modification techniques having widespread, long-lasting or severe effects as the means of destruction, damage or injury to any other State Party."

It continues: "the term 'environmental modification techniques' refers to any technique for changing — through the deliberate manipulation of natural process — the dynamics, composition or structure of the Earth, including its biota, lithosphere, hydrosphere and atmosphere, or of outer space."

18. *Here, there, everywhere.* — Seabed treaties, ABM and ICBM, biological, even Moon Treaties and Weather Conventions. Why so many treaties? And why is there so much faith placed in them? Could it be that urging us into so many empty gestures makes the gestures more mechanical, more knee-jerk? Is it a form of conditioning, whereafter, at long last, we sign, amidst heaps of paper, something vital, dangerous and irrevocable? And with the proliferation of so many undreamt of weapons: how many more treaties must there be? Can minds grow ever softer and softer, with treaty after treaty, with absurd clause after matter-of-fact semi-colon? Where does psychological warfare end and the decisive technological advantage begin? Or will we sign a Psychological Warfare Treaty and put an end to *all* our worries?

19. *Macabre anniversaries reconsidered.* — SALT II was signed by President Carter and General Secretary Brezhnev in Vienna on 18 June 1979. President Carter transmitted this treaty to the United States

Senate on 22 June. Curious thing, this 22 June popping up again. More irony? More laughing up the sleeves by Kremlin bosses? Coincidences in dates, with treaties? Ominous bloodsoaked remembrances from the past associated with the cordial treaty-making of the present? But don't calendars exist to remind people of specific dates? And isn't it true that we mark our calendars idiosyncratically? Twenty-two June is a date on the Soviet calendar which signifies to *them*, most dramatically, that treaties are pieces of paper which can be broken at any time. Therefore, as a way of reminding themselves of this eternal truth, the Soviets have signed on this date. And then there was the signing of the INF Treaty on 8 December. President Gorbachev arrived in Washington for the summit on 7 December.

20. *Soviet Backfire Statement does not backfire.* —
"The Soviet side informs the US side that the Soviet 'Tu-22M' airplane, called 'Backfire' in the USA, is a medium-range bomber, and that it does not intend to give this airplane the capability of operating at intercontinental distances. In this connection, the Soviet side states that it will not increase the radius of action of this airplane in such a way as to enable it to strike targets on the territory of the USA. Nor does it intend to give it such a capability in any other manner, including by in-flight refueling. At the same time, the Soviet side states that it will not increase the production rate of this airplane as compared to the present rate."
Scout's honor!

21. In the mid 1980s the United States Senate ratified, and President Reagan signed, the Genocide Treaty, which now is part of the supreme law of our land. But the principal victims of the coming genocidal war will *not* save themselves thereby, but only make themselves ridiculous: that is, as laughingstocks and weak tenderfooted freaks of nature, unable to deal competently with their enemies.

We are talking about a law which admits that we have entered an age of mass extermination. Nonetheless, it is a law that denies the necessities of such an age. Truly, it can now be said that most every child has his pacifier while the United States Senate has its Genocide Treaty. The bleak reality of modern war stands before us, and look at our manly way of dealing with it. We reach for a pen and sign our names on a piece of paper. One can see the reaction in the Kremlin. They are laughing at us. Tears of mirth are streaming down their faces. The stupid Americans have done it again. Stalin fooled them, Khrushchev fooled them, Brezhnev fooled them, Gorbachev fooled them, and Yeltsin is making jackasses out of them!

America ought to look at the world around it: crowded, hungry, and mean. Under these circumstances can a nation endure when it seriously

----

renounces its chief method of self defense (i.e., to exterminate in turn)?

As for the treaty itself: it is a ridiculous jumble of vague and contradictory words which stupidly contest the primacy of murder in world affairs. But here, in the United States, we swoon and rant; trying to put forward a *good impression.* Words! Words! Words! Empty, vacuous, conceited, arrogant, high-sounding placebos built up from alphabets into syllables, punctuated by ironical pauses. And that is all one can ever make of such internationalist rubbish.

"Article III
"The following acts shall be punishable:
"a) Genocide;
"b) conspiracy to commit genocide;
"c) Direct and public incitement to commit genocide;"

—*This entire book,* for example, is now made illegal with the passage of the Genocide Treaty. For in these pages I advocate a strong national defense in an age when national defense is inescapably genocidal in its implications. Therefore, in accordance with Article One, the United States is obligated to suppress this book and punish its author. He has violated Article Three, paragraph (c) of the Genocide Treaty. Senators: I defy you. I defy your Genocide Treaty. I violate it by demanding that the United States win every genocidal war that may be forced upon it. I publicly incite our generals to unleash their nuclear rockets in the event we are attacked. Come senators! Arrest me! I am breaking the supreme law of the land! *I am urging the defense of my country!*

22. This adoption of new laws, this berserk passion for treaties, this rampant moral hyperbole, demonstrates that the majority of our senators are unfit to lead a great nation; that they have lost their hard edge; that their morality is the morality of actors and sentimentalists. Add to this that they have passed into law a treaty by which they themselves may be tried and shot.

23. As America's government became increasingly irritated at ongoing treaty violations under Mr. Gorbachev in mid-1991, there occurred that staged incident, the Potemkin coup, which brought in Mr. Yeltsin. Thus, while the violations continued we again received assurances. Yet there appeared an Associated Press story on 24 November 92: "Russia to Increase Spending on Arms," which said that Russian President Yeltsin announced a ten percent increase in military spending on "arms and equipment." No eyebrows were raised. Everyone

----

slept soundly, and the West continued to disarm.

In January 1992 President Yeltsin promised—once more!—to halt the Soviet biological weapons program. By September of 92 there were press stories about chemical, biological, and nuclear weapons violations. Promises were renewed once again, and the West believed in them. Then it was reported, in the 1 February 93 issue of *Newsweek* magazine, that the Russian biological weapons violations were continuing. The only substantial change had been the closing of a Russian test site.

In early April of 1993, an American reporter, Will Englund of *The Baltimore Sun*, was arrested by the Russian secret police and detained for two days of questioning because of a story he had written on the Kremlin's chemical weapons program. The story was based, in part, on information obtained from Vil Mirzayanov, a Russian scientist who has been charged with disclosing state secrets. It seems that Mirzayanov accused the Yeltsin government of testing a new and very powerful chemical weapon in violation of previous agreements.

24. *Real nuclear disarmament.* — When every last rocket has been fired.

7

Critique of Education

Anyone who has taught in a typical American college is unlikely to be impressed by the urgency of student desires for more education. He may even be painfully aware of their resistance to, and evasion of, education. Of course it is still true that large numbers of people would like to be in college, for reasons which range from the sublime to the ridiculous. Most of them see college as a way to get ahead.

— THOMAS SOWELL [1]

American schools could do with more discipline and more hard work. The students I have met too often seek out the easiest way to get through school and college, instead of setting out to learn something. Too often they are only interested in money.

— PETER DERIABIN, former KGB official [2]

In history, the way of annihilation is invariably prepared by inward degeneration, by decrease of life. Only then can a shock from outside put an end to the whole.

— JACOB BURCKHARDT [3]

Along with its natural protectors and guardians, learning will be cast into the mire, and trodden down under the hoofs of a swinish multitude.

— EDMUND BURKE[4]

1. My first note on education, as a former educator, should not be misunderstood. I believe that a process is underway and has been

---

[1] Thomas Sowell, *Education: Assumptions Versus History*, (California: Stanford University Press, 1986), p. 107.

[2] Peter Deriabin and Frank Gibney, *The Secret World* (New York: Ballantine Books, 1959), p. 332.

[3] Burckhardt, *Reflections on History*, P. 57.

[4] Edmund Burke, *Reflections on the Revolution in France* (England: Penguin Books, 1986), p. 173.

underway for many decades. And what is this process? According to recent findings, 135,000 American schoolchildren take guns to school every day.

2. The educational cliché of our age, that history should not be the memorization of names, places and dates, leads us to history as an amorphous mass of Wherevers and What's-His-Names, chaotically arranged without regard to When—and a generation that cannot locate Europe on a map.

3. *A generation at risk?* — In 1990 the National Association of State Boards of Education and the American Medical Association created a joint thirty-six member panel to study the youth problem. The findings of this panel were so shocking that one of the participants, Roseann Bentley, said: "We are absolutely convinced that, if we don't take action immediately, we're going to find ourselves with a failing economy and social unrest."

According to the joint commission formed by the two groups: at least one million teenage girls became pregnant in 1989. The suicide rate for teens has doubled since 1968 and teenage arrests are up three thousand percent since 1950. Of high school seniors, nearly forty percent admitted to recent drunkenness, and the leading causes of teenage death are alcohol-related.

In response to these and other findings, the joint thirty-six member panel was quick to propose a solution. They suggested that community health centers, financed by local or state governments, be set up for adolescents. In turn, the schools would be responsible for initiating "a new kind of health education—a sophisticated multifaceted program that goes light years beyond the present lectures about personal hygiene."

Perhaps my comment here is unduly cynical, but are not these proposals somewhat self-justifying on the part of the aforementioned health and education officials? In the name of addressing the calamity of American youth, these organizations are hoping to acquire jobs and money. If not for the possibility of such jobs and money, one doubts that the "problems of youth" would ever be mentioned at all.

4. The fact that one might enrich oneself in the short term by paying lip service to social problems has itself become a social problem. The name of the game is "Careers." To correct a tragic situation, or to deal with it realistically, is to lose the game. For once in place, a social bureaucracy has a vested interest in keeping various social problems alive.

The idea is to milk them, but not to milk them dry.

5. Michael Josephson, who runs the Joseph and Edna Josephson Institute for the Advancement of Ethics asserts that "an unprecedented proportion of today's young generation lacks commitment to core moral values such as honesty, respect for others, personal responsibility and civic duty." According to the Josephsons, seventy-five percent of high school students and fifty percent of college students admit to cheating in school.

6. *Civics lesson, student to teacher.* — "Why should I learn the Constitution? I know my rights. I know how to scream. My lungs are strong. Therefore: Why should I learn the Constitution?"

And: "Civics is boring. I cannot remember it. I cannot remember it because it is boring. It is boring because I cannot remember it."

And: "Chitter chatter, chitter chatter, chitter chatter, ha ha ha."

7. Spare the F and save a fuss. Save a fuss and strengthen the bureaucracy. Strengthen the bureaucracy, strengthen oneself. Strengthen oneself and take it easy. Take it easy and live longer. Live longer and collect social security. Collect Social Security and get revenge. Get revenge by sparing the F.

8. A thirteen-year-old student sneeringly accuses her English teacher of incompetence. Another student openly berates this same teacher for being "negative," and for making them read sad stories. Yet another wants to know the teacher's religious affiliation. The teacher refuses to say. A student blurts out: "You need God." "You shouldn't dwell on negative things," says one of the girls. The teacher replies: "For you there is God but no Devil." They snicker and joke, and one girl says, "You're right." Another—"Who cares? What's it to you?" "You talk propaganda. I think you are out to brainwash people." The students burst out laughing and snickering. The teacher reprimands a boy for being out of his seat. The boy smirks, then recites a dirty poem. The class bursts forth in unconstrained howling.

Such a despicable teacher!

9. *Other teachers.* —

"So! You're reading Dostoyevsky!" says the literature teacher. "*Crime and Punishment.* I don't know how anyone could stomach that book."

"It's very good," replies the visitor.

"When I read it I practically broke out in a fever, like the main character. I felt as if society were crushing me, and closing in all around. I was terribly depressed afterward. I would never waste my nights like that again, except for college credit. It's a work of art, but it's really terrible."

Another literature teacher, a woman, interrupts: "I tried to read that book a couple of times but I could never get through it, much too depressing."

"Depressing?" asks the visitor.

"*The Brothers Karamazov* is a much better book."

"But *Crime and Punishment* has a happy ending."

"But there's too much grief on the way."

10. An English teacher says that George Orwell's *1984* should be avoided. "There's not a shred of hope in it."—Which means, as a matter of course, that bitter truths should remain in the shadows and that flabbiness ought to prevail everywhere. This is, at bottom, essential to the fabric of America's cultural optimism.

11. Progress, as the progress of fat, must needs have consequences: It zips and zooms through overpeopled landscapes soon-to-be moonscapes; looks for the limits of itself and discovers that as the fountainhead of decadence it comprehends no limits. It grows and swirls, permeates everything, corrodes all definitions and formulations. Every area of national life is contaminated, trashed, and corrupted; creating an abyss of ignorance and puerility, it breeds and interbreeds—*with itself.* Mass public education from its very beginning has jerked spasmodically toward its ultimate, logical, necessary, undecreed END: it is, and becomes, *education to make stupid.*   Professor Allan Bloom did not go far enough. He only scratched the surface. Who then will give America an idea of the new and misshapen soul of today? Who now dares explain educational deformity to the educationally deformed?

12. *Education.* —

The dirtiest lie of our age is the euphemism "education," which refers to our concentration camp for the child. We say that we value family, children, and morality; but we sacrifice all these to urges, to pecuniary gain, to momentary thrills. We want everything to be easy. We want to have our cake and eat it. So we allow our children to become brats. For discipline is hard work. In place of hard work we have words, mere words, nice words, as we drown in words—like "education." Let us own up to the fact that we don't want to be bothered with our children.

13. *In a typical high school.* — The teacher notices that many of the students are cheating if they are doing anything at all. Outside the class room the halls are clogged with trash; drowned each day in a surfeit of smashed cakes, soda pop cans, candy wrappers, and other student-

generated garbage. The principal has a supple spine. Most of the teachers have given up.

The teacher rises to speak: "This is wrong. You aren't learning. And further, you know that we cannot make you learn. Everybody in this class, except two or three people, deserves to fail. Add to this the monstrous difficulties placed in the way of our goal. I must take roll, cope with loudmouths, play policeman and baby-sitter, and you resist every inch of the way. If something peaks your interest it cannot last. For that would mean an exertion of effort and concentration, which you despise and resent. So you drop it immediately in favor of a joke or smart remark.

"Hardly any of you can draw a simple world map. How many times have I told you to study that world map? How many times have you refused? How will you cope? How will you judge, vote, think? Weapons are pointed at you. People are lying to you on TV. You haven't any idea of what's out there. NO IDEA."

But the students think the teacher is a fool.

14. *High school.* — An unproductive, government-financed, baby-sitting center, providing weary adults with so many years of respite from the youthful horde pressing up to replace them. Narcotics retailers see a ready-made market amid these enervated, blank, and impressionable minds.

15. It is bureaucratically incorrect to flunk the seventy percent of the students who do next to nothing. One may, perhaps, flunk the three percent who do nothing BADLY; but for the rest, everything is graded on a curve. A very warped curve. Therefore, the *practical* teenager is sometimes known to drop completely out.

16. The textbooks are written for the dullest brains. Moneys are extorted by spendthrift legislators and the students are compelled by mandatory attendance laws: all based upon the theory that the child will learn something.

17. One day you might play teacher. You might notice a boy spitting on a girl's chair. There will be 37 children all squirming and shrieking and sassing and smart-alecking. Send seven students at a crack to the vice principal and they still won't shut-up. There isn't any corporal punishment available and so they laugh at you. Why should we improve our behavior, they ask? Why indeed!

18. *Without respect.* — He's a big man, a fat man, a coach. Someone says he's funny because he tells dirty jokes in class. But no, he

----

isn't funny. For while a dirty joke can win laughter, it cannot win respect. And what, in the final analysis, counts more?

19. In the world at large the average person has no need for books or learning. The typical individual considers himself amply knowledgeable without recourse to official instruction. And the average student's deep resentment against forced-feedings of hack textbook-writers is quite often justified. Reading is not a popular thing; and *this* kind of reading *most of all.*

20. *A 12th grade economics class.* — A student insists on going to the bathroom and returns laden with Twinkies, nuts, candy-bars, and soda pop. The teacher tells him not to eat in class. The student rips open the Twinkies and begins to eat. The teacher takes it away and throws it in the trash. The student proceeds to open something else. The teacher again throws it in the trash. The student is sent to the vice principal. Then a girl loudly asks about the teacher;s sex life.

21. Every year, day after day, America's children are herded into gigantic fenced camps wherein roll call occurs, like clockwork, upon every hour because prisoners are bound to escape, to get loose and make trouble; little brutes soon-to-become big brutes, torment each other with open cruelties, persecutions, and mockeries; even tormenting teachers, especially substitute teachers, with vexatious insolence, faked inabilities, rampant cheating, vandalism, pencil-breaking, paper-crumpling, and— above all— constant, unpunished (and perhaps unpunishable) sniggering.

Think of it this way: The students are locked in with one another, to corrupt and interfere with one another; to stunt one-another's growth; to pester and poke one another; but at all costs, to be kept away from the civilizing influence of adult society, until, at long last, adult society becomes *yet another question.*

We have constructed an enormous confinement, a ghastly existence in which children, both bright and dull, are slowly crushed by all-encompassing horseplay, tedium, and petty tyranny—which are all unavoidable elements in a "mass" system. The brightest students, of course, have the most to lose, while the rest become slaves to peer pressure; which is, the pressure to smoke dope, to drink, to mock teachers, parents, police; to take "uppers," "downers," hallucinogens; to sniff, snort, inject, copulate and impregnate themselves into adulthood. This environment, this situation, is called "preparation for the real world"; *these* the human beings, the raw material of tomorrow, shaped in a setting where the principal reality is the group and its demands; a group led by the most appealing, "coolest" children. No longer do such children believe in good and evil, authority or truth. For the vast majority only social acceptance and social rejection have significance.

22. Modern education, as an establishment, has certain prejudices: (1) there are no moral absolutes; (2) all prejudices are bad, except educational ones; (3) minority studies must be crammed down everyone's throat; (4) anyone can be educated; (5) all should receive education; (6) the failure of education is due to inadequate funding or reactionary home influences; and (7) children should be "socialized."

23. Universal free education means that the government determines which individual is to be educated, who is educator, and what is worth learning. This type of arrangement also becomes mixed up in the governmental machinery. The end result is: 1) a society slavishly adhering to government seals of approval; 2) a society with bureaucratic instincts inculcated from the age of five or younger; 3) a society hardened against culture and riddled with bogus career "goals."

24. *We economists.* — Nietzsche once called the state that "coldest of all cold monsters." If the characterization is apt, then why let the state take on the role of parent? The answer, of course, is that motherhood has become economically "inefficient," and mothers must be encouraged to pursue "careers." The answer also has to do with the decline of fatherhood. Also, there is the "single" mother who *must* work. And so it has come to pass that only six percent of the children now attending school have mothers who are exclusively homemakers. Before criticizing this arrangement, one must consider its efficiency. Only one government official per twenty children is thought necessary to watch over, socialize, and educate a batch of preschoolers. Think of how spendthrift it would be to allow a mother to stay home with two or three children. Imagine the economic waste of it!

25. One ought to mention television, which further alienates children from their parents. And the parents acquiesce because television—like the state—is a convenient baby-sitter.

26. It is little wonder that the state increasingly accepts responsibility for bringing up children while the parents become increasingly lax, easy-going, and permissive. There is a definite laziness here. There is a secret desire—if not a demand—that somebody else do the dirty work. Meanwhile, the state-certified teacher goes forth to slay the triple-headed dragon of reactionary guilt and ignorance concerning "safe sex," substance abuse, and ethnocentricity.

----

27. *Our solution?* — Take away all crutches for the parent. Liquidate the public schools and pull the plug on television. Make the family *necessary* again.

28. Aristotle said that habit must precede reason in moral education. Here is where we have most failed our young people. We have neglected the inculcation of honesty and justice *as habits.*

29. *What today's 12-year-old students want (from a teacher's questionaire):*
a. I'm happy (usually) when I'm with my friends. But not with my family.
b. Having lots of people who care about me.
c. Money.
d. Money, girls, sex, surfing.
e. What makes me happy? When I have a good day and get a new girl friend. Rich. Famous.
f. I could be the happiest man in the world if someone could give enough money to be the richest man in the world. If someone bought me three million computer games.
g. It makes me happy when people are considerate and don't care about appearance. After that I feel everything else would fall into place.
h. Something that makes me happy is money.
i. Money, girls, surfing, more girls, GIRLS (SEX) SURFING (BIG WAVES), money, lots of.
j. Being rich and evil.
k. The thing that would make me happy would be riches, people that are homeless to get homes & food, money, guys, parties, music.
l. A leprechaun.
m. What makes me happy is when I get good grades on my tests.
n. Coming home and relax. Just have fun.
o. It would make me happy if I can be the best in every school I go to, because I want a good education and have a good job.
p. Life is happiness, surfing, girls, school.
q. A rad teacher who gives no homework and sex rad surf good friends.
r. Surfing, girls, (sex most important), money.
s. I wish I had the most awesomest chick in the world. And also a lot of money. Sex.
t. Money don't go to school. If you go don't have to do anything and girls and a Big house.
u. I am already as happy as I can be. Last week I was baptized as a dedicated servant of Jehovah God. The only way my life could be any more complete is if I became a pioneer or helped at our headquarters in

----

New York as one of Jehovah's Witnesses.

30. What do we make of these students as they cry out for money, sex, girls, money, more sex, etc.? Certainly one understands the dislike of homework. This is merely typical. Also, it is perfectly understandable that knowledge does not thrive in them. But the thing which shocks us, especially in children of such tender years, is the fact that country, religion, and family have a hold on so a few. Everything that might counterbalance sensuality, selfishness, and impudence is conspicuously absent.

31. *True-False as answered by 7th graders (from a teacher's questionaire);*
    1. I have cheated on a major test this year—15 say false, 6 say true.
    2. Communists are bad—16 say false, 5 true (laughter at question).
    3. Good and evil is a matter of opinion—4 say false, 17 true.
    4. Cheating is wrong—9 say false, 12 true.

32. *Answers from the same grade class: —*
Arrange the following names in chronological order:

Moses
Hannibal
Caesar
Jesus
Charlemagne
William Pitt
Lincoln

Only one student could answer. He had for the last six years attended school in Bolivia.
The same test was given to students at a major American University. Result? Of the 90 college students, not one could arrange the names correctly.
Conclusion: No Bolivians.

33. *A typical seventh grade disruption.* — Irrepressible giggling over the fact that Sumerians maintained "dikes."

34. henry James hatched a story which grows, day by day, into the story of our American youth.. It is the story of Daisy Miller. We find, in every classroom, the essential elements the same: 1) She has no

imagination; 2) she doesn't know any history or care to know any; 3) she spurns parental authority, even as her parents are absurdly lax; 4) she is bored and yearning for excitement; 5) empty-headed; 6) innocently immoral; 7) cruel, disrespectful, and naïve.

Daisy Miller's attitude is: I want to have fun. There is no time for a good job. Let us do a bad job and have a good time at it. Let us not be "stiff."

35. *What a teacher has to say.* — "I think the students are bright, as long as they receive encouragement from home. What they lack is discipline. They don't show respect. They are not used to doing what adults tell them."

36.   *Ongoing conversation between a substitute teacher and students in a Physical Education class —*
Subsitute teacher: If a person murders someone out of envy, isn't that evil?
First Girl: No.
Second Girl: No
Teacher: Then you don't believe that evil exists?
First Girl: Who are you to say what's good or evil? You don't have the right to judge anybody. You're just negative.
Second Girl: Yeah, you're just negative.
Teacher: No! No! You've got me wrong; I'm merely trying to understand the implications of what you're saying. [The shower bell rings].
First Girl: Our regular teacher always lets us leave at the first bell.
Second Girl: Yeah.
Teacher: But that's against the rules.
First Girl: I'm telling you the truth.
Teacher: I have to follow the rules.
First Girl: You don't believe me, but I'm not a liar.
Teacher: I never said you were a liar.
First Girl: You won't get into trouble.
Teacher: I am forbidden to let students go at the first bell.
First Girl: What does that matter?
[A boy comes up to the sub].
Boy: Are you going to take roll again before class ends?
Teacher: Why do you ask?
Boy: I just wanted to know. Are you taking roll?
Teacher: I don't know.
Boy: Come on, tell me.
Teacher: No.
Boy: You better tell me.

Teacher: No.

Boy: F--- you, man. [And he walks off].

Teacher: What a nasty kid. Hey! Come back here! What's your name?

First Girl: Maybe his parents beat him.

Second Girl: You can't blame a person for being bad if they were abused. Maybe that's all they know.

37. Self-esteem has become the new catchword for what today's children are lacking. Self-esteem, as the cult of the unfettered self, teaches expansiveness and the destruction of all limits, the corruption of all rules, and the elimination of all punishments. You can become anything you want. You can achieve your wildest desires. We will not stand in your way. And what is more: we ask *nothing* of you, as you have no responsibility, no duty, no honor, no need to adjust yourself to the older view. If we punish you, then *we* are wrong. For punishment is inherently vicious. Therefore, we say unto the young: Make your own view. Create a culture of youth, of sensuality, and of good times. For we have taken away the rod, the stick, and the belt. We have stopped the military draft. We have ceased to tutor you.

—Tutor yourselves!

38. Since rules and punishments have largely disappeared, and since there is no longer any true guidance, today's youth are experiencing a crisis of direction. Where to now? Having never climbed the mountain of discipline one is unable to climb anything at all. A vague feeling of impotence creeps into a soul which yearns to hear itself praised, which yearns to hear the chorus sing: "You can do anything." "Self-esteem is what you need." "Don't be anxious." "Be a winner." "You can do it."

—Since we cannot find direction in rules, we must bolster indirection with slogans.

39. *The political question of our time.* — Why do we need these universities, these poisonous wells and toxic dumpsites of the spirit? There is not *one* sound reason for them to continue in existence. I defy this prejudice of our age which unquestioningly accepts the value of state-financed higher education. All our state-run universities should be converted into libraries. All these tenured professors should be given the boot. The administrators, too, ought to look for *real* jobs. Redirect university funding to retire the national debt. Send the president of the American Political Science Association to Mars. Give outer space something thick and unreadable.

40. *Twinkle twinkle, little star.* —
Author: How I wonder what you are.
Professor: A human that lives in the 1990's.
Author: I could get that answer from a truck driver. You are supposed to be an intellectual.
Professor: A truck driver has just as much reality as I do.
Author: Are you sure?
Professor: Well, you can't be sure of anything.

41. Something snapped inside his head and he became a sociologist. —Yes, I'm the product of a certain kind of toilet training. No, I haven't any free will. But yes, I believe that people make decisions. *Do I contradict myself?* Yes. Conclusion: I should have been a plumber.

42. We fool ourselves about the meaning and purpose of higher education. Today we say that such an education involves "learning how to think." But how does one teach "thinking"? Suppose that thinking is forever hidden from us. Suppose that the dark foundation of introspection is an impenetrable mystery. What noble note could the schools trumpet then?

43. A professor was lecturing to a small band of graduate students: "You need to learn how to think. You are no longer undergraduates. It's time to grow up."

After the meeting one of the students said to the professor: "But education is not about learning how to think. Education is about indoctrination."

The professor frowned: "That doesn't even deserve a reply."

"Education is indoctrination," continued the young man. "The fact is unavoidable. In the end you will find yourself merely indoctrinating people. So why lie about it?"

"If you really feel that way," replied the professor, "then you'll never make a good teacher."

"No," said the graduate student, "I'll make an honest teacher, which is far better than a dishonest one."

The professor shook his head. "I'd hate to be one of your students. You've thrown out everything worthwhile. Who could learn how to think from someone so narrow-minded? It is exactly *this* attitude which must be eradicated. People want to develop their minds. They want to learn how to think. They don't want to be preached at."

The student answered by saying: "While it is true that people don't want to be preached at, you are mistaken when you assume that they want to develop their minds or learn how to think for themselves. What

---

they want is a career. In other words, they want to learn ideas that will get them accepted. It is not profitable, in a society like ours, to think. That would raise too many eyebrows and generate too much animosity. Every student instinctively knows that indoctrination in 'accepted ideas' is what they need. As for 'techniques of thinking,' such are merely formulas routinely applied by those who are constitutionally incapable of figuring things out for themselves. As for the value of such 'techniques,' I feel obliged to point out that thinking is a living act and not a formula. It cannot be taught. It is a predisposition in favor of clarity. One cannot teach a predisposition."

The professor was dumbfounded. He was caught off guard. "But there are certain secrets, certain methods"—

"No. There are no methods," interrupted the student. "If there were such methods then thinking could be taught and everyone could do it. But something as wonderful as thinking is not like that. "Okay," said the professor, "if you're so smart, then teach me how to think."

"Can we teach a baby how to focus its eyes? No. It's up to the baby. The same goes for thinking. It absolutely cannot be taught. Besides, thinking is not merely a matter of method, but of character. All I can do is give you some empty phrases or formulas to memorize and ask you to repeat them back to me. But this would be a foolish way to teach thinking. Any student of these methods might pass the course by flattering his teacher with the mere regurgitation of these selfsame formulas and techniques. And how could the teacher tell if the student was 'thinking' or mechanically parroting a formula?"

"Here's my advice to you," said the professor. "Keep your opinions to yourself. You are not well-served by them. Your job here at the university is to absorb the teachings that *we* offer. Save your opinions for later. After a while, you'll be in a better position to judge. Your teachers have worked hard and know a great deal. Until you accomplish similar work you haven't any right to draw conclusions, especially as far-reaching as the one you've just expressed. Your job here is to learn from us. Then, after a while, you will be ready to think."

"This is your method?" smiled the student. "But you are not alone, of course. Nobody likes to hear other people's thoughts. You dislike mine and think I have no right to them. You therefore agree with me that indoctrination is best. You merely call indoctrination by another name. You call it 'learning how to think'—which is perfectly understandable. People are quick to realize the disadvantages of allowing others to think for themselves. If somebody dared to think for himself, and if he dared to oppose *your* views, you'd feel quite badly about it. Therefore, the independent thinker must be careful and keep his thoughts to himself, immersing, even drowning his own thoughts in the thick soup of your doctrines; this you call 'learning how to think.' For example, just now you dismissed my thinking altogether. That clues me into the fact that I must change my tactics. For the game is made as follows: *Your* thinking is *my* indoctrination. My work might earn a C+ or an A, depending on how closely it follows your methods and formulas. Of course, I can disagree with you, but only after a preapproved fashion. I may be as stupid as a cow, but if I've a sufficient memory you'll thrill that I've learned to 'think'—as you call it. How dare any of us run ahead of the instructor and think for ourselves. And besides, how can thinking be graded? What standard would be used? Do we look for originality, truth, structure, logic—what? And who is qualified to judge of these things? Mr. Test, of course! And what is Mr. Test interested in? Grammar and memory. So what happens to 'thinking for oneself'? It disappears in the twitching of a neuron. For thinking is a useless skill from the student's point of view, as well as irksome to the teacher. Then why should one risk one's career by daring to think when all that is required is a good memory? No sir. Far from teaching us how to think, you can do nothing but the opposite. You yourself have admitted as much. The institutional arrangement itself dictates the nature of the learning process. And there isn't any way around it. Thinking means a break with one's teachers, while teaching means the handing out of grades. Until we prefer the truth to an A, until we put thinking ahead of career, we will remain intellectually mediocre. Thus the primary prerequisites to thinking are *courage and independence.* Now let us ask the question which follows: Who can teach courage? Given what happens to us from kindergarten to college there is no reason for us to esteem courage over conformity. We don't want to stick our necks out. We're *all* far gone in that regard, having lived our entire lives under a conformist educational regime. Do you suppose that our graduate seminars will suddenly, at this late hour, instill character in us? No. The situation is clear. You cannot teach people how to think, because you cannot teach courage and independence."

The professor fumed and was about to reply. Then he walked away.

44. In the nineteenth century Friedrich Nietzsche wrote that education bred nothing but industrious scribblers who do not learn from nature but from the sham that is culture. Today one might say that education breeds industrious humbugs who do not learn at all.

45. Higher education is a career path, a way to secure one's fortune, to establish credibility with the "little people." It is a grand bluff comprised of big words and even bigger ideas.

46. In terms of student output, most professors want some kind of formatting or number crunching, especially of the kind they have built

----

their careers upon. This might be called "enforced homage."

47. *The professors alone with themselves.* —

We, the cowards of contemplation, who command through our pens while the unlettered masses sweat and expire, we live as the parasites' parasite; and, like every other kind of morbid insecurity, look contemptuously down upon those who are better off than ourselves.

We sneer at the moral failings of the capitalists and, perhaps by way of intellectual intimidation, extort our daily bread. The capitalists, in turn, pat themselves on the back for being broad-minded and liberal. We thereby assist in the neurotic maladjustment of the blood-sucking vampire; we, the hypocrites and purveyors of institutionalized remorse, every one of us a "Sister Do-good," proving by nondeeds that social justice vindicates cynicism as pastime. Our holy mission? To turn the sons and daughters of the bourgeoisie against the bourgeoisie.

We lament the abject servility and complacency of the credulous proletariat, flattering ourselves that *we* know better how to deal with the duplicitous capitalists who eat out of our hands like tamed tigers. We never play the toad. Oh no, not us—never. Of course, the establishment we serve, as everyone knows, expects us to be unserious; to defer on important questions; to be clowns, cultivated poltroons, pedants and bean-counting monomaniacs. And then there is our teaching. To us—it's kid stuff to keep everyone entertained. Meanwhile, let us bloat the student body with the conceit that they actually know something, that they've learned how to think. Yet, while we tickle these juvenile fancies, let us also eliminate every visible trace of our mercenary motives. Let us bite the hand that feeds us.

We professors (and other so-called intellectuals of leftist persuasion) believe that the more craven you are, the higher you rise in the capitalist system. So perhaps we too are up-and-coming. Of course, that doesn't prevent us from sneering at everything in the world, nor does it keep us from talking about social injustice (encouraging young minds into the appropriate forms of protest). Don't ask us to manufacture patriots and other "war criminals." Our job is to stuff our students full of whatever we have on hand, that is, with "stimulating ideas" and the general conviction that everything is exceedingly vague and unjust.

And mind you, we're out to prove the social Darwinists wrong. Our goal is the survival of the unfittest (i.e., ourselves). Evolution and development are *not* our cup of tea. We want to bring man back to his primitive innocence. Our method is the negation of the negation. In each sphere we see the denial of the sphere itself. Is it not clear that in a few decades something entirely new, terrible and exciting will burst forth from this compost?

We professors are optimists.

48. *A lecture by Professor X on the sociology of Late Capitalism.*
Heraclitus asserted that the universal principle is change. Cratylus
pointed out that if Heraclitus was right, then not even the permanence of
the Law of Change could be maintained. Soon thereafter a Macedonian
bugmonger asserted that the "good" ought to make the laws. This is
called Aristotle's Law, which gave rise to another law: namely, that the
good get rich. This is called Calvin's Primary, which has many
secondaries, including, the Iron Law of Wages (the poor get poorer) and
the Fat Farm Paradox (the rich get skinny).

Still there is another axiom at work which says: God is dead. This
means, in principle, that religion declines. This is called Nietzsche's
Syntax (to be differentiated from taxes on wine and cigarettes); which
leads to the Jimmy Bakker Corollary (the clergy get sex); and also the
Jimmy Swaggart Effect (the clergy beg forgiveness). Gresham's Law
then comes into play and the bad drive out the good. This is the decisive
law for Late Capitalism and it especially applies to governments, schools,
books, music, professors, women, and movies, continuing until a critical
mass of "bad stuff" accumulates in the cultural lymph nodes of the body
politic. Next comes Pluto's Law: At which point the bad blow up the
bad, which means universal destruction and Hell on earth. This solves
Cratylus's paradox because when everything blows up there remains
nothing to change; ergo, change itself proves to be impermanent, which
only goes to show that—contrary to the Law of Excluded Middle—you
can be wrong and right at the same time. Thus, to summarize the
aforementioned dialectical points:

1) Only change is permanent; 2) the good make the laws; 3) the good
get rich; 4) but God is dead, so 5) the bad drive out the good; 6) the bad
blow-up the bad; 7) change stops changing, rendering change
impermanent; therefore, 8) no Law of Excluded Middle.

In this way, not only are all the contradictions of capitalism resolved,
but so are the contradictions of universal metaphysics and constructionist
bourgeois epistemology.

And one more thing. You are expected to know this for Friday's
test.

49. *Nondeist.* —
Believer: Are you an atheist?
Professor: I'm a nondeist.
Believer: What is a nondeist?
Professor: Religion doesn't mean anything to me.
Believer: What about the implications of nondeism?
Professor: I'm not ideologically concerned with that.

50. *The professor as conversationalist. —*

Man: How do you know if what you say is true?

Professor: I don't.

Man: So you can't know about anything?

Professor: Not about the big things, no. I guess I look at things not in the sense of whether they are real or not (that doesn't mean anything to me) but whether they are useful for the social organization of the times.

Man: So you are an epistemological pragmatist?

Professor: I guess.

Man: But if you can't know things —

Professor: You can know things, but only within your society.

Man: Then how do you say somebody is wrong?

Professor: Things are labeled wrong by the people who have power in the society.

Man: I'm not asking how society determines right or wrong. I'm asking how you do it.

Professor: But I get my concepts of right and wrong from society. If not, then nobody would understand me. For example, you get your ideas from people who all think the same way.

Man: I do?

Professor: Yes.

Man: But I thought *you* were the conformist.

Professor: No, I'm a maverick.

51. *Yet another actual conversation.*

Man: What do you think the result of your ideology will be for the world?

Professor: Basically, it will make people less arrogant, less nationalistic; and it will stop people from using categories such as capitalism and socialism.

Man: And what if the Soviet Union attacks us?

Professor: The Soviet Union can't even conquer Afghanistan [Laughing]. I'm not afraid of the Soviet Union. I'm afraid of things like economic breakdown because corporations are exploiting cheap labor overseas and we don't have the money to buy back the products, so we get a cave-in, a crash.

52. *Again. —*

Man: Do you ever see yourself getting political power?

Professor: No, I don't want it. I don't want any power whatsoever. I distrust power. I was a military brat. My dad was an intelligence officer for this country. He was like most military types. He was very brutal and not bourgeois.

Man: How so?

Professor: They basically believe in making the body react in certain ways by using force on it, like in military training. They train people to use force on other people's bodies.

Man: Doesn't that have its place?

Professor: Of course it has its place. But they use it against people who are labeled "communist," but they might be any type of person.

Man: What if they are communists?

Professor: I don't think there is anything wrong with communism.

53. *Again.* —

Professor: Reagan is a murderer. He's as bad as Hitler.

Man: Reagan?

Professor: Well, when he says people are communists he is saying that they don't have as much right to live as someone else. So he hires hitmen, like in Nicaragua.

Man: But the Sandinista's *are* communists, and communists are big-time mass murderers wherever they take power.

Professor: The Sandinistas don't call themselves communists.

Man: But they're self admitted Marxist-Leninists.

Professor: They don't call themselves that.

Man: Of course they do. Haven't you read their writings? And besides, I don't see how that makes Reagan the equivalent of Hitler. Reagan is fighting *for* freedom and against evil.

Professor: No he's not.

Man: I think that's what he's fighting for.

Professor: Well, Hitler thought the Jews were evil. He thought they were the most evil people in the world. And Reagan has the same feeling about communists as Hitler had for Jews. Hitler is just like Reagan. He wanted to free the world from communism, too.

Man: Yeah, but Hitler was proposing something just as evil as communism.

Professor: Anything Reagan would propose would be evil, too. When you use evil means you have an evil end.

Man: What are you talking about?

Professor: Well, when you try to destroy a country you are being evil.

Man: But the communists are the destroyers. They are the evil ones.

Professor: Not really. What if *you* are actually the evil one. The Nazis thought that they were the good guys.

Man: They were wrong.

Professor: That's only because we destroyed them. If they'd won

---

then they would have been right. Might makes right, baby.

Man: Might makes right?

Professor: That's right.

Man: Is that so?

Professor: As you know, Britain declared war on Germany in both World Wars. The Germans didn't attack them. You do know that, right?

Man: Of course.

Professor: Well, you've got to put it into context.

Man: But Germany attacked allies of Britain, in both instances.

Professor: No, Britain attacked allies of Germany first.

Man: What? Where? What allies?

Professor: Colonies in Africa, allies in Africa. This is what we call the "double standard."

Man: I know nothing about this "allies in Africa" business.

Professor: That's because you're crude and stupid. If you knew anything, you'd know that people take their "right and wrong" from the winners. Since the allies won the war, they wrote the history. And that makes them look like the good guys.

Man: But that doesn't make might into right.

Professor: I'm just saying that history is written by the winners.

54.   Would the university retain a geologist who professed the flatness of the Earth, an astronomer who denied the heliocentric model, or a physician who promoted the bleeding of patients as in olden times?

But oddly, there's this whole school called "social science."

55. *Another conversation. —*

Professor: All great philosophers are full of contradictions. That's what makes them interesting.

Rationalist: But then that makes them wrong.

Professor: No it doesn't. It just makes them full of contradictions.

Rationalist: No! It makes them wrong. If you contradict yourself then something you said was wrong.

Professor: No, it just means that you have a blind spot; because every time you develop a philosophic system then you're going to leave out some realities and sometimes, to handle those realities, you make a contradiction. Systems of thought cannot handle the total reality, so they must have contradictions which are interesting.

Rationalist: What is the contradiction in logical thought?

Professor: Possibly there's none, that's why it's a zero. It doesn't answer anything. Something without contradictions answers nothing. There are contradictions in all great thinkers. That's why they're interesting. You try to get those tensions between those contradictions to work something, to get something together; even though you never do.

But a flat thinker—a one-dimensional thinker—has no contradictions. He counts for nothing. Do you know what a one-dimensional person is? Well, a one dimensional thinker is the same thing: a polemical tract. Basically, such thinkers try to take out the ambiguities of life and the contradictions out of reality.

Rationalist: There are contradictions in reality?

Professor: Of course there are.

Rationalist: Show me one.

Professor: Okay, gravity.

Rationalist: How so?

Professor: Gravity takes you down to earth where we are, right?

Rationalist: Yes.

Professor: But when you go far away, the gravity is gone.

Rationalist: How is that a contradiction?

Professor: It is a contradiction because at certain places and in certain eras you don't have gravity, and yet we have gravity.

Rationalist: You mean that at the same time, in the same place, you can both have gravity and *not* have gravity?

Professor: Yes, like in a dive-bomber. You have gravity, yet in the bomber you don't have gravity.

Rationalist: So you can break the law of gravity?

Professor: Yes, if you just do something else, yeah, sure.

Rationalist: Can you give me another example?

Professor: Plenty of them. How do you think change happens? It happens because of contradictions.

Rationalist: Could you define what you mean by *contradictions*?

Professor: You believe in reality, right?

Rationalist: Yes.

Professor: Well, aren't atoms very unstable entities because they have contradictions?

Rationalist: It is impossible for objects to contradict themselves. A contradiction refers to a discrepancy of language, not a discrepancy in the things themselves.

Professor: Have you ever heard of ambiguity? You can be ambiguous because the concepts you use are not precise.

Rationalist: But still, you are talking concepts and not reality.

Professor: [Pausing] You have to bring in history then.

Rationalist: No, just give me your definition so I can better understand what you mean.

Professor: Some people are rich and other people are poor.

Rationalist: That's a definition?

Professor: Yes. The poor people want to change that situation.

Rationalist: I thought a contradiction is when you say that everyone

----

is rich and yet everyone is poor. Now that would be a contradiction.

Professor: I know what you are. You're a dualist! Old Anglo-Saxon logical dualism. You separate everything into either-or. I see things as a monism. All is One.

56. Notice how the academic loves his scholasticism, his sophistries, his complications and circumlocutions. To him they are interesting, beautiful, absorbing. The idea is to fascinate oneself by building an intricate maze, *so* intricate that one can hardly find one's way. This has been the tendency of the scholarly world since Medieval times. Today this tendency has grown increasingly perverse, resulting in a very mild type of schizophrenia. From the university it extends ever outwards, inevitably to taint—for all his want of education—the man in the street.

57. *The great curlicue, continued. —*

Professor: You can love and hate somebody. You know that, right?

Rationalist: Again, you are only speaking of contradiction in the sense of thoughts and words which do not agree.

Professor: Thoughts are facts of existence, especially if you act on them.

Rationalist: Thoughts and statements are realities which claim to represent other realities.

Professor: You're not looking at the holistic thing. You are just looking at one thing and saying: "aha! that's reality!" But people live in history.

Rationalist: And they also die in history; and, as it turns out, they are either alive or they are dead.

Professor: No, they may be dying.

Rationalist: Yet a dying person is still alive.

Professor: But life requires both life and death. They both need each other.

Rationalist: Need? Let us just say that they imply each other.

Professor: You want to make everything one-dimensional.

Rationalist: No, I just want to be consistent.

Professor: In physics they have found ten dimensions so far. Now, with ten dimensions you could find somebody both dead and alive at the same time. But you aren't even three-dimensional. That's why you are so confused.

Rationalist: But you are the one who believes a contradictions.

Professor: If you go into more than one dimension it is possible. Physics has mathematically and theoretically proven that these other dimensions exist. Therefore, you can both be alive and dead.

Rationalist: Given your method of thought I can't resist asking if you know yourself to be alive or dead?

Professor: You don't even know anything except what's here and now—and who cares?

Rationalist: So you cannot know anything except immediate sensations, like an animal?

Professor: You can only know how your consciousness structures your perceptions.

Rationalist: And I take it that you don't even determine that.

Professor: No, you don't. It's put into your head before you even know anything.

Rationalist: And what does that say about human life?

Professor: It says a lot of things. It says that life can be very interesting if you don't make it one-dimensional.

Rationalist: But if your dimensions are determined beforehand then what can you hope for out of life?

Professor: Myself? I'd like to feel less fears about things, without giving way to one-dimensional thinking. People who are afraid want to have a handle on how they can escape their fear. They usually do it by hooking onto some sort of one-dimensional thinking, either religious or ideological; and they think this will save them from their fear. But the fear is still there.

Rationalist: So you think that I'm afraid?

Professor: Everybody is.

Rationalist: But you're not.

Professor: I have lots of fears.

Rationalist: But you want to free yourself?

Professor: I'd like to deal with them so they don't control my life.

Rationalist: Are you afraid of death?

Professor: I don't know about that. I'm afraid right now, just existing right here and now. And also my past—I'm afraid of that. I'm sort of afraid of the future.

Rationalist: So you're afraid all the time?

Professor: Yeah. Most people are, unless they're one-dimensional and think they know it all. I know how fragile life is because I've seen people die—very easily—without much pushing over, and very unlucky too. They didn't have much individual will about it.

Rationalist: That can happen.

Professor: It happens all the time. That's the modern world!—with things happening like that all the time.

Rationalist: Well, it happened in antiquity, too.

Professor: No, much more now because things can come and hit you from afar, like an atom bomb.

Rationalist: What you're saying is that you feel powerless.

Professor: Somewhat, yeah. If somebody accidentally lets go of a nuclear weapon, sure. You can't stop it.

58. He is scared all the time. A chronic case. The essential state of a whole generation enmeshed in a morbid, self-absorbed orgy of fearfulness, its scholarship painted over with the greenish hues of envy—as hatred of reality, suspicion of achievement, and the moral condemnation of power. These are but lackluster excrescences born into bastardy from the coupling of many willful self-deceptions, from a sissified squeamishness which buries its head in the sand, all the while complaining of bad air. All this from a tiny shrunken spirit that needs a kick in the ass and someone to tell it: "Be a man."

59. *Envy.* —

Common Sense: Then you are a determinist?

Professor: Most of the time you strive for predetermined goals.

Common Sense: You mean that I cannot determine my own goals?

Professor: You can, but you'll pay an awful price for it. Look at the way people go to school, to college. Look at the kind of courses they take. Are they really the schools that people picked or are they just the places to go for greater and greater monetary reward?

Common Sense: Well, that could be a reason to pick a school.

Professor: No, that might not be what they really want.

Common Sense: It might not be a reason that you recognize, but it's a reason they recognize.

Professor: Why can't they get a possibility of success and security out of a musical gift? Why can't they get as much reward out of that as being a business major?

Common Sense: Life isn't Disneyland.

Professor: Most people go into business administration or engineering to make money and not because they made a choice.

Common Sense: But that is a choice.

Professor: No, they could have other choices that they've totally ignored because there's no money attached to them.

Common Sense: But maybe their choice is money.

Professor: Why is that? In another society there might not be a money economy and so they'd make different choices.

Common Sense: Yeah, like which piece of rock to make the first tool out of.

Professor: In our society only a few choices are rewarded.

Common Sense: Blame Mother Nature.

Professor: Money is not a natural thing.

Common Sense: So what? Monetary rewards aren't the only rewards in life.

Professor: Oh! Well! Along with monetary rewards come sexual rewards and social rewards—and everything else, too. Especially in a very, very bureaucratized society like this one.

Common Sense: Then money is an attractive choice, isn't it?

Professor: The only choice, and it is totally dictated by society.

Common Sense: But what about self-satisfaction? What about the true dedication of the artist? Of the man of letters who is satisfied with a small sum of money?

Professor: Well, many people don't feel self-satisfaction when they get badly rewarded by the society for doing what they like to do.

Common Sense: What is this whining crybaby stuff? The world doesn't exist for our convenience. It sounds like you want to be rich. You aren't really satisfied in a humble station doing what you like. You want to have fun and make lots of money at the same time. If you want to make ugly music or bad poetry —

Professor: How do you know its ugly music? Maybe it's beautiful music that just doesn't pay.

Common Sense: Okay, fine.

Professor: Do you think rock is beautiful?

Common Sense: No.

Professor: But it is the biggest music there is, isn't it?

Common Sense: That's right, if you're measuring by money.

Professor: So then what should I do? Should I do rotten music?

Common Sense: That's up to you.

Professor: It pays the bills.

Common Sense: Get a part-time job and do your own kind of music.

Professor: No, then that takes away from my creative efforts.

Common Sense: Well, life isn't free.

Professor: If I was born a Rockefeller life would certainly be free. I could be mentally retarded and still be a millionaire if I were born into the Duponts.

Common Sense: I don't understand the point you are making.

Professor: For rich people life is free; they can do what they want. They own it all.

Common Sense: Okay, I'll go along with that. If you inherit millions then you're rich, of course, that's true. And being born rich you could devote your whole life to making beautiful music. So? What's the point?

Professor: But there are people who are poor who have just as much talent, and can't do those things because they haven't got the money. So they haven't got any freedom.

Common Sense: Yeah, but they don't have the money.

Professor: Right, they don't have any money.

Common Sense: And their dad didn't make it.

Professor: Well, should they pay for what their dad didn't do?

Common Sense: This is a very odd way of thinking. You say that everyone born to poor parents is unfairly "paying" for what their fathers did not do? Isn't it the case that children born to rich parents are merely the beneficiaries of what their forefathers *did* do?

Professor: His father has just ripped off workers, that is all.

Common Sense: These successful entrepreneurs create jobs and organize increasingly efficient means to supply our wants. This is not ripping off workers.

Professor: Wrong! In the Soviet Union the workers produce things and they don't have capitalists.

Common Sense: In the Soviet Union they don't have capitalists and the whole country is miserably poor.

Professor: They have the second or third biggest economy in the world.

Common Sense: Have you ever driven a Soviet car? Have you ever eaten Soviet agricultural products? Does anything of Soviet origin—besides propaganda—ever enter your life?

Professor: Not many places produce cars in this world.

Common Sense: How many places have capitalism?

Professor: Most of the world is capitalistic.

Common Sense: Nonsense! Even America is becoming socialistic.

Professor: Japan is more socialistic than we are.

Common Sense: Okay. So what?

Professor: I think what you do is look at the national unit and separate the society from the government. Isn't that what *you* do? You think capitalism is in the nation-state unit?

Common Sense: A nation-state makes laws for itself. And aren't the laws of property extremely important for economic development? In fact, such laws are decisive for determining whether a society is socialistic or capitalistic. I speak here of laws respecting property rights.

Professor: Property rights? No such rights are ever respected! They are not protected in any country that I know. In Norway, for example, there is much more freedom of expression and allowing of people to come into their country to make speeches.

Common Sense: I am talking about property, not speeches; and besides, we have free speech in America.

Professor: No we don't. There are plenty of people who aren't allowed to come to this country because of their political beliefs. I know that for a fact. Recently the head of the Communist Party of Italy wasn't allowed in, but the head of the Fascist Party was.

Common Sense: The Fascist Party in Italy?

Professor: There are two of them, actually.

Common Sense: They are called "fascist parties"?

Professor: They like Mussolini. They dig on him. You can take it from there. There are plenty of left-wing playwrights that can't get into this country. As a matter of fact there are movies that have won awards in Canada that are not allowed here.

Common Sense: Yet I saw Mr. Gorbachev on TV talking to the American people.

Professor: He wasn't allowed to speak at our Congress.

Common Sense: And therefore, according to your argument, we haven't got any free speech?

Professor: Hardly any.

Common Sense: Nor the freedom to choose a career?

Professor: Hardly any freedom, unless you're rich.

Common Sense: So what social system do you advocate?

60. *Paranoia.* —

Professor: Don't you know that we live in the age of surveillance? We judge what is harmful for everybody. If they think you are a communist, like they did Martin Luther King, then they will watch you.

Anticommunist: Well, the communists are our enemies. There is a certain amount of danger from them.

Professor: So we persecute them. We make sure they cannot get good jobs. We harass them. We make sure that they cannot speak at certain places.

Anticommunist: Martin Luther King spoke all over this country.

Professor: But he was assassinated, wasn't he? And we don't know how that happened, do we?

Anticommunist: Some crackpot shot him.

Professor: Oh, that's a good one; we always have certain crackpots shooting at people who are against the system.

Anticommunist: Well, crackpots shoot people. It can't be helped. A communist crackpot named Lee Harvey Oswald shot President Kennedy. How about that? There was a *crackpot against* the system, shooting the chief of the system.

Professor: You're sick.

61. *The music of today.* —

Objectivist: What do you think of Arnold Schoenberg?

Professor: I like him a lot. He was good for his time, too. He's very romantic and very passionate.

Objectivist: What do you think of his twelve-tone scale?

Professor: Nobody uses it except some Germans and some French. It's gone way beyond that now. Like Boulez. Pierre Boulez was influenced by Webern. He's more of the influence of that kind of thing than Schoenberg. Schoenberg was an initiator, but he didn't go all the way.

Objectivist: What do you mean when you say that something—like Mozart—was good for its time but not for today?

Professor: You can't compose like that today and expect it to mean much. It wouldn't be serious music.

Objectivist: Do you think the music composed today is of the same quality as Mozart's?

Professor: Who knows? Mozart didn't live in a capitalist society.

Objectivist: Then you don't believe there are classics? Or that Beethoven and Mozart possess a kind of immortality?

Professor: I think that John Locke has a sort of immortality. So does Montesquieu—but for their time. You can't use their stuff in a complex world like in the world of today.

Objectivist: So we need to have atonal music today because we live in a complex world?

Professor: Most of that Schoenberg stuff is very old-fashioned, emotional, good. It's of its time: Germany in the 30s.

8

Critique of Ideology

MARXISM-LENINISM — The revolutionary teaching of Marx, Engels and Lenin, is an integral scientific system of philosophical, economic and socio-political views expressing the outlook of the working class. It is concerned with the revolutionary reshaping of the world and with the laws governing the development of society, nature and human thought.

— K. H. SABIROV[1]

... within the next decades, will be decided for generations whether all mankind is to become Communist, whether the whole world is to become free, or whether, in the struggle, civilization as we know it is to be completely destroyed or completely changed.

— WHITTAKER CHAMBERS[2]

Once someone has proclaimed violence as his METHOD, he must inexorably select the lie as his PRINCIPLE.

— ALEKSANDR SOLZHENITSYN, *Nobel Lecture on Literature*

Our age is indeed the age of the intellectual organization of political hatreds. It will be one of its chief claims to notice in the moral history of humanity.

— JULIEN BENDA, *La Trahison des Clercs*[3]

1. On this subject my first note reads: *What was built on faith cannot be salvaged by reason.* Julien Benda was right about the treason of the intellectuals. Our modern writers and thinkers, to a great extent, have destroyed the tranquil spell of objective discourse the ancient philosophers handed down. Modern intellectualism, if one dares to generalize, has left wisdom and goodness in the dust. To humanize a basically inhuman standpoint, the intellectuals have struck many poses in

---

[1] K. H. Sabirov, *WHAT IS COMMUNISM?* (Moscow: Progress Publishers, 1987), p. 289.

[2] Whittaker Chambers,*Witness*, p. 7.

[3] Julien Benda, *The Treason of the Intellectuals*, trans. Richard Aldington (New York: W. W. Norton & Company, 1969), p. 27.

favor of the poor and the downtrodden. But who has not penetrated the insincerity of it all?

The fact is, from my experience, the revolutionaries and ideologues of today are impressed with the tragedy of their own insignificance. It is a rude simplification, but there is an element of truth here. For I have met the tormented little revolutionists of the day, and I have seen their lives up close; they have imagined themselves to be insects, as in the Kafka story. In horror they recoil from this strange self-vision. Their sense of proportion, of right and wrong, of deeper and more spiritual realities, has left them. A right-wing ideologue once told me: "I am determined to be somebody important. I will *not* be an insect like my father." Using more indirect language, with greater subtlety, I have heard the same refrain from acquaintances on the left.

The mistake of the ideologue is an inner one. Life teaches loss and humiliation. It teaches us to be good losers. The finest things in the world are of the spirit, and can never be taken away from those who inwardly possess them. Our ideologues and revolutionists are somehow incapable of digesting this basic truth. Pity these sad rebels, for they are the least able to appreciate what is genuinely good. They are lost souls, prisoners of a mistaken notion. Their essence is poor sportsmanship, which always gives itself away in terms of its fixation on "winning at any price." Such people lack faith in life's underlying meaning. Reason wants solid things, mathematical proofs, scientific methods. Yet the soul, in its journey, discovers something else: an inward proof of a higher perspective, the perspective of the saints and the prophets. The poor ideologue, so modern in his ideology, has no faith in that finer world, and so, instinctively, he is a materialist in pursuit of the main chance; a dangerous Machiavel, a schemer and a wretch. Woe to him. If he avoids living as an insect, he will do so as a beast. It would seem that in either case, his humanity is forfeit.

2. "The world," said Renouvier, "is suffering from lack of faith in a transcendental truth." This is the obvious diagnosis. Our doctors of ideology have come up with other remedies—non-spiritual truths—to renew our senile world and to redirect our energies. But *these* remedies only make the world sicker.

3. *How to sell ideology.* — Make it simple so that anyone can grasp it. Make it attractive, palatable, and positive. Or make it difficult, hazy, and complex. Make it promise the moon. Offer benefits, solutions, placebos. It is better, by far, to solve all problems on paper, with theoretical flourish, than to speak realistically. Always pander to expectations and prejudices. Do not rely on proof alone. Hold out

hopes, *glorious hopes.* For hope is attractive and proof is dull. Hope is closer to life, to something that breathes and has a heart-beat. Think also of the usefulness of hope, which attracts the fanatic who will solve our problems by eclipsing them—*by making worse problems.*

4. Ideology has come to take the place of those supposed dinosaurs of the spirit: religion and philosophy. Ah, how the carcasses and skeletons of bygone ideals fill up the landscape. Poor old beasts, unable to adapt themselves to this sudden drop in temperature. How agonizingly they die!—frozen in the snows of our spiritual ice age, to serve as food for the snow rats, those devious little creatures whose sum of grandeur coalesces in the term "rational self interest" or "class struggle." Ah, such coziness of conception. And look! There he is!—that furry face, those myopic eyes, that one-sided little brain wondering if its stomach can digest all this frozen meat. But not to worry. The little snow rat's digestive juices contain ideology. And ideology can dissolve whatever exists. It can integrate contradictions, prophecies, gods, devils, and every type of pseudoscience. Therefore the snow rat can swallow anything—and does!

5. We modern men are ideological creatures. That is, we were invented by ideologists. For if we removed all ideology from the world, we ourselves would (in large part) be removed. That is the low state we are in. It is not the extent to which we have absorbed *ideology*, but the extent to which ideology has absorbed *us.*

6. And have the whirling dervishes of modernity discovered the cure for their nihilism? Or have they a placebo, a finger in the crumbling dike—in social ecology, class struggle, Reagonomics and economics? Are those who grasp at such straws men, or are they corpses animated by the Will To Believe, propelled by the need for faith, for nonsense, for a hope that springs eternal—an intellectual wheelchair? Not whirling dervishes but whirling canes, crutches, Seeing Eye dogs in a wilderness of circular logic, surging with excitement, the blood rushing through all-too-pale cheeks: little lives transformed into shallow crusades against so many deep (nay, fathomless!) realities. Are not the economists, the Objectivists, the socialists, and the democratic asses exemplars of decadence? Are we not ripe? Overly ripe?—That is, rotten to the core?

7. We are so bland and dead that we have even tried to make patriotism into an ideology. But *real* patriotism is not an ideology. It is a flesh-and-blood instinct of loyalty to one's own larger community, an extension of the family tie. But today, in a world of broken homes and swinging singles, family loyalty is badly shaken. Therefore, patriotism,

in the most advanced countries exists only in theory—and *as* theory it is but a vapor.

8. *How one conquers with ideas.* — An academic philosophy (like that of Immanuel Kant) does not conquer the world. It conquers pedants. The envious are most readily conquered by an ideology that predicts the victory of envy. Scientists are most easily won over by the scientific style. To conquer the power-luster, one merely talks as if "power" were the end-all and be-all of existence. One conquers artists with artistic flair. All those who conquer with ideas are, in some sense, flatterers. Therefore, flattery is the propellant of ideology.

9. A Devil Theory is a kind of narcotic, a stimulant that orients the energies of the whole person. It combats nihilism with adrenaline, and becomes our temporary answer to the collapse of positive views. In the hands of an ideologue it becomes a technique for jump-starting dead batteries.

10. A Devil Theory finds its most radical employer in the fanatical ideologist who prides himself in the casting out of demons. This ideologist believes in demons because he is possessed by them himself.

11. Ours is an age in which every institution grows senile: the family, the state, the church, *and* the individual.[4] This senility is most in evidence whenever some new thing crawls into the world and lays claim to truth. Then our instincts tell us: "This too shall pass away." Thereupon we blink. And behold! Wrinkles, grey hairs. Then a moment later: white hairs on the same head. Truth has become something for yesterday's papers. Everything ages rapidly. Everything grows tired, or else *we* grow tired of everything. For us, nothing is permanent; nothing is eternal and nothing is transcendent. There remains only the sensation of the moment, the urge of the day; the desultory and the irregular; the husk of a burnt-out civilization made ready for the demon of ideology, who cannot help but take possession of us.[5]

12. *A note to the Libertarians.* — We have taken freedom too far. Today's freedom: nothing but soil for the cultivation of dictators. For what is freedom but a tyranny in conscientiousness? And what has become of this tyranny in conscientiousness? *It is gone.* Freedom has now become synonymous with the absence of guilt, the abdication of self-control, and a decline in moral standards. Freedom and

---

[4] Yes, the individual *is* an institution.

[5] The accusations against demonology now stick fast to the accuser.

licentiousness are now indistinguishable. Thus is freedom discredited. Thus do we make ourselves unfit for liberal institutions.

13. Usually the party leader believes the party slogans, *but not stupidly.* The art of interpretation allows him to refine the most idiotic ideas into respectable things, especially with help from sharp arguments. Never underestimate the pragmatism of the dogmatist. If ideas and slogans are more often tools of the moment, then belief itself is also a tool.

14. Suppose you have an ideology which is only tentative versus an ideology which has become bigoted? Which ideology is more suitable? Clearly, only the latter produces willingness to die, to sacrifice everything. In other words, only the bigoted ideology has utility for mass politics.

15. *A problem for the ideologist.* —Always remember Machiavelli's Corollary, which says: Never tell a lie unless you know what the truth is.

16. For the deep man, *as* Machiavel, let him find only rich soil, a soil of dupes. For soon the deep man finds that everywhere shallowness prevails, rules, and is rewarded, that depth is odd man out, suspected and defamed. They tell the deep man: "Thou art morally deficient." Therefore, demerit for his merit. The world spurns him and heaps its laurels upon those with easygoing smiles, mechanical skill, good looks, dumb luck, diligence, energy, conformity—spitting into the deep ones, and laughing. For the deep are treacherous, abnormal, and monstrous by nature. Under these circumstances the deep man, drinking from this bitter cup, embraces sarcasm and becomes distrustful. He learns to conceal himself, to dissemble and deceive. An embryonic cynicism forms at the center of his spirit. So the deep man, the *profound man*—as a man entirely alone, defeated, bypassed, demeaned, and persecuted— eventually becomes a true villain. He comes to view the success of superficiality, in all its forms, as a fact worthy of exploitation. Joyfully he embraces the world, laughs at it, plays with it, and makes mischief in it. Perhaps he even becomes a *maker of ideologies.*
Superficiality, he soon discovers, is plastic and pliable. He comes to the bottom of it. He uncovers its springs and gears. He soon is able to predict it and orchestrate its movements. The deep man, as psychologist, can now avenge himself. It is possible for him because he is fathomless, because nobody can find the spring *in him.* Nobody can find *his* motive or *his* process of thought. He believes in free will for himself alone. All shallow men, he says to himself, are predetermined men. Thus continues

----

the Machiavel who shall never lack for dupes, the whole world brimming over with useful materials, ideas, pretenses, poses, self-delusions. The whole shallow lake—*his* pond.

17. Ideology simplifies, abridges, and stylizes reality. And most of the time we haven't the leisure to check our ideological premises. At some point we must stop checking and live out our political commitments.

18. What we see everywhere is an incapacity to call things by their proper names. War has become "police action" and "cold"; compromise is called "arms control"; abandonment of allies translates as "diplomacy"; accepting the Russian and Chinese arms build-ups is "balance of power" because "they can't feed themselves"; while the financing of the "former" Soviet Union goes under the name "cultural exchange," and is performed for the sake of capitalism. Our national interest is subordinated to holy words and phrases like "peace" and "new world order," while stockpile by stockpile we dilute our great arsenals of mass destruction. The name which shall next appear on men's lips, but which cannot be euphemistically improved upon is: Third World War.

19. We despise violence, and make up convoluted excuses to avoid its employment. But violent methods are often necessary. And we have yet to realize that necessity is, after all, necessity. In dealing with international criminals we have tried every conceivable nonviolent method; while it remains obvious, even to the simpleton, that violence is the only satisfactory answer to violence.

20. *Liberalism.* —This void in search of a void; this weakness incapable of conviction and endurance, yearns to hear the authentic voice of authority; yearns for order and direction precisely because it hasn't any. And in the final analysis, when our civilization has been critiqued to death, the only voice will be the *iron fist*; its knuckles—pure eloquence. The capitalist system, undoing itself, shall give over its power to monsters. And then shall come the great revival of authority and authoritative values. The only question remains: what shall the new values be? We will only know the answer to this question when news of millions upon millions of corpses puts us in the correct frame of mind.

21. Those writers who have plundered Nietzsche, especially in order to prop up some flabby ideological edifice, are too myopic and short-ranged in their thinking to profit from such depredations. For Nietzsche wrote in terms of many centuries. Therefore, how can men who haven't

----

anything to say about the next ten years make serious use of him?

22. *The impostor phenomenon.* —Insecure people need constant reassurance that they are great. Illusion: that one must be "great." Illusion also: greatness itself. Illusion again: that one must *do* something. The underlying true confession? That one is insignificant. Answer to the problem: stop posing stupid questions.

23. Carl Jung said that our society tends to reward achievements won at the cost of self-immolation and the diminution of personality: the surrender of soul in exchange for financial consideration, security, position, etc. Perhaps his observation is merely the product of a grudge held by Jung against modern social arrangements. Perhaps it is also due to the conceit that one possesses a soul. Certainly, the business world does not share such a conceit. All around us self-immolation is promoted on the basis of its commercial utility. And we ought to recognize the value of all these ambitious people who have no sense of self-violation. I think we should be grateful that so many people are willing to sacrifice themselves on the careerist altar, even while they smile and call themselves "successful." Thanks to them our stores are filled with many good things to buy. The real problem comes when the careerist discovers his own wretchedness—and turns to ideology.

24. Today we employ ideas as substitutes, surrogate parents, and wombs for big babies. We are frightened because old institutions are collapsing. We hear news of the "death of God," of family, of society itself. We *must* grab hold of something. Let us begin by grabbing hold of ourselves.

25. *Seeming paradoxes of our age.* —That pacifism brings war, that the war on poverty brings poverty, and the war on drugs empowers the drug lord.

26. *What is evil?* —Evil is *not* chaos. Milk turns bad, not evil. We say to our pet: "Bad dog!" We do not say: "Evil dog!" Only through calculation does the merely bad descend into evil; and then only by choice, by means of its knowing rejection of righteousness. Evil is willful *and* diabolical.

27. *Of the progress of Statism.* —
In the beginning was the Word, and the Word was with the State, and the Word was the State.
The same was in the beginning with the State.
All things were made by It: and without It was not any thing made

----

that was made.

In It was life; and the life was the light of men.

And the light shineth in darkness; and the darkness comprehended it not.

Thus arose the need for secret police, firing squads, labor camps, and torture chambers.

28.   Positing a moral standard is highly problematic.   Moral pronouncements hurt the ears. And then there are rival moralities, which often appear ridiculous and discredit the very idea that right and wrong exist. We often see all of this as a confirmation of moral relativism. But this is an illusion because civilization cannot survive for very long in a relativist way. Therefore relativism is refuted. For in the final analysis man needs his right and wrong; and we must, with limited knowledge, find the courage to form moral categories.

29.   There is, of course, a grave danger in loosening one's moral principles in favor of a situational ethic. While the discerning man may occasionally justify an exception to the rule (because the rule is an imperfect approximation), he will soon founder if he persists in being clever; because men are incapable of sustaining such cleverness over a long period of time.

30. Reason is not a foundation, but a method. What we really want is tradition. But reason has destroyed tradition. *This* is the barbarism of reason, a barbarism that says: "Tradition is stupid—away with it!" But stupidity has its place, and serves an important social function by stubbornly preserving that which is foundational.

Reason, on the other hand, breaks things down. It cannot preserve because it is flexible, ambiguous, and multisided. It cannot leave anything alone. It cannot establish a foundation, but only a critique of foundation—because every foundation, at bottom, is irrational and therefore unacceptable to reason.

9

Critique Left

> How ludicrous I find the socialists, with their nonsensical optimism concerning the "good man," who is waiting to appear from behind the scenes if only one would abolish the old "order" and set all the "natural drives" free.
>
> — NIETZSCHE, Will to Power # 755

> Socialism has not consciously willed the destruction of society. It believed it was creating a higher form of society. But since a socialist society is not a possibility every step towards it must harm society.
>
> — LUDWIG VON MISES, *Socialism* [1]

> ...there is little reason to believe that...socialism will mean the advent of the civilization of which orthodox socialists dream. It is much more likely to present fascist features. That would be a strange answer to Marx's prayer. But history sometimes indulges in jokes of questionable taste.
>
> — JOSEPH A. SCHUMPETER, *Capitalism, Socialism and Democracy* [2]

> ... although our socialist system is still imperfect and has suffered disruption, it is much better than the capitalist system.... Our system will improve more and more with the passage of time. By absorbing the progressive elements of other countries, it will become the best in the world. Capitalism can never achieve this. It is absolutely wrong to lose faith in socialism and think that it is inferior to capitalism just because we have made mistakes.
>
> — DENG XIAOPING [3]

1.   Out of the last Dark Age sails Columbus, Renaissance, Enlightenment, Industrial Revolution, American Revolution, and then: materialism, a slackening of religion, the inner life diverted to

---

[1] Ludwig von Mises, *Socialism* (Indianapolis: Liberty *Classics*, 1979), p. 450.

[2] Schumpeter, *Capitalism, Socialism and Democracy*, p. 375.

[3] *The Collected Works of Deng Xiaoping* (Peking), p. 320.

microscopes and telescopes. Now begins a process of despiritualization. Priestcraft gives way to guillotined kings, bicameral and unicameral legislatures; a bewildered otherworldliness searches for a new religion, a new faith, and a new Dark Age. At last we arrive at formulas which eventually blend all vile ingredients into one great curriculum, into one great body of well-crafted morbidity, ready to take center stage as God is edged off.

—Enter, Karl Marx.

2. Jesus versus Marx, theology versus ideology, Christ versus Antichrist. One is worldly, the other transcendent; one crucified, the other militant. Between the two, a radical difference in content. Yet there are similarities, too. Each promises salvation, each trades in absolute answers, each has the other as enemy. Hammer and anvil, with man in between. The final battle between materialism and religion.

3. *Marx the flatterer.* — To call the bourgeoisie a ruling class is to flatter those who are by nature the antithesis of a ruling class.

4. The communist is an ingenious self-deceiver who somehow avoids, for the time being, committing suicide. Leave suicide, as a specialty, to the Gerondists, anarchists, Objectivists, Libertarians, conservatives and liberal Democrats, (*i.e.*, to the most ineffectual types). Suicide is not for the communist. He would rather have the whole world die than his ideology lose its place of power. That is the definition which suicide assumes in the communist lexicon.

Marxist-Leninist doctrine derives its prestige from the following: 1) it determines ultimate goals; 2) it frees from moral inhibitions; 3) it justifies acts of aggression and terror on the basis of promises concerning the future; 4) it believes in the inevitability of its own victory.

5. We impracticals and ineffectuals think to ourselves: "Communism is doomed because it cannot deliver a satisfactory standard of living to the masses."

This is completely stupid. Communism in Russia would be doomed if it actually delivered such a standard of living. For under such circumstances the Soviet here-and-now would soon eclipse the Soviet utopia at the end of the holocaust, and all human sacrifices to the future would be unnecessary; thus the totalitarian system would collapse.

6. *The humanitarian.* — Let us look at Karl Marx: the dirty-fingernailed man who put Hegel right-side-up, the phrenology-believer

who took various bizarre propositions and created out of them the so-called doctrine of scientific socialism.

Born in Trier in 1818, Marx grew up a spoiled child, bullying younger sisters, taunting schoolmates—a budding ruffian. He was not popular, even then, since sharp sarcasm does not make friends. But who needs friends? His family was well-off. At Friedrich Wilhelm Gymnasium Karl received high marks for German, Greek, and Latin. He received poorer marks in history, mathematics, and French. He eventually went to the university at Bonn to study law; and played the part of enthusiastic student, drinker, and brawler. He participated in duels, got into trouble with the police, squandered his "allowance" and ran up debts. He wrote nihilistic poems about wandering "godlike and victorious through the ruins" of the world, about Devil-possessed and Hell-doomed fiddlers. He even wrote a play. Its leading characters were satanic and corrupt, overspilling with curses, homosexual fantasies and other dark passions. In this style Marx wrote a love poem about murdering his belovéd if he could not possess her. This was very characteristic. He burned with the desire to destroy everything he could not own. And since Marx could not own the world, he had a peculiar faculty for relishing the destruction of the world. It seems he was obsessed with the idea that he would either be a ruler or a destroyer. Great deeds would transform him into the equal of God—or, at least, he might rank with the Devil. Karl's father, Heinrich Marx, began to wonder about his son's odd behavior:

"What is all this?!"

Heinrich Marx decided that the University of Bonn was too permissive; so he sent Karl to the University of Berlin, where the young man became a "bohemian" student, ditching class, sucking beers, jawboning with radicals. The aforementioned poetry continued and was published. Old Heinrich Marx, vexed, perturbed, critical of Karl's ideas, wrote:

"Frankly speaking, my dear Karl, I do not like this word, which all weaklings use to cloak their feelings when they quarrel with the world because they do not possess, without labor or trouble, well-furnished palaces with vast sums of money and elegant carriages. This embitterment disgusts me and you are the last person from whom I would expect it. What grounds can you have?...Yet the first untoward event, the first disappointed wish, evokes embitterment! Is that strength? Is that a manly character?"

Poor Heinrich, in despair, nearing the grave with only a few weeks left to him, wrote ever-harsher letters to an ever-colder son, complaining of Karl's "complete disorder," "stupid wandering through all branches of knowledge," and "repellent unsociability."

Wrote the dying father:

"I will not be weak now, for I feel that I have been too indulgent in the past. I poured out my complaints too rarely, and so, in a way, I am guilty toward you. I will and must declare that you have caused your parents much chagrin and very little—or no—joy."

But for Karl Marx there must be no honoring of father, and especially no honoring of mother, or gratitude, or love. Heinrich died on 10 May 1838, funeral unattended by son.

Who was Karl Marx? Of what stuff was he made? *Cruel and implacable stuff.* As a child he tortured his younger sisters, putting ropes around them and riding them as though they were donkeys, forcing them to eat his filthy dirt-cakes. Marx embodied an uncompromising malevolent passion. Didn't Engels describe him as "an unleashed monster" with "a thousand devils gripping his hair"? There is evidence that Marx wanted to be an aristocrat, a prince—even a god. Poor Marx, not obeyed or worshipped, but a mere bourgeois with delusions of grandeur, never to be satisfied in *this* or any other world. Ignorant, ungrateful world. Angry, vengeful Marx.

After five years and thirteen university courses completed, Karl had ditched too many classes and drunk too many beers. He couldn't graduate from the University of Berlin. So he went, instead, to the diploma mill at Jena for his Ph.D., becoming a journalist when his widowed mother refused to pay him an allowance. Therefore, he cursed his mother, hoping she would lurch forward into her grave, so that he might get his hands on the family estate. For Karl's debts were enormous, ballooning, debilitating. He wrote to an associate that his family was quite rich and out to block his career. Men of character must not be blocked!

Marx's brand of journalism on the *Rheinische Zeitung* was nothing special. Just sneering. But he rose to the editorship, rubbed shoulders with that new breed—the socialists—and became a living testament to the dangers of free speech. Eventually he got into trouble with the Prussian censors, and in the end was compelled to resign his editorship. Out of work, out of money, Karl then married the girl next door: Jenny von Westphalen, who also happened to be the sister of an Interior Minister and the daughter of a baron. Next came the honeymoon in Switzerland where Marx squandered a legacy bequeathed by his mother-in-law. After this followed a spell of mooching off friends and relatives. Then, finding himself without substance, he became a communist, moved to Paris and conspired against private property, was booted from Paris and went to Brussels. He penned his way into a leadership position among revolutionaries, ruthlessly bullying, blackmailing, and browbeating. His goal was to get power in *The Movement.*

Pavel Amenkov described Karl Marx as a man who never spoke but to make judgments without appeal. Those who did not believe his doctrines and theories he called "traitors." He bitterly envied and despised anyone with talent who might compete with him for leadership. Therefore Marx calumniated, hissed and spat venom. He indulged in character assassination and libel. And then came Engels, a willing tool, foremost of the Marxian creatures, paying homage to the one true shepherd, Karl Marx: a Red messiah, who ruthlessly abused friendships with well-known intellectuals in order to elevate himself, projecting his faults onto others while preaching destruction and extermination. Proudhon cautioned Marx: "It would be bad politics for us to present ourselves as exterminators."

Marx became enraged, raised his poison pen in fury and attempted to exterminate M. Proudhon!

Between attacks on compatriots he threw punches at civilization, property, God, family, church, state, laws, democracy, Jews, Russians, Kalmucks. "Nothing existed which wasn't worth destroying." —his favorite line from Goethe's *Faust*, from the lips of his hero, Mephistopheles. Marx venerated the playwritten demon and sometimes even signed himself "Old Nick" or "Devil." His own son once addressed him in a note: "My Dear Devil." His wife once referred to him as her "black master."

But why worry about these darker signposts when Marx was so obviously a man of many gifts? For example: the gift of idleness, and also the gift of drunkenness which urged him on pub crawls. And let us not forget the gift of paranoia, for he read cheap French "conspiracy" novels, which whetted his appetite for intrigue.

Then the fateful year arrived—1848. With help from Engels he wrote the *Manifesto of the Communist Party.* It sputtered and exploded against property, against justice, against civilization and equilibrium. From the filthy Marat he stole phrases like "The workers have no country" and "The proletarians have nothing to lose but their chains." The "dictatorship of the proletariat" he swiped from Blanqui. Progressive income tax had already been proposed by the younger William Pitt in 1799. From Karl Schapper was taken the slogan: "Workingmen of all countries, unite!" The *Manifesto*, nevertheless, shall endure *because* it is vulgar.

Meanwhile, troubles in Switzerland became fashionable elsewhere. Unrest and revolution came to Europe. Marx, then thirty, was booted out of Belgium and fell back to Germany, to Cologne, becoming editor of the *Neue Rheinische Zeitung*—not merely editor, but god-editor, intolerant bully, and generally unpleasant person. Engels called it the dictatorship of Marx (—Engels, vice-dictator). They cheered along the sidelines while Austro-Hungarian ministers of defense were being lynched by attorney-generals of the lamp-iron. Marx howled with glee, and slyly encouraged more of the same. Marx: humanitarian, lover of children, dogs and old people. It turns out he was a hater, too. A very pronounced hater.

When Denmark proved conservative, Marx called them "brutal, dirty, piratical Old Norse," vilifying Scandinavianism for violence toward women, "permanent drunkenness, and a tearful sentimentality alternating with berserker rage." Imagine such abuse applied to Denmark. Could anyone take it seriously? Marx called for a quick solution to the "Danish Problem." All allies of Denmark must be smashed. Marx called for TOTAL WAR, hoping that a general conflagration would spawn communist revolution and land him the job of dictator.

Marx took steps: he formed, after the French style, a Committee of Public Safety. In the midst of strife he grasped for power, but power would not be grasped. So back at the *Neue Rheinische Zeitung* Marx incited further bloodletting, in a manner subtle and indirect. But the authorities were not stupid. They brought Marx to trial on charges of sedition and treason. Poor, civilized, jury-scrupulous Germans. Marx easily tricked an acquittal out of them. Nevertheless, an order was signed to kick him out of the country, no longer to incite bloodletting from his cozy editorial perch. On its last day of publication, the *Neue Rheinische Zeitung* declared to the world: "We are ruthless, and we ask no quarter from you. When our turn comes, we shall not disguise our terrorism."

Not a man to mince words, this Karl Marx.

To Paris he went and from thence was promptly ejected — landing, feet first, in London (still huffing and blowing on the embers of the revolution). Since he was denied his German dictatorship there was no choice but to take up residence in a slum. The only revolution around: the Industrial Revolution. The only nation that would accept him: liberal, bourgeois England. He was penniless, destitute, having spent all his money on guns and propaganda. His wife and children were threatened with hunger and a gutter existence. Yet he still furiously worked for revolution into the year 1850. He formed alliances with French revolutionaries and Chartists, formed a Central Revolutionary Committee, formed a Union of Revolutionary Communists. Marx and Engels wrote a secret call to arms: "A Plan of Action Against Democracy," which proposed an alliance with bourgeois liberals in order to eliminate the ruling princes of Europe. Afterwards, the bourgeois liberals would be liquidated. Five deluded cranks expected to be future dictators of a communist Europe: Marx, Engels, Willich, Harney and Vidil. Willich was to be generalisimo of the Red Armies. But Marx did not trust Willich and wished to counterbalance him with a soldier-adventurer named Gustav Techow. On 21 August 1850, Marx got drunk with Techow. First they guzzled port, then red Bordeaux, then champagne. Marx staggered drunkenly, dominating the conversation in his usual manner. Techow held his liquor better, saw an uninhibited Marx displaying unconcealed contempt for humanity and for the communist parrots of "that class shit." Marx couldn't hold his liquor and he couldn't hold his tongue.

Techow later wrote to a comrade about the incident: "It is a matter of regret...that this man [Marx] with his fine intellect is lacking in nobility of soul. I am convinced that a most dangerous personal ambition has eaten away all the good in him. He laughs at the fools who parrot his proletarian catechism, just as he laughs over the communists ´*a la* Willich and over the bourgeoisie. The only people he respects are the aristocrats, the genuine ones, those who are well aware of their aristocracy."

Techow had seen the *real* Karl Marx. He had seen Marx in a drunken, honest, uninhibited state and did not appreciate the evil greatness he found there. So Techow became disgusted and ceased to cooperate. Later, during a meeting of the committee, Marx and Willich locked horns in argument. Both had wild tempers. Willich, who was a crack shot, challenged Marx to a duel. Marx refused. But a crazy disciple named Schramm offered to duel in his place. The duelers—Schramm and Willich—went to a beach near Antwerp. Marx made no serious effort to stop them; and besides, he didn't care if they blew out one another's brains. Willich shot Schramm in the head. But Schramm was a true-believing communist and consequently the bullet glanced off his thick skull. The duelers broke up: Willich passing back across the channel, Schramm passing into temporary unconsciousness. And so ended the Central Revolutionary Committee, *not* in world revolution but in Antwerp-beach farce.

Marx was then without his revolutionary following; without money, without job, without citizenship. He begged Engels for help. Good Engels, nice Engels: bark Engels, sit, roll over—give money. That's a good dog, Engels. And with help from this good dog, Marx's wife and children went to reside in a small shabby apartment on Dean Street: six people living in two rooms. Amidst this squalor three of Marx's children died, his wife suffered a nervous breakdown, and he was smitten with boils.

A Prussian spy infiltrated Marx's apartment and made a report on it for the Berlin government, perhaps for the perusal of Marx's brother-in-law, the interior minister. Accordingly, the spy reported that Marx was, in private life, "an extremely disorderly, cynical human being" and that "Washing, grooming and changing his linen are things he does rarely, and he is often drunk." The report continues: "In the whole apartment there is not one clean and solid piece of furniture. Everything is broken, tattered and torn, with a half inch of dust over everything and the greatest disorder everywhere."

The observant Prussian agent further reported that Marx's dominating trait was "a limitless ambition and love of power." Adding, "He is extraordinarily cunning, crafty and reserved." (if sober). We learn from other sources that Marx still had a ferocious temper, sarcastic tongue, intolerant opinions, was feared rather than loved. He remained, in the final analysis, *a bully*. During this period, Marx said: "The mind of the criminal has more grandeur and nobility than the wonders of the heavens."

While living in this slum, Marx had a maidservant named Helene Demuth, who eventually became pregnant with Marx's child. On 23 June 1851 Helene gave birth to a boy. Marx cast off the child and would not give a penny for its support. He even denied being the father and tried to put the blame on Engels—which Engels, good dog, accepted; that is, until his deathbed whereon the truth was finally told.

Throughout all of this, Marx was eaten by self-doubt; eaten also by headaches, ulcerous sores, liver complaints, and insomnia. But he was strong, and sustained himself with thoughts of revenge, of worldwide economic collapse and bloody revolutionary wars. The most delicious thought of all was his hopes for a Marx-Engels dictatorship. In this regard, Marx was quite an optimist, predicting revolution forty times in thirty years.

During these long days of hopeful waiting, Marx never left off writing splenetic tracts and books. He spat rain clouds, even whole storm fronts, of invective upon his adversaries. He even stooped to criticize noses, ancestries, religions, mannerisms, cranial formations, etc.

Cranial formations?

An associate of Marx, Wilhelm Liebknecht, reported that Marx studied phrenology: the analysis of cranial protuberances which allegedly determine character, intelligence, and ability. Marx even ran his fingers over Liebknecht's skull. But Marx was not an expert in this area, and the Communist League had its own in-house phrenologist, Karl Pfaender. Evidently, getting into the League required the correct kind of cranium. Said Liebknecht: "My skull was officially inspected by Karl Pfaender and nothing was found that would have prevented my admission into the Holiest of Holies of the Communist Alliance."

Yes, it's all quite bizarre. But is anything too bizarre for Karl Marx?

Come to think of it: why would Marx be attracted to only one kind of quackery? Isn't phrenology the same as the stuff in *Das Kapital*?—The only difference being that Marx didn't believe in *Das Kapital* while phrenology was something quite credible to him.

Eventually, as time passed, Marx indulged in further revolutionary intrigues. He competed with anarchist Bakunin for control of the International Working Men's Association. He bamboozled, infiltrated, subverted, and rewrote its declaration of principles by means of a conspiratorial trick. To Engels he bragged, "I was only obliged to insert two 'duty' and 'right' phrases in the preamble, ditto 'truth, morality, and justice'; but these are placed in such a way that they do no harm."

Marx's books were written with a similar method in mind. And since his biography grows tiresome we shall merely say that around 1883 Karl Marx died, never tasting of dictatorship or revenge. But he left behind a life's supply of poison, which is not an insignificant legacy considering the future course of communism; its gulags, committees of state security, politburos, purges, and malproductions. Such a legacy—as dramatization—goes farther than any academic criticism. The history of Marxian communism proves to be more than criticism and better than mere rebuttal or invalidation. Let us clarify a point for the benefit of the theoretical-minded: that the biography of Karl Marx, coupled with his complete writings, shows us a man less scholarly and more sour in his eloquence than we should expect from one so widely venerated. He personified the arrogance of science, the shallowness of our "big" ideas, and the meanness of our modern spirit. After all this one cannot help wondering: Why have we, for so long, read Karl Marx the theoretician when Karl Marx *the man* is so much more to the point?[4]

7. *Das Kapital*, the Marxian Bible, self-destructed almost as soon as it emerged from Marx's hellish pen. But with time the book succeeded because its author was deeply evil and his critics were shallow. They were concerned with theoretical niceties, while Marx was out to give full "scientific" expression to his feelings of resentment, revenge, and frustration. All those who share Marx's feelings cannot care much about the correctness of his logic. They march together under the banner of hate, as an exalted and inexorable movement of history, sanctified and blessed. What an exhilarating, liberating, empowering moment when the envious discover that envy is righteous.

8. A man hellbent on destroying civilization is a strictly modern phenomenon. In ancient times there were occasional impulses toward the

----

[4] Robert Payne, *Marx*. Biographical details taken from this work.

----

destruction of tribes or cities, sometimes impulses for the looting of whole provinces and peoples, but never a conscious attempt to systematically wipe out an entire civilization. Even the German tribes, who slowly broke up the Roman empire, never intended to destroy civilization. Yet the new barbarians, our Karl Marxes of today, are not the hardy product of the frozen north, but the denizens of a spiritual sewer flowing with the blackest arrogance.

9. *Karl Marx's epitaph.* — a psychologist without introspection and a prophet without foreknowledge.

10. Dare we say that Lenin is to Marx as Paul was to Christ? — that an idea perchance falls into the hands of a "genius of practice" who equips it to dominate an age? Considering how much was at stake, and how crucial the developer to the development, one is tempted to wonder: *what if Lenin had died in his cradle?*

Yet Lenin did not die in his cradle. He led the first successful communist revolution and built the Soviet Union. And once created and endowed, who can resist this Thing that seems so well adapted and which exploits every peculiarity of its age? Cannot we detect, in all of this, a principle of natural selection pertaining to ideas and to states? Notice how it is: that a peculiar species of thought or practice finds itself advantaged under certain conditions, and then, as with the destruction of the dinosaur, something better adapted emerges to fill the gap, eating out the yoke of the old lizard's egg, eventually hatching something of its own.

11. Marx spoke for history, but Lenin outwitted it.

12. Lenin once read Chekov's "Ward No. 6," a story about a psychiatric patient who talks a weak-minded doctor into insanity. About this Lenin is alleged to have said: "I was absolutely terrified when I read the story. I couldn't remain in my room any longer. I had the feeling that I myself was shut up in Ward No. 6!"

Lenin's biographer, Robert Payne, tells us that "this same feeling would recur at intervals in...[Lenin's] life."[5]

Was Lenin tormented by the feeling that he was going mad? Did he have bizarre dreams? Did he see UFOs, goblins, angels, ghosts?

What could lead a Marxist to question his own sanity?

13. Lenin had a tremendous gift which put him far above most other ideologists. This gift was partial deafness. And with this gift it was all

---

5 Payne, *Lenin*, p. 91.

----

the easier for him to hear only his own thoughts.

14. The most dangerous enemy of the Soviet Union is not the one whose enmity springs from humanitarianism. All such enemies are worthless and end by being communism's unwitting accomplices. He who destroys Soviet Russia will necessarily meet fire with fire.

15. *Stalin's secret.* — The Soviet people know enough to admire Stalin, even if such admiration admixes with dislike. In the end, the world trusts strength and despises weakness. The swindler is infinitely more attractive to us than the swindled, the oppressor more envied than the oppressed. It is the sickness of the West to imagine that human nature is otherwise.

16. One day it happened that certain theologians admitted an end to the "Age of Miracles." A similar event is transpiring in politics, only in reverse. We are now expected to believe in new miracles and in the idea that the age of conquest and war is over, that all warlike spirits have been cut off so that the earth has suddenly become, if we are to believe our eyes, *a world of shopkeepers.* What, then, is the Leninist Party? Have they become shopkeepers too? —Daniel Ortega, Fidel Castro, and their friends in the Kremlin—*all shopkeepers?*
What a pleasant thought!
As Nietzsche once said: "A little poison now and then: that maketh pleasant dreams. And much poison at last for a pleasant death."[6]

---

[6] Nietzsche, *Thus Spake Zarathustra*, trans. Thomas Common (New York: The Modern Library, no publication date), p. 12.

10

Critique Right

In the ear of the Conservatives. — What was formerly not known, what is known today or could be known—a *reversion*, a turning back in any sense and to any degree, is quite impossible. We physiologists at least know that. But all priests and moralists have believed it was possible—they have *wanted* to take mankind back, *force* it back, to an *earlier* standard of virtue. Morality has always been a bed of Procrustes. Even politicians have in this matter imitated the preachers of virtue; even today there are parties whose goal is a dream of the crabwise *retrogression* of all things. But no one is free to be a crab. There is nothing for it: one *has* to go forward, which is to say *step by step further into decadence* (—this is *my* definition of modern "progress"...). One can *retard* this development and, through retardation, dam and gather up degeneration itself and make it more vehement and *sudden*: more one cannot do. —

> — NIETZSCHE, *Twilight of the Idols*

We need to acknowledge, fatalistically, that the assault on the very idea of permanent things is by no means something that happened only yesterday, nor something done only by infamous names.

> — WILLIAM F. BUCKLEY JR., Nov. 18, 1986

A Conservative government is an organized hypocrisy.

> — DISRAELI, March 17, 1843

1. The Right is a fiction. Everyone is on the Left.

2. All our anticommunists, antileftists, antitotalitarians: mere talkers, merely flatterers of the things they oppose; shallow ponds filled with dead fish; not clear, but stagnant, sour, and unable to sustain anything vigorous. Where went the bloody, fertile reactionaries? Are they not in disrepute? We cannot have enough scorn for all these reputable "conservatives" with their toothless bite and their cool-toned sentences. They make us ready for captivity. We sneer at their half-baked formulas; nay, insolences posing as formulas! We despise the

cowardly optimism which lurks beneath their stupid exterior; —the optimism of anticommunists *without bomb shelters.* Our nose is excellent for smelling out hypocrisy and ineptitude enamored of limp-wristed Cold War oxymoronism. The fact that NATO tanks have not overrun Moscow, that the CIA has not seen through the fake Soviet collapse, speaks volumes against the reputable anticommunists. In the last analysis they signify a nullity.

3. And what have our cherishers of old bones not done to breathe life back into various dead bits and pieces? What of our so-called conservatives who dawdle as political Frankensteins, each with his own grave robber's collection of impolitic body parts, trying to sew up a complete corpse? Can they actually bring anything back to life?

No, of course not. For there is not any wholeness or any wholesomeness in what they have assembled; no functioning organ of nutrition, no unity of style, no agreement on method or purpose; no organic cohesion except as necessitated by common enemies; namely, by communists and nihilists. It turns out that the enemies of conservatism are the glue that holds the conservatives together—which is ominous.

4. *To elaborate further.* — Modern conservatism is an anarchy of ideas and poses stemming from our nostalgia for what is gone. The conservative, superficially, is a worshipper of old ruts. But underneath he is modern, he is liberal; employing liberal means which are but homage to the liberal end. Our conservatives no longer have anything to conserve. Conservatism, therefore, as it fails to regenerate dead tissue, has become the work of political undertakers whose job it is to make the corpse appear better than it did in life. But despite all this cosmetology, the corpse grows riper and riper. We hear the cries for more and more perfume: for drug czars, education reforms; commissions on corruption, pornography, and crime. In the final analysis, the valiant campaign against decomposition becomes increasingly shrill as the body politic continues to deteriorate.

5. *And what of our moderates?* — They need a good kick in the teeth; for theirs is almost always a moderation out of weakness, flabbiness, and self-satisfaction. Let all these fat middle-of-the-road sheep wake up to what it means for them to be standing squarely on the double yellow line, where they can be run over from *both* directions.

6. We need to make the golden mean ever meaner, even to the point of bloodthirstiness. We need to educate our moderates on the question of extraordinary measures, lest they lazily give way to the closet bolsheviks. Our moderates must learn that it is sometimes proper to be improper. In

other words, they must adapt to what is coming, and master the art of prudent immoderation. For moderation will not suffice when politics itself has become an extreme. The imperative will then be clear, though paradoxical: that we must sacrifice our principles in order to save them.

7. To pronounce oneself nonideological is merely to pronounce yet another ideology. The centrist, halfway between two lies, imagines he has found the truth. More often than not, the ideology of centrism is merely a rationalized lust for respectability which stigmatizes all else as "cult" or "fringe." The centrist congratulates himself after the following fashion: "I am not unusual. I am not ridiculous. I am respectable. For I am in the middle."
—In the middle of what?

8. As the middle gradually loses ground to the extremes, men shall learn to loathe the uncertain and equivocal character of centrism. They shall become wary of excessive reasonableness. They shall begin to suspect that moderation is cowardice. Thus a moderate age always lurches toward an immoderate age. Afterwards, the immoderate age bleeds its way back toward the moderate.
—History: an unhealed wound in the soul of time.

9. How dark, how evil, are the counsels of crisis, when all that happens is extraordinary and morality itself proves to be immoral. In such times, if the moderate man is moderate by precept rather than by judgment, then the particulars are bound to turn against him and suicide will be the result of his policy. The historical example of Cicero is instructive, for he was the archetype of misapplied moderation. In dealing with the conspiracy of Catiline, it was Cato—not Cicero—whose unyielding firmness cut the floor out from under the conspirators. Cicero's many orations against Catiline cannot compare with Cato's brief but poignant speech, in which he characterized the Roman leadership under Cicero as "each waiting for someone else to act." In this way Cato, ridiculed by Mommsen as the "Don Quixote" of the aristocracy, shamed the Senate and Cicero for their want of bloody steadfastness. Being stung by the words of a self-righteous extremist, the Senate cast its timidity aside and the Republic was saved.
In Caesar's assassination the impotence of the moderate appears again, as Brutus's dagger proved its point far better than Cicero's pleadings. When one had need of steel, cruelty, and distrustfulness, the moderate man of antiquity—the man of promise—failed; and in the end, Mark Antony's assassins got the better of Cicero's "Philippics." So what we find in Cicero, as in many moderates, is chronic impotence with

----

reasonableness as a pose. And, therefore, it should not surprise us when the modern centrist deals with today's Catilines and Caesars by way of that same out-of-place mildness and sense of delicacy that Cicero used; a sense of delicacy which ended in the Second Triumvirate, the death of the Republic, and Cicero's severed head fastened above the rostra in the Forum.

10. The type of the moderate politician is temperamentally incapable of understanding that all states are born in blood, renewed in blood, and sustained by blood. There has never been any other way; not for George Washington, not for Abraham Lincoln, not for anybody. To shrink from violence is to shrink. The difference between Abraham Lincoln and Josef Stalin is not that one was bloody and the other was white as snow. For both these rulers sent hundreds of thousands of people to untimely deaths. The difference is found in their values. Both men sacrificed lives so that a type of government might live. But all types of government are not of equal moral worth. A government might embody a new birth of liberty and virtue, or it might embody bigotry, licentiousness, and unscrupulous ambition.   Can we suppose that violence in defense of the former is the same as violence for the aggrandizement of the latter?

11.   The Iraqi dictator's first name, Saddam, means "one who confronts." It is an auspicious name. Yet centrists would spurn this name. It is easy to predict from this the fate of everything that tries to find a middle way, imagining that all differences can be settled amicably and without confrontation. Every conflict, for the centrist, is therefore unnecessary. Caught in the grip of crisis a moderate will procrastinate. He will play for time, saying to his comrades: "If only we wait, then things will resolve themselves peacefully. If only we wait, everyone will think twice."

But what if time isn't on the side of peace? What if time, instead, is hurrying us toward the slaughterhouse? Then, with each passing day butchery looms larger and larger. Under such circumstances hesitation only increases the carnage, while bold preemptive action might save millions of lives.

12. The moderates should consider the moderation of God, who has reportedly wiped out a considerable number of men; not only by drowning them in the Great Flood, but by various other catastrophes, sometimes called "divine chastisements." In this we can clearly discern that God is by no means a liberal democrat, like some of his modern spokesmen. God is an autocrat possessed of limited patience. And today His patience is being put to the test, which brings us to the winepress of

the wrath of God:

— "And the winepress was trodden without the city, and the blood came out of the winepress, even unto the horse bridles, by the space of a thousand and six hundred furlongs."[1]

And then there are the words of Christ, as he speaks to all moderates, centrists, and other sharp reasoners: "I know thy works, that thou art neither cold nor hot: I would thou wert cold or hot.

"So then because thou art lukewarm, and neither cold nor hot, I will spue thee out of my mouth."[2]

13. Every middling expedient and half measure now leads us to catastrophe. Kindness reaches the point of absolute cruelty, reasonableness becomes unreasonable, concern for the commonwealth becomes party spirit. We enter into a paradoxical crisis. Now must we unsheathe our steel and harden our hearts. Now must we become evil to do good. This is our revelation: that when someone is out to annihilate you, there is only the choice: annihilate or be annihilated.

14. The neoconservatives are even more naive than the moderates. Their talk about economic freedom and individual rights is nonsense because they have no idea what these terms signify. The words they use, so rich with meanings and implications become, in their mouths, *gibberish*.

15. The neoconservative politically calculates in terms of individual rights. And what are individual rights? Metaphysics. But the neoconservative does not believe in metaphysics. He believes in economics. Even so, he still maintains his "rights"—as a sly dog steals toward the chicken coop.

16. And where comes this marvelous free market, Mr. Laissez-Faire? Out of which dreamcloud does it drop?

Mr. Laissez-Faire stares blankly at the camera. He stammers out a formula deriving economic growth from freedom. But we stop him, and ask: Wherefore is this freedom? He does not even understand the question. He stands there, muttering that the free market is free, that he found it at the bottom of a cereal box. His wide eyes stare innocently. He smiles and mutters something about "truth." He cannot grasp that the free market is not free. He cannot understand something above and beyond supply and demand. He does not know that liberal institutions need *illiberal* supports. He cannot grasp that blood is above money, that

---

[1] *Revelation*, 14:20.

[2] Ibid., 3:15 and 16.

consumer values are not ultimate values because they cannot stand alone. In order for markets to be possible one must look higher, to the warrior who protects markets, and who sheds his blood in the struggle of empires. On hearing all of this Mr. Laissez-Faire grins slyly, rolls his eyes and says: "My blood is too valuable to spill. That is why I am for a volunteer army." And then he adds: "My money, somebody else's blood."

17. Edmund Burke was correct when he called economists "the little, shriveled, meager, hopping, though loud and troublesome, insects of the hour."

18. And so, yet another dilemma confronts the latter-day right wing; namely, who will die so that fat money cows and junk bond dealers might prosper. —Fat cows who say: "Whatever befalls, we are not obligated to fight and die for our country. Our sons will not go to the front!" And here, in all its splendor, shrinks the will of the capitalist state to take up arms and bridge the Yalu, to cross the DMZ, to go beyond Checkpoint Charlie and kill the Butcher of Baghdad. Somehow we always seem to stop at the edge of *real war*. Ours is an exercise in restraint, to be distinguished from the "domino theory" as "domino history."

Once upon a time the right wing sat in castles, cultivated war and hand-to-hand combat. In those days the dominant class had no need of theories. It was willing to kill or be killed to maintain itself. But now, since the ruling class is bourgeois, one defends oneself theoretically, with Ciceronian orations. In other words, one wants *something* for *nothing*. One wants cowardice on an equal footing with courage. When a class is no longer willing to die for its political ascendancy then it will sink ignominiously back from whence it came, and someone else will take up the reins.

19. *What the Right lacks.* — Throughout the last century, as the Left continued its irrevocable advance, the Right smugly assumed that the old institutions of state and church were its strongholds. But this assumption was wrong. For in reality there was nothing inherently right-wing about state and church once they were exposed to the cultural power of money, which follows its own inexorable laws. And these laws are anticonservative to the point of malice. From all of this, by looking closely at the money process, the Right must recognize the current unsuitability of its neo-conservative trenches.

Meanwhile, behind the left there lies a truly efficient organ of power: the underground communist cells and various left-wing front organizations, backed by highly disciplined foreign intelligence services that have infiltrated the drug cartels and other criminal groups. In conjunction with these, the Kremlin spymasters continue to saturate our government and media with moles and agents of influence, like Aldrich Ames. This well coordinated fighting array, pursuing a long range deception strategy, strengthens the American Left, providing direction and cohesion, promising inevitable victory to all "progressive forces." The Right has no comparable instruments of attack and defense; nothing so single-minded or comprehensive, nothing so authoritative or terrible. Indeed, it is remarkable to see how effectively the Left disguises its growing power and influence at home and abroad.

If the Right hopes to save the country, then it must develop its own clandestine machinery. It must acquiesce in the creation of a militant right-wing octopus, whose tentacles reach into every sphere, and whose nerves are steeled against every hard necessity. For in the present war against Antichrist, if we do not bring ourselves to acknowledge our right of self defense—our right to answer in kind—then we might as well salute the Devil and pack for the gulag. It can reasonably be argued that without a special instrument of our own, we cannot expect to keep the field. We can only expect to lose. Let us then consider how much murder and destruction will ensue our present feebleness. Let us consider how many souls will be lost. Can we, in good conscience, continue as mere parliamentarians— penning Letters to the Editor, or to a Congress filled with men whose aims are daily twisted by secret forces of subversion and sabotage? The sad fact is: the patriotic cause doesn't even have a counterintelligence capability. Therefore, we cannot begin to name all those domestic facilitators who stand with the enemy.

The need for counterintelligence—as one weapon among many— dictates our course of action. We need a hidden hand that reaches out for other hidden hands, to feel our way in a world of hidden things.

20. Our cult of democratic moralism weakens us greatly. According to this cult, war is seen as an unnecessary evil and strategy as a black art.

Nietzsche, foreseeing the danger of this, rebuked the "essential demand...that mankind should under no circumstances do harm or desire to do harm." He called this "the castration of all possible enmity" which can only result in "the unhinging of all instincts of ressentiment" leading to "peace of soul" as a chronic disease. [3]

21. Joseph Schumpeter wrote that when facing direct attack the bourgeoisie "talk and plead—or hire people to do it for them; they snatch at every chance of compromise; they are ever ready to give in; they never put up a fight." He further says that the "only explanation for the

---

[3] Nietzsche, *Will to Power*, #351.

meekness we observe is that the bourgeois order no longer makes any sense to the bourgeois itself."[4]

Nietzsche anticipated this also, where he writes:

> There is a point in the history of society when it becomes so pathologically soft and tender that among other things it sides even with those who harm it, criminals, and does this quite seriously and honestly. Punishing somehow seems unfair to it, and it is certain that imagining 'punishment' and 'being supposed to punish' hurts it, arouses fear in it. 'Is it not enough to render him *undangerous?* Why still punish? Punishing itself is terrible.' With this question, herd morality, the morality of timidity, draws its ultimate consequence. [5]

22. Liberal democracy eats its own entrails. Hard work, family values, farsightedness and frugality are slowly eroded over time. All order is crumbling. All sense becomes nonsense. In this context, Schumpeter explains that "the capitalist order not only rests on props made of extra-capitalist material but also derives its energy from extra-capitalist patterns of behavior which at the same time it is bound to destroy."[6]

23. What are we to make of the words "them" and "us"? But these are precisely the words which are today maligned. No sooner does the word "them" slip from your mouth than the liberal is screaming bloody murder. The idea of an *inside* or an *outside* has been taken away. Multiculturalism, internationalism, and that "global village" nonsense merely tells us to stop drawing boundaries, dividing lines and such. It is a view which sees its own interests in the vaguest and most bloodless terms, if it sees them at all. Worse yet, these interests are supposedly tied to "humanity" and "progress." Here we find an absence of solidity. At the same time: race, religion, and culture are decried or undermined precisely because they are solid; precisely because they arouse deep feelings.

The idea of "them" and "us" is intrinsic to human life. Here we are not speaking of rationalist categories, but of basic societal feelings which bind men into communities, which bind them to laws, and cause them to look suspiciously on anything which threatens that "binding." And here the modern spirit, which is diametrically opposed to everything that binds, confesses its decadence.

---

[4] Schumpeter, *Capitalism, Socialism and Democracy*, p. 161.

[5] Nietzsche, *Basic Writings of Nietzsche*, trans. Walter Kaufmann (New York: Modern Library, 1968),   p. 304.

[6] Schumpeter, *Capitalism, Socialism and Democracy*, (New York, 1975) p. 162.

24. Because war is usually fought over "higher" things, over questions of the future, over national power and ruling ideals, the latter-day bourgeoisie often fails to understand it, to make sense of it, to *want* it.

25. The rhetoric of the "New World Order" rings hollow. Perhaps it is the ring of our crazy internationalist altruism—the ring of a hollow head about to collapse upon itself because the pressure of outside reality is too great.

26. The bourgeois concept of "righteous man" as "useful man" contributes to the mental conditioning of an "ideal herd animal." What is referred to here is a ripeness for totalitarian institutions: i.e., "Chinafication." Point of correction: "Righteous man" is something far above "useful man.". The fact is, if you serve mammon, your righteousness is a nullity. The argument, as ever, boils down to a question of transcendent values versus career advantage. And capitalism (read "consumerism") teaches us that career advantage is life's ultimate end.

27. Today the family is not really an institution, but a mere device of convenience—like everything else. Its authority is lost. No authority, no institution. Here the conservatives are merely offering something along the lines of lip service.

28. The sociological analysis is clear. Capitalism needs a protector. Capitalism needs to be placed in a subordinate position if it hopes to survive. Of course, the capitalists will never acquiesce. Whether they are establishment liberals, or pseudoestablishment conservatives, they pride themselves in their opposition to any idea or movement that has a nonbourgeois orientation. Therefore, any fundamental criticism of our crumbling democratic system is out of bounds.[7] Thus, any serious effort to ensure our national survival can only come from outside the all-powerful establishment elite, which instinctively regards our first line of defense—i.e., military discipline—as fascist, sexist, and homophobic. This cannot be denied or glossed over. The recent creation of whole classes and bureaucracies of antinationalists and anticapitalists under a form of society which is fundamentally nationalist and capitalist, only goes to prove that the current establishment is determined to commit suicide. Only a patriotic group, working outside the establishment, can

---

[7] The Japanese novelist Akiyuki Nosaka recently said that watching America is like watching "a test run for the decline of the human race."

forge a true fighting spirit. As it stands now, the money power has only produced a career-oriented elite; a selfish and myopic bureaucracy.

To clarify the above point: the country is in the hands of individuals who are sharply disconnected from any patriotic base. Careerist attitudes affect even our best national leaders. Worse still, the mass media is often hostile to patriotism. Cultural nihilists actively employ ridicule, slander, and censorship against all those who would speak forthrightly about national survival and national interest.

29. The new right-wing morality is selfishness. The bourgeoisie no longer finds it necessary to see things in religious terms. Now it can be utterly forthright. It can sing an ode to greed and cut its irksome ties to self-restraint and Victorian prudishness.

30. *Under the present circumstances:* If the so-called right wing seriously attempted to stand for self-control, it would collapse within a year. That is why I say that the Right does not exist at all. *Everyone* is on the Left.

11

Against History and Futurity

> People will not look forward to posterity who never look backward to their ancestors.
>
> — EDMUND BURKE

> What is attacked deep down today is the instinct and the will of tradition: all institutions that owe their origins to this instinct violate the taste of the modern spirit. — At bottom, nothing is thought and done without the purpose of eradicating this sense for tradition. One considers tradition a fatality; one studies it, recognizes it ...but one does not *want* it. The tension of a will over long temporal distances, the selection of the states and valuations that allow one to dispose of future centuries — precisely this is antimodern in the highest degree. Which goes to show that it is the disorganizing principles that give our age its character.
>
> — NIETZSCHE, *Will to Power*, #65

> Behind all this lies that sleek god of affluence, now proclaimed as the goal of life, replacing the high-minded view of the world which the West has lost.
>
> — ALEKSANDR SOLZHENITSYN [1]

1. All that we know derives from history. Even our interpretations of the Here and Now are historical, and our predictions too. We cannot escape the past. Of all the animals in this world *man remembers*, and glorifies what he remembers. When man ceases to remember he ceases to be man. He forfeits his place in the present. He forfeits his relationship to the future. In fact, man becomes deranged when important moments are forgotten or passed over. Imagine therefore, how much danger we are in, that we have missed the sociology of the bomb, that have we missed the significance of totalitarianism. Imagine how great our forgetfulness must be. Realize, from this, how great must be the danger that follows.

We have failed to remember. We have failed to be men.

Today, when we look at the wars of the past, we do not see these

---

[1] Aleksandre Solzhenitsyn, *The Mortal Danger* (New York: Harper Torchbooks, 1980), p. 70.

wars with an eye to the future. We somehow imagine we are living in a different universe, a universe which stands above the barbarism of the past. This, of course, is an illusion. The barbarism of the past remains.

When I first began writing this book, my only thought was to warn people, to get them to take a second look, to examine the nuclear dilemma from another angle. But our memory—as a people—was so atrophied that no warning was possible. The voice of alarm was heard only as an alarmist is heard, not as something genuine, but as a form of chilling entertainment.

The sociology of knowledge, in this case, teaches that only something consistent with commercial civilization can be understood by commercial people, that is, by consumers. As recent events show, the commercial herd does not accept or reject something on its merits—true or untrue—but on the basis of its economic utility.

"It's the economy, stupid!" is the slogan of our time.

Where does that leave ICBMs and hydrogen bombs? Somewhere in Russia a high-ranking general is laughing to himself, saying: "It's nuclear war, stupid!"

To remember the past is to know that war always comes. This is part of the historical process. Our inability to reflect on this process defines and dooms us. As the Russian generals have long said, a future world war will be a nuclear war, involving the mass use of nuclear missiles. In the United States nobody wants to acknowledge this possibility. Conservatives imagine they are opposed to the utopian idiocies of the liberals and leftists. But the socialist paradise conservatives oppose is, at bottom, a capitalist dream. Peace and plenty for everyone—the illusion of all illusions—dominates conservative thinking to such an extent that any serious talk of nuclear war is unacceptable to the conservative. He will not tolerate it. The idea that world war is inevitable threatens *his* utopian project.

The very nightmare that socialism produces in practice, the very war it inspires, is only possible in the context of a materialist and commercial civilization. The left is a business enterprise that stands against business. As such, it is careerist and opportunist, just like the so-called conservatives. The left does not foresee a nuclear war, but dreams of political power and prosperity. It does not realize that its goals are impossible and its methods are evil. It does not suspect that its peace accord with Russia must lead to war. In this, the left and the right share the same stupidity. Presentism has corroded everyone's understanding. Taking a broader view, most modern ideas are wrong because today's "ideologists" have dropped the very context of modernity, which is not merely the history of the past two hundred years, but the history of the last twenty-five centuries.

Fourteen years ago I began reading history from the earliest recorded times, starting with the ancient Greeks. I encountered countless wars and massacres. My belief in world peace was shaken. I read about Athens and Sparta. My democratic illusions fell away. My faith in human nature and progress did not survive *The Decline and Fall of the Roman Empire*. War is the law of history. The armed man, under the discipline of a mixed system, under a moral law undergirded by a belief in the supernatural, has always been the principal stabilizing, progressive basis of every age. Modern ideology, so far as it ignores this basic truth, is dangerous to mankind. The idea that we are somehow different, that we stand above history (as suggested by Francis Fukuyama) is absurd.

With twenty-five centuries of war and empire behind us, the future is clear. America's chief military rival is violating nearly all of the arms control agreements it has signed. Why? Yevgenia Albats, Anatoliy Golitsyn, Jan Sejna, Andrei Navrozov, Stanislav Lunev and Andrei Codrescu provide the clues. Their books suggest that something dangerous is going on behind the alleged "collapse of communism." And what is more, their books better fit the context of history than the CBS Evening News.

I do not mean to make the faithful old communists into one-dimensional villains. Don't mistake me. Things are not so simple. Lenin's followers never intended, for the most part, the destruction of so many countries. The fact is, these poor people are too practical-minded to see backwards and forward in time. And despite their claim of being the champions of history, they *also* lack historical sense. Many of them probably embraced communism because they could not embrace God. They could not believe in supernatural forces at work behind history, so they embraced materialistic forces. In fact, they rejected supernaturalism out of historical ignorance. For even Machiavelli, the cynical author of *The Prince*, treated the supernatural as an established fact, as something that historians and politicians must take into account.[2]

But our modern materialists, of the Left and Right, have no sense of history.

2. In politics, the ancients took a genuinely conservative view. They thought of progress in terms of decay; for all living things, as anyone can see, progress inexorably toward old age and death. Therefore all monarchies are progressing toward tyranny, all aristocracies toward oligarchy, and all democracies toward anarchy. The ancients were careful observers. They saw the evils of decay, the disruptions and bloodlettings that result when a political mechanism grows senile. Therefore they suggested techniques for arresting decay. In this regard

---

[2] Niccolo Machiavelli, *The Discourses*, trans. Bernard Crick (Middlesex England: Penguin Books, 1985), pp. 249 - 50. See Book One, Discourse 56.

----

their political science was entirely practical, and concerned with how to stabilize, settle, and retard the forces of change. The solution, of course, was found in the notion of "mixed institutions" wherein each function checked the decay of every other.

3. But Time, that old vagabond, broke out of its ancient constraints during an age of industrial and social revolution, which politicized that fickle goddess, Reason. Vain was the hope that Reason might provide new and stable machinery. For in practice, Reason intensified every tremor. And so there was a conservative backlash against the Revolution. Yet this reaction and its reactionaries could not long hope to maintain their power. For Reason had allies: Commerce and Science. Behind these marched the bourgeoisie: new money, new values, new ideas, and liberal democracy. Then did Reason triumph, arrayed in purple and decked with gold, riding a scarlet-colored beast, holding up the banner of universal suffrage and free public education. In her wake Time became a hurricane. The masts of civilization snapped, its sails went into the drink, the helmsman fell overboard, and we were driven into the sea of storms: the twentieth century. And as we rose and fell with the mountainous waves, we saw — dead ahead — a rocky shore. But the passengers just whistled a tune, ignoring the danger.

Illusion took the helm. It severed man's ancient ties with the grace of Heaven. For the type of rational inquiry that came into vogue, and the methods for carrying out that inquiry, tended to deny divinity its place in the soul of man. To grasp the extent of this internal calamity, observe that only societies with belief in the divine have continued to grow and extend their prosperity. Materialism and hedonism have always been proofs of impending decline and societal dissolution. This is true whether or not we admit the reality of God.

4. If there is such a thing as learning, then the past is our principal teacher. And however the past misleads us about the future, it is nevertheless our only possible guide, excepting God Himself. In other words: a thing can impress us only after it has happened to us, provided it hasn't killed us.

5. Today we no longer think in terms of history or futurity. We think of ourselves as the Be All and End All. Therefore criticism, under our regime, really is in bad taste, for we don't recognize any historical standard by which to judge; and God's standard is no longer decisive or authoritative as a whole. So when a book appears and pronounces judgments, as this one does, we find it distasteful. We say to ourselves: "This author is behind the times." And yes, he *is* behind the times, but also *ahead of the times.* In this sense, history and futurity are *one.*

Our journalists, who today crowd the throne of latter-day discourse, find no oneness in the world. And they do not properly relate things to history because they have not studied history. They are therefore clueless when it comes to futurity. Subsequently their lives, their writings, and their effects on the world, are utterly disjointed. They report facts and sometimes interject hedonistic preferences. More they cannot do.

6. The expectation of apocalyptic catastrophe following from a general collapse of moral values, is the surest ground for our twilight perspectivism. And besides, every compass points in this direction. All ships are driven to this rocky shore. Here, at last, is terra firma. Here at last is a Yes and a No: a vision of the future.

7. And so these observations on "futurity and history" are not *merely* moralistic. They are panoramic. Notice how full of questionable implications they are. But notice, also, how full of unquestionable ones as well. Give heed then, if you can. If you cannot, then smile, breath easy, and enjoy the good things that licentiousness has to offer. Your time is short.

8. *For those who are with me*: — how to begin? How does one uncover modernity's enmity with past and future and develop the theme: "Against History and Futurity"? Let us start by considering the "greatest story ever told," which describes Christ's death on the cross. Whereas Christ suffered for the sins of the world, we now believe that suffering itself is an impertinence. For in our view, suffering can be sensibly avoided. And in addition to being impertinent, suffering inconveniences those who are compelled to notice it. Therefore it has now become, on the most subtle level, *an evil thing to suffer*, whereas previously, it was helpful to the soul.

9. In light of this, the question for us becomes: how do we forgive our predecessors their sacrifices and sufferings, namely, the Great Depression and the Second World War? How do we forgive them for boring us with their tales of hardship: going without luxuries and doing backbreaking physical work? It's enough to fill us with absolute horror. And then, of course, they were spanked. Worse still, as children they were seen and *not* heard. Undoubtedly our parents were born in the Dark Ages. The fact is, we can *never* forgive them. The thing to do is—*forget them*.

10. Rather than the toil of the father possessing moral significance, it is the consumption of the son which now sanctifies. All of history is

therefore seen as the story of continual progress towards a regime of bread and circuses in which the redeemer, as Final Man, says to himself: "History culminates in my sensualism." For this is the modern gospel, an unwritten ideology that expresses itself in the sneer of the young against the values of the old, a sneer as declaration of war against history, and which, in a new generation of parents, gives rise to the neglect of children and a war against futurity.

11. Wherefore this concept, this invention, this newest philosophy which expresses itself in the term "unwanted pregnancy"? Are we not approaching a day when *every* pregnancy shall be unwanted, when the expression "unwanted pregnancy" shall ring with redundance? One sees, even now, that "unwanted pregnancy" is itself a pregnancy threatening to give birth to a mother that devours her own children.

12. I think that pregnancy itself has become synonymous with disease, as all pregnancies are increasingly a source of irritation. Anything is preferable to parenthood. People are realizing this more and more. The secret dirty thought of today is: "Liberate me from my children." —a viewpoint that posits sterility as good luck. Only when they become old and frightened do people adhering to this viewpoint rush off to find pathways back to fertility. But sometimes it is too late. And then there's the wreckage of so many past "relationships" behind one, a series of regrettable pedestrian accidents mucking up the soul. And a woman with direct experience of this cynical new world cannot be sure that her husband won't cashier her for a newer model when midlife crisis takes hold of him. On the other hand, women ought to be independent— right?—and learn to live like bachelors. Everyone knows that the traditional role of housewife is to be sneered at. The age-old safeguards, the age-old chivalries, are but masculine condescensions and should be rejected out of hand as patronizing and arrogant. Such trappings diminish the feminine personality. Therefore, an alternative to the old ways has been proposed. Its name is "women's liberation." Yet whatever we call this newest of creeds, the sexual urge of the man seems to be the *real* winner. For up until recently, the slogan of civilization was: "Women and children first."
—Now changed to: *Every man for himself.*

13. *The war against tomorrow.* —
In America we slice millions of babies out of millions of wombs every year. And unaborted children are, in a sense, left to abort themselves retroactively. About this fact there exists a high degree of ambivalence mixed with lip service to various shades of righteous indignation. Juvenile crime statistics for the last fifty years are up over

three thousand percent while SAT scores have plummeted. But, as Stalin once said: "One death is a tragedy, one million is a statistic." So it really does not change anything if, in the last few months, many hundreds of babies have been tossed in dumpsters, garbage pails, plastic bags, sacks; if increasing numbers of teenagers are crammed into Juvenile Hall. Then, of course, there is molestation, abuse, neglect, divorce and, to sum up, the public school system; that is, institutionalized molestation, neglect, and abuse—a dumpster for the whole lot!

And who really wants children? What little bores they are. How messy, frightful, disgusting, expensive. What possible utility are they?—helpless, ungrateful, stubborn, unruly; and again, but pardon me, *expensive*. I'm planning on a peaceful death, a ripe old age, a nice retirement. Kids would sack my savings, drain my health and energies, spoil my romance, ruin the furniture. In other words: it's best to cancel the future generation and make a war against tomorrow. Why not? We will issue bonds and bolster up the Social Security system, transforming our neglected children into beasts of future tax burden. In essence, it is to our advantage. The little jerks can reap the whirlwind after we are gone. It is the rational thing to do; and we are, nowadays, so *terribly* rational.

Meanwhile, we send the kiddies behind the chain-link fences of a state-run concentration camp, and call it "school." We give them over to bureaucrats and wonder why they graduate so ill-disciplined and stupid. How could it be otherwise when Mr. Lackluster is given to teach from dull textbooks under a regime of keen peer-group vulgarity?

And again, we ask: Who needs the brats? Lengthen the school year, hire more hacks, put fewer difficult words in the textbooks, and wage a phony war on drugs. That will fix things as far as we are concerned.

That is us, and we don't mind admitting it. Abort the babies—or if we don't, saddle them with debt. Load those youngsters like beasts of burden. Snooze comfortably into ripe old age. We won't be here to worry about tomorrow's consequences.

And also, there is our revenge against those younger than ourselves.

14. Put a rat in a box and give it three levers: one for food, one for sex, and one for cocaine. What will the rat do? After learning what each lever brings, the rat pushes the cocaine lever until it dies.

Next, we try the experiment with human teenagers.

15. That which *feels* good begins to transcend that which *is* good, begins to usurp the position of ruling principle and becomes, without doubt, the transvaluation of all values: *man as pawn of his gonads*. Where we once saw the brutal overlord and disciplinarian we now see the rule of sensual impulses, democracy as the immediate gratification of preponderant lusts.

The consequence of this system? An offended future. A future
insulted as mere continuance of orgasm into eternity, insulted because
"good sex" has come to think of itself as possessing more grandeur, more
importance in the pettiest offices, than Time herself. Therefore, a new
point of departure: our ship leaves port without compass, without charts,
sailing into an icy north wind.

16. We find ourselves caught in larger feuds when we provoke the
future. (For the future is a part of Time, and the whole takes umbrage at
the insult to its parts.) We've also stirred the temper of Time's monsters
who emerge from the black and bloody depths. Foul-breathing History,
for example, snarls, foams, rages. It is angry because we can no longer
learn from her, because we say to ourselves: "Who needs the past? Who
needs that bitch, History?" And as for the future, it is inevitable death
and nothingness. Therefore, we narcissists, we hedonists, are better than
the past, we are wiser than history, and we care nothing for posterity.

Of what concern is it that men have lived before and shall live
hereafter? We see nothing worthwhile in such trivia.

17. Disregard for the past is a corollary of disregard for the future.
It means the neglect of children and old people. It is expressed through
culture, as journalism instead of the thoughtful elucidation of facts, and
also, as a loose segregation by age as opposed to a time when the
generations lived together. It means contemporary "theories" instead of
ongoing traditions.

18. *The disease diagnosing itself.* —
Francis Fukuyama, a "Sovietologist," writes about the coming end of
history. By the "end of history" he means the liberal-capitalist Golden
Age (i.e., "last history"). Upon closer examination, however, this Golden
Age turns out to be nothing but the continuance of economic prosperity
ad infinitum.

The widespread, if momentary, interest in Fukuyama is due to the
fact that as pale optimist he hinted at economism's victory, which is
nothing more than telling the mob what it wants to hear.

An overnight celebrity, Fukuyama was dumbfounded at the attention
he received. "Frankly," he said, "I wasn't expecting this kind of reaction.
I wanted the thing to be quite speculative and thought provoking." But
he should have realized that any wishful thought, when given thick
expression by a Harvard Ph.D., will generate interest because sickness
always yearns for its pill.

19. The system is decrepit and about to die, not because of pauperization, as Karl Marx predicted, but because the system worked all too well, by making the masses affluent. What we never figured was the ultimate implications of this affluence, which broke down piety, family, virtue, and citizenship. Our tendency toward making economic values into primary values is a cancer which has gradually eaten away all transcendent concerns. There are also the vulgar, plebeian, and egalitarian tendencies inherent in the social development of economism, its intellectual and moral vacuousness, its reliance on rationalized (i.e., bureaucratic) authority, its uncertainty in the face of the future and its ignorance of the past. Specifically, what proves to be the most disturbing symptom of the "shopping mall regime" is its subordination of politics to economics. Without qualification, this arrangement is dangerous because where the market-place rules there can be no maintenance of spiritual and political standards, but a general and continuous decline. Our republican political system has been so weakened by the nexus of economics that nothing can save it short of mass religious conversion. But now we have reason to fear that religion, too, has fallen prey to economism; so that the two pillars of order—church and state—have been chewed through by green-backed termites. It seems that our religious and political instincts have dissolved into one grand economic instinct.

Other dangers emerge from this: namely, that these passionate economic forces, now triumphant over state and church, will begin to engender totalitarianism as they shake every pillar of that which is order, of that which is binding, of that which is static. For the static impulses of society—towards order, meaning, and eternal truth—cannot be cast aside without engendering some kind of *reaction*. But the capitalist state is now so stupid, its brainpower at such a low ebb, that the current apparatus can only save society by committing suicide, which it seems to be doing.

20. We live in an Age of Anxiety, an anxiety which begs for certainty, authority, and a father image. But alas, no fathers. No fathers in the main. Only an occasional accident, a father by chance—here and there. Nothing surefire, nothing intrinsic. To a large extent the socialists and the communists, the racists and traditionalists, are lashing out, fearfully attempting to bring under control all those unpredictable and frightening forces unleashed by liberalism. These forces have torn morality to shreds, crippled authority, and severed continuity. These forces, which our socialists and reactionaries are attempting to control, are so anarchic and explosive that the danger of societal collapse and regression cannot be overestimated.

21. Today people have a lust for recreation as opposed to serious

leisure activities. Leisure time, as the fountainhead of all previous high culture, cannot withstand the assault of modernity, the race of rats, the busybusy of the faster and faster hurry-up. Add to this the detrimental effects of money. We find commercial interests pandering to a populace exhausted by tedious forms of labor where the need for relief, refreshment, and stimulation is all too powerful. It is only natural that people should prefer comedy to tragedy, the light to the heavy, the sensational to the profound, so that comedy, light drama, sex and violence necessarily absorb the off-hour attention of the masses and, in turn, accelerate the process of widespread despiritualization. Mass culture cannot be otherwise.

22. *The feminization of man.* —
One modern woman says: "He was cute at first and then he began to bore me. I started fixing him up, changing his hair style, picking his clothes, but he still wasn't very good-looking."

23. *The Progress of Fat.* — Through many centuries of tedium, war, disease and anguish civilization progressed. And with civilization fatness also progressed, from the hollow-cheekéd look of the primordial cannibal toward the big-gutted look of the modern bourgeois. Today big-guttedness represents enervation and decrepitude, decadence, softness, and lack of self-control. They say, in America, that the current generation is the fattest yet known in history.

Though past generations have celebrated fatness, the present generation faces the grim side effects of narrowed arteries and choked hearts, of clogged veins, poor circulation and sudden death. Fatness now kills more people in the West than war, pestilence, and famine. Fatness is typical-archetypical of modern capitalist life. It dramatically exemplifies all that is wrong in us. We are soft and flabby, in mind and body—and in body politic. While we grow in physical corpulence, and its attendant diseases, there appears a parallel in civilization as a whole; that is, our tendency to indulge in thoughts the same way we have indulged our grosser appetites. In other words, we seek out what is palatable instead of what is healthful. We refuse the nutritious but bitter-tasting truths. We yearn instead for a high-cholesterol plate of love, peace, utopia, brotherhood, quick cures and equality for all human beings. We yearn for chocolate mousse humanitarianism. Fat has not only filled our hearts, but plugged our ears and closed our eyes.

24. Since the advent of masses and the demise of social classes we have found that in political and moral terms it is easier to destroy than to build, easier to corrupt than to purify, easier to break than to fix. The

----

masses are Midas inverted. Whatever they touch is turned to muck. Whatever they meddle in is ruined. The *state*, which has fallen into their clutches, is the prime example.

25. *Survival of the unfit.* —
Sitting at the desk of a clerk, shrunken down into an ugly speck; thoughts also shrunken, and the world limping insanely toward a typhoon. No captain, no officer of the watch, just billions of nonentities elbowing one another. This is the great whirring machine in which each part must give over its substance to the doomed destiny of the whole. Those parts which refuse to whir, those revolutionists against continuous revolution who cease revolving in order to think, are cast onto the junk-heap. To cease whirring would mean an end to the smallness and shallowness born of dizzying rotation. It means that one no longer fits and is no longer fit for licking the bottom side of the next company memo or committing to memory the intellectual ditchdigger's catalogue of dreary procedures; and it also means that one ceases to earn the pay.

26. The question: "Am I a bad person?" now means "Am I liked?" And a related question: "Do important people like me?" to the point where: "Am I successful?" "Am I given opportunities?"
What happens to morality and decency when these formulas reign supreme?

27. Item of wishful thinking: The Chinese government will back down in Tiananmen Square. They won't massacre the student demonstrators.
Symptom: belief that the "people" always win. Reality: force wins. Origin of belief? Democratic ideology. Corrective? Read Lenin.

28. *Reading.* —
Reading is important. But this does not drive the modern man to read, and if he reads, to read the right things. He sometimes reads predigested summaries, or newspapers, or trendy magazines, or trashy romance novels. But for the most part, he does not read at all. He does not read because reading requires effort. It requires muscle, discipline, a regular commitment to the nourishment of consciousness.
This raises far too many difficulties, wastes precious time, and is not commercially profitable.

29. Some have said that conformism is the product of a certain kind of education (i.e., socialist). Some have blamed conformism on dictatorship, on collectivism, on tribalism, etc. But conformism is very bourgeois. Conformism is as American as apple pie. And democracy is

----

institutionalized conformism.   Blaming conformism on collectivist ideology simply won't wash.   The middle class has always believed firmly in the universality of its own perspectives and has therefore been the engine of conformism from the beginning.

30.   The peer group rushes into the modern vacuum.   But the peer group is only the sum of drift and aimlessness, the hub of fashion.   The peer group is a creature of sensuality and not of authority.   Though it has taken the place of authority, it cannot perform the function of authority and is not an adequate substitute for definitive values because the peer group does not believe in anything eternal, transcendent, or sacred.   The peer group is always extemporaneous, flighty, and fluctuating.

31.   Authority cannot exist without morality.   For who would follow an authority which failed to make a convincing moral claim?   It is also true that morality cannot exist without authority.   For who would adhere to a morality which lacked authoritativeness?

32.   If we are to judge from history: the day of the dictator is only dawning, because every era of exaggeration brings despotism whether in ancient Egypt, Mesopotamia, or Weimar Germany.   And ours is an era of exaggeration to end all eras of exaggeration.

33.   After many centuries of discovery and development we arrive at the regime of convenience.   And this regime has its problems.   For as convenience is king, neither honor, nor truth, nor justice can have much weight.
Why?
Because convenience declares itself honorable, as a matter of convenience.   It declares itself rational.   It usurps truth, both in business and politics, as a matter of convenience.   To break a contract today is as nothing.   Bankruptcy is as easy as divorce.   To allow allies to fall under the conquerors boot is considered peace-loving.   On the other hand, we are quick to oppose tyranny when our supply of gasoline is threatened.   Once more—*convenience!*[3]

34.   During this era of the transvaluation of values, our psychologists have reported a growing void inside the human psyche.   They have detected an emptiness, a meaningless space, a lack of internal structure, a gnawing nihilism.   No order above, no order below.   We no longer have answers to fundamental questions.
We are therefore empty and weak.   We are ready for conquest.

---

[3] Consider the Gulf War, fought in 1991.

35. Structure is the essence both of biological life and social life. It takes us some time to grasp its universal importance. Every living thing has need of bounds, and requires hierarchical arrangement in addition to horizontal arrangement. Hierarchy in the human world means authority, moral values, rank order. Nietzsche once said: "For institutions to exist there must exist the kind of will...which is anti-liberal to the point of malice." Once this antiliberalness ceases to exist, the human material becomes unfit for institutions.[4]

36. The amoralist scoffs at the idea of American decline. For him the idea of decline is discreditable precisely because it is a moral idea, and moral ideas—as he will tell you—are nonsense. The amoralist believes that humankind is naturally selfish, that selfishness is good and wickedness is not really a problem. He'll say that everything is going to be okay because the free market works wonderfully, that liberty is the true religion and Christianity is a bad influence. Divorce, abortion, prostitution, pornography, drug trafficking, petty theft, and other "victimless crimes" should be facilitated. If the schools are bad it is no big deal. Book learning is a dubious enterprise anyway.

To these shallow optimists and libertines I deliver the following riposte:

Every day an average of 7,742 American youngsters become sexually active; 623 contract gonorrhea or syphilis; 2,740 become pregnant; 1,105 have abortions; 1,293 give birth; 369 miscarry; 684 attempt suicide; 2,989 witness the divorce of their parents.[5]

37. The prophet Isaiah, sent to foretell the doom of God's people, was told by God that the people's ears would be heavy and their eyes would be shut "lest they see with their eyes, and hear with their ears, and understand with their hearts, and convert, and be healed." The philosopher Nietzsche also described these people. He said that when confronted with the truth they "blinked thereby." And Nietzsche wrote: "They understand me not: I am not the mouth for these ears."[6]

The only mouth for these ears, it seems, is a mouth deceitful and flattering. Such ears yearn for the cult of sweet promises, which spurns as "negativism" all hard truths. We are speaking of a complacency which makes a virtue out of accepting oneself *as is*. Ignorance thus finds its bliss and the people cry out against all higher strivings as if such strivings were so many tyrannies. They mock the idea of raising themselves up off all fours: "Give us this last man, O Zarathustra, make us into these

---

[4] Nietzsche, *Twilight of the Idols*, p. 103.

[5] "Children's Lack of Power Leaves Needs Unmet," *Los Angeles Times*, 16 May 1991, p. A1.

[6] Nietzsche, *Thus Spake Zarathustra*, p. 12.

last men! Then will we make thee a present of the Superman!"[7]
Today we find this plea sliding playfully off people's tongues, posing in store windows, on TV, in books and magazines, seducing us with music, with girls, with sex, with more girls, with more sex, etc. America has embraced last-manism with a will, as if nothing else mattered. We want to *be* the last man. And this ambition—as lack of ambition—signifies that nothing can be done to make us understand.

Then why give out prophecies? Why bother with such people? Albert Jay Nock, a commentator on American decline, wrote an essay attempting to answer this question, called "Isaiah's Job." In it he said that Isaiah, by giving out prophecies, was not concerned with correcting the grammar of mankind, but wanted only to nurture the remnant, a dispersed minority who alone might comprehend the humane life and its vision. To reach this remnant one had to preach a general message because the remnant is hidden in the crowd, solitary and cut off. One might add that the prophet also accomplishes his task by speaking posthumously; in other words, after one's own death and after the death of the age, in a voice designed to penetrate the ears of future time. This is practical insofar as the substance of prophecy is not merely that it predicts the future, but that it has special meaning *for* the future; because a prophet, proved by history, becomes an indisputable source of authoritative wisdom for posterity. And posterity, emerging from the flames of holocaust or captivity, is sometimes improved by a meditation on wrong turns taken, opportunities missed, on truth and consequences. Considering these things, men will have reason to cherish the words of the prophet. He reminds them that history makes sense, that there is justice in it. Meaning and morality thus restored, posterity cannot help feeling affection for a man who showed fatherly concern for these orphans, these lost children, yearning for some word from the past.

From such a posterity there might conceivably spring "first man," the antithesis of "last man." One might honorably venture a life of penury and rebuke in order to leave something of value for such men.

_____

[7] Ibid.

12

Scholars and Intellectuals

Intellectuals are in fact people who wield the power of the spoken and the written word, and one of the touches that distinguish them from other people who do the same is the absence of direct reponsibility for practical affairs. This touch in general accounts for another — the absence of that first-hand knowledge...which only actual experience can give. The critical attitude, arising...from the fact that his main chance of asserting himself lies in his actual or potential nuisance value, should add a third touch.
       — JOSEPH A. SCHUMPETER, *Capitalism, Socialism and Democracy*

In the wilderness have ever dwelt the conscientious, the free spirits, as lords of the wilderness; but in the cities dwell the well-foddered, famous wise ones — draught beasts.
       For, always do they draw, as asses — the *people's* carts!
       — NIETZSCHE, *Thus Spake Zarathustra*

One of the principal lessons of our tragic century, which has seen so many millions of innocent lives sacrificed in schemes to improve the lot of humanity, is — beware intellectuals.
       — PAUL JOHNSON, *Intellectuals*

1.   *Neurotic* is a far more sinister adjective than people realize. Sigmund Freud once suggested that neurotics are poor sports; that they are unable to lose gracefully. And the worst poor sports of all, it seems, are the intellectuals.

2.   Freud observed that every civilization *must* coerce people and make them renounce their instincts. This coercion might be subtle, involving the threat of parental or peer group rejection; or it might be heavy-handed, like corporal punishment, jail, or public execution. Whatever the specific mechanisms involved, *coercion remains necessary.* Freud wrote that the "masses are lazy and unintelligent; they have no love for instinctual renunciation, and they are not to be

convinced by argument of its inevitability."[1]   In this way Freud
rebutted the utopians, optimists, and other forward-lookers.   New
generations brought up in kindness and reason would be no better than
previous generations.   Freud denied that the human soul had improved in
modern times.   All that has happened, he explained, was that external
coercion had gradually become "internalized."   Man had thereby
developed a conscience, which Freud called the "super-ego."   Only the
super-ego makes man a moral being in the human sense.   Strengthening
the super-ego, said Freud, is essential for the survival of civilization.

3.   Robert A. Heinlein, in his didactic novel *Starship Troopers*,
argued that corporal punishment is a necessary aspect of moral training.
Pain, said Heinlein, leaves a deep impression on the human nervous
system, and is therefore wonderfully suited to reshaping human behavior.
For example: a man reaches for a cigarette and receives an electric
shock.   After repeatedly experiencing this association between cigarette-
smoking and pain, the man begins to lose his craving for cigarettes.   Pain
can break down all kinds of bad habits.   In the case of punishing
criminals Heinlein also pointed to the importance of humiliation, which
serves to combat the solipsism inherent in criminals.
    Here again, the word is *coercion*.

4.   Paul Johnson's book on intellectuals suggests that a great many of
them were spoiled children.   One finds, in Johnson's work, a parade of
arrogant and willful individuals, maladjusted and amoral, self destructive
and destructive of others — a gallery of neurotics.   Were they properly
punished as children?   Were they humbled?   No.

5.   Irving Babbittt, the American thinker and moral philosopher,
believed that modernity was witnessing the triumph of "naturalistic
philosophy" over "moral philosophy."   He argued that man desperately
needs moral philosophy, which consists in the cultivation of self control
and the checking of our darker impulses.   Babbittt also argued that the
entire modern movement runs counter to this, tending to favor the
impulses, spontaneity, and naturalness.   The result is the deconstruction
of man's conscience.   Babbittt said that this deconstruction could only be
reversed if we returned to a moral discipline that emphasized humility.
Only *this* could bring man's lawless urges to heel, while the naturalistic
standards of scientific thinking put pride in the place of humility,
negating humanity's moral development and encouraging what Babbitt
called the *libido sciendi*.   The implications of Babbitt's analysis are
fascinating, for the *libido sciendi* turns out to be a mild and characterless

---

[1] Sigmund Freud, *The Future of an Illusion*, trans. James Strachey (New York: W. W. Norton &
Company, 1975), p. 8.

magalomania. This is exactly what Paul Johnson shows in his book. Our writers and artists are increasingly sinister in their instincts. It is a phenomenon which can no longer be ignored. And as Babbitt warns: any attempt to found a governing class on such an intellectuality would lead in practice to the death of civilization.[2]

6. Søren Kierkegaard had an interesting way of explaining liberalism's course of degeneration. He called it "leveling" because liberalism means relativism and relativism means the end of authority (and hierarchy). Thus, with authority shattered, the higher self loses control over the lower, the good man loses advantage over the bad man. Humanity's worst impulses are then released from the shadow world, no longer repressed but free to wreak havoc. Thus we hear the voices of envy, spite, and malice as they grow louder and louder *from within ourselves.* Next, there arise irrepressible urges, crime waves, sexual explosions, the collapse of the family, of individuality, moral authority being supplanted by an anarchy of backbiting and second-guessing. Kierkegaard's vision was of a regime from which nothing positive could come.[3]

7. Today's scientific specialist is mentally lopsided. Nevertheless, we look up to him. We listen carefully when he makes political or philosophical pronouncements. It is hard for us to realize that in fields of endeavor other than his own, he may have nothing to offer.

8. When men toil away their lives in the labyrinths of specialization, then the liberal tradition which preaches the equality of men proves itself a lie.

9. Our overproduction of intellectuals means "intellectual Malthusianism": too many intellects and too few careers. But intellectuals are ingenious. In a democratic state they always seem to find work for themselves by agitating for various causes. This is one reason why the welfare state continues to expand.

10. The professional intellectual first appeared as a significant phenomenon during the Italian Renaissance. In older times those who wrote books were generally amateurs like Thucydides, Polybius, Cicero, and Tacitus. These were men of wealth and leisure, or retired politicians, aristocrats interested in practical problems, generals and lawyers,

---

[2] Irving Babbitt, *Democracy and Leadership* (Indianapolis: Liberty*Classics*, 1978), p. 285.

[3] Søren Kierkegaard, *The Present Age,* trans. Alexander Dru (New York: Harper Torchbooks, 1962), pp. 33 - 75.

----

appreciators of noble deeds, men imbued with notions of civic duty, prudence and tradition. The sobriety of the ancient Roman writers is particularly impressive.

11. The position of the intellectual has always been tenuous because he is commercially underprivileged. Unless born into money he faces bleak prospects for livelihood, for he is competing in an arena where few can succeed. Thus his place in society is questionable and his stake in the status quo is small. All these factors tempt him to become a rabble-rouser. Even so, he resents having to prostitute himself before a vulgar crowd. He resents having to lower his standards. Perhaps this explains his tendency to become a demagogue. Perhaps this also explains his elitist tendencies, which come out in the all-too-common preference for socialism.

12. Jacob Burckhardt confirms some of this in his celebrated essay on Renaissance culture, where he writes of the "natural alliance between the despot and the scholar."[4]   Burckhardt says that the intellectuals of the Renaissance were permeated with a spirit of negation. He tells of "a poisonous brood of impotent wits, of born critics and railers, whose envy called for hecatombs of victims."[5]   The famed economist Ludwig von Mises, speaking of our times, refers to the "vain arrogance of the literati" and "frivolous intellectuals" who are "a nuisance."[6]   Many social thinkers seem to agree: the intellectual tends to be a bad egg. Julien Benda thought the intellectuals had betrayed civilization by becoming advocates of violence, revenge, and upheaval. They were the organizers of political hatreds. As Benda tells us, the intellectual sits at the heart of every *modern* problem.[7]   For the intellectual finds pleasure in exacerbating our difficulties, in sowing confusion, in turning brothers into enemies.   With the inception of freedom the black tide of intellectualism rises ever higher—a generalized pornography of the spirit: *in art, in literature, in music.* Joseph Schumpeter, commenting on the sociology of the intellectual, explained how "impossible it is to stem the tide" of the intellectuals "within the framework of capitalist society." He further adds: "Only a government of non-bourgeois nature and nonbourgeois creed—under modern circumstances only a socialist or

4 Burckhardt, *The Civilization of the Renaissance in Italy*, trans. S. G. C. Middlemore (New York: The Modern Library, 1954), p. 162.

5 Ibid., p. 121.

6 Ludwig von Mises, *The Anti-Capitalistic Mentality* (Spring Mills, Pennsylvania: Libertarian Press, 1981), p. 107.

7 Julien Benda, *The Treason of the Intellectuals*, trans. Richard Aldington (New York: W. W. Norton & Company, 1969).

fascist one—is strong enough to discipline them. In order to do that it would have to change typically bourgeois institutions and drastically reduce the individual freedom of all strata of the nation."[8]

13. The most fanatical part of the fanatic is his intellect.

14. What Camus calls "metaphysical rebellion" is definitely a part of the modern movement. One rejects not merely God, parents, tradition, morality, reason, but also—*reality*; because reality is tyrannical. It puts brackets around us. We rebel against brackets. We despise the truth. All truth threatens to oppress.

15. Theology has come to represent the progressive degeneration of religion, an attempt to put the tool (reason) before the user of the tool (soul). Therefore we have, as Russell Kirk said, put the soul out of business. Where a soul used to be, now one finds mere reasons. And Reason, in supposing the body to be more palpable than the soul, often aligns itself with sensualism. One can hear the intellectuals objecting; so I ask: Since when have our modern intellectuals shown themselves to be anything but sensualists?

16. Another question occurs to us: Does man possess a nature? No, no, no, and a thousand times — no! That is the answer one hears in the lecture halls of the universities. This denial of human nature helps explain the political incompetence of our intellectuals. It is an essential ingredient in their utopianism and a backdrop for their leftism, subjectivism, neuroticism, etc. Lacking a clear notion of human nature, the intellectuals cannot grasp man's need for authority. They cannot order punishments with a clear conscience. Under their direction military strategy lapses into bungling and education *makes* stupid. In their way of thinking, human nature is so misunderstood that the carrot is now thought better than the stick. But the carrot without the stick is useless and uninstructive. The abdication herein revealed is an abdication of authority in terms of the willingness to inflict pain. Our hedonism puts its emphasis on pleasure, not pain. Go to a society which puts the emphasis on self-control and one finds physical punishments still in practice. This observation leads us to wonder whether the demise of authority in the West is connected with the demise of corporal punishment and hellfire. Please note that the loving but angry God has dropped His anger only to find Himself declared "dead."

---

[8] Schumpeter, *Capitalism, Socialism and Democracy*, p. 150.

13

Organized Crime and the Fifth Column

The basic revolutionary strategy took shape in the years 1954 to 1956. As detailed by Sejna, there were five principal thrusts in the modernized strategy. First was the increased training of leaders for the revolutionary movements....

The second step was the actual training of terrorists. Training for international terrorism actually began as 'fighters for liberation.' The term 'national liberation' was coined to replace revolutionary war movement as a two-way deception: to provide a nationalistic cover for what was basically an intelligence operation and to provide a label that was semantically separated from the communist revolutionary war movement.

The third step was international drug and narcotics trafficking. Drugs were incorporated into the revolutionary war strategy as a political and intelligence weapon to use against the bourgeois societies and as a mechanism for recruiting agents of influence around the world.

The fourth step was to infiltrate organized crime and, further, to establish Soviet Bloc sponsored and controlled organized crime syndicates throughout the world.

The fifth step was to plan and prepare for sabotage throughout the whole world. The network for this activity was to be in place by 1972.
—JOSEPH D. DOUGLASS, Jr.[1]

1. A couple of decades after America stopped believing in hell, the soon-to-be President of the United States, William Jefferson Davis Clinton, suddenly abbreviated himself—William Jefferson Clinton.[2] After all, Clinton is a new man. As such he doesn't need the past. The new man, the pragmatic man, is made up entirely of appetite, which only knows the here and now. For him, as scientific materialist, power remains the sole aim of all political activity. The rest is illusion and mythology. He wants only the solid thing itself (with which to dominate). And being so streamlined, so perfect in his focus, he knows very little about history. He only studies that which promises immediate

[1] *Red Cocaine*, p 10.

[2] See the *Concise Dictionary of Biography* (London: Tiger Books International, 1993), p.78.

results. Beyond this, there is only the residue of slack sixties socialism, the long abandoned polemic of a half-educated draft evader, and a self-righteousness better annunciated obliquely by the first lady. (Why take chances oneself?)

Thus we find ourselves governed by a man who seldom reflects, who always emotes, who never acts but reacts. A man without history or futurity, too weak to play Antichrist, too blind to see the threat of Russian power, and too corrupt to avoid being the target of international blackmailers.

Is Clinton a man of the center, as he pretended during an election campaign, or is he a man of the left who hides his true ideological view, which now and again is glimpsed through the intellectual fog?[3]

Or maybe he is nothing but a puppet.

And what of the first lady's flirtations with Marxism? In days gone by Mrs. Hillary Clinton has worked to assist extremist groups, including the Black Panthers, CISPES (which supported communist insurgents in El Salvador), and the communist-controlled National Lawyers Guild.[4]

At the close of one NLG meeting the delegates sang the communist *International*, which states:

> 'Tis the final conflict, let each stand his place.
> The International Soviet shall be the Human Race.

Should we suppose that Hillary Rodham Clinton disagrees with the words of the communist *International*? In fact, there is reason to suspect that she's as red as a fire truck. But for those who insist that our first lady is by no means subversive, let them read what David Mark Price has written on Hillary's ties to radical groups.[5]

2. For those who think this is paranoia, I have news. There is an ideological struggle taking place. It is not some figment of an

---

[3] Socci, "Compagno Bill," *Il Sabato*, August 8, 1992, p. 22ff.

Clinton said in the Socci interview: "I went there [to the communist co-op of Legga] to study. I came five years ago to the province of Florence to find out how the cooperatives...and the micro enterprises function. Then I went back to Arkansas and I helped put together about seventy youth cooperatives."

Socci then asked: "Don't tell me this is your economic prescription for the States?'"

"Absolutely." Clinton said.

[4] While working as the Director and Chairman of the Board of Directors of the New World Foundation from 1987-1988, Hillary Clinton oversaw the funneling of money to communist fronts and various far left organizations. See Daniel Wattenberg, "The Lady MacBeth of Little Rock: Hillary Clinton's hard-left past and present," *The American Spectator*, August 1992, p. 32.

[5] David Mark Price, *Secret* (Witchita, Kansas: Sunset Research Group, 1993).

overwrought right-wing imagination. It is something real, which any thinking person who is alive to the world of ideas will find if he but attend a leading American university. Those who assume that Marxism is a relic (that only professors toy with) should be reminded that the average college graduate unconsciously takes more of Marx with him into the world than anything else. We cannot begin to estimate the hold which Marxist thought has on the country's elite. It pervades our institutions. In fact, scientific socialism has wormed its way, however camouflaged, into our business schools. We should not be surprised that this oh-so-gentle cosmological insinuation fails to sport a Stalin mustache or speak with a thick Russian accent. After all, we are not the czar's peasants. The West is more sophisticated; therefore, a more sophisticated type of propaganda tends to prevail here, and a different feeling about socialism than what prevails in backward countries. As for those who imagine that Marxism is dead, a side note: Try getting an advanced degree in political science today while denouncing Marxist ideas. See how far you get before you find half a dozen unexpected obstacles placed in your path. The war of ideas has its ideological warriors. They cannot stop a person from getting a degree, but they can make it costly. Certainly, if an aspiring academic has the least sense of career advantage, his ideological predisposition must be adjusted accordingly.

As it turns out, our American subversives and revolutionaries do not ambush people on mountain roads or lead revolutionary armies as they do in Third World countries. Here, in the land of Jefferson and Lincoln, they seize institutions and promote their friends from the ranks. Therefore they congregate in education, publishing, entertainment, and government service. In this they are not stupid. In fact, such activism should recommend itself to our lazy right-wingers.

3. The Russians are preparing for war. Meanwhile, domestic socialists in the executive branch have given away our nuclear and missile technology to Red China. What is being done to protect us from this twofold danger? Nothing. Former House Speaker Newt Gingrich, a Republican, was a hawk. But alas, he said, "I am a cheap hawk." He declared himself to be for impeachment in the event of improprieties. But in the end it was Mr. Gingrich who resigned. The impeachment of Clinton did not work. Instead of focusing on the president's dealings with Chinese spies, the Republicans focused on a sex scandal.

Think of it! Republican politicians, homosexuals and adulterers themselves, said Clinton had committed perjury and obstruction of justice to hide his affair with Monica Lewinsky. The country was tititlated. Which Republican would resign next? Clinton's ratings went up. Questions related to national security were ignored.

The real issue, the bottom line, is national defense in an age of mass destruction weapons. What can we afford to tolerate from the nation's leader?

Mr. Clinton wants to improve America. But these improvements will lead to a disastrous defeat, to an unprecedented calamity for our people. To be precise, Mr. Clinton is against ABM defense. He is against civil defense. As such, Mr. Clinton is a hazard. If we are to trust the testimony of Terry Reed and Larry Nichols, he is much worse. Perhaps our leading politicians are useless timeservers. Many in Washington are corrupt, but Clinton is in another league altogether. In this context, what explains the recent rash of corpses, which invariably pop up in the wake of clandestine operations?[6]

If you want to understand who Clinton is, you must watch him closely. You must see how he reaches for power, how he weakens the national defense in the face of Russia's ongoing treaty violations. With every move, Clinton strengthens Russia and China as he weakens America.

People ought to ask why.

4. It was not so long ago that Liddell Hart wrote about a new kind of warfare, involving intellectual weapons. What he did not foresee was that his principle of "the indirect approach" could be carried into sociology, that an attack could target deeper social structures, creating and exploiting otherwise harmless deformations. In this context, crime and corruption have always been with us. The Bible states that man is a fallen creature, easily led astray. Even good men are tempted. Therefore, the organization which would exploit corruption in an opposing social system (i.e., the KGB) builds its own opportunity for such exploitation, especially through narcotics trafficking. Here is a trap for the big fish — for politicians and government officials of every kind. The bait is the money, the vast sums of cash that are generated by selling dope. It is far more efficient, by every measure, to corrupt the enemy leaders and blackmail them, than it is to harass them with slogans and the threat of nuclear attack. (If one is going to use nuclear weapons, it is best

---

6 See, especially, *The Clinton Chronicles Book*, ed. Patrick Matrisciani (Hemet, California: Jeremiah Books, 1994). See also Terry Reed and John Cummings, *Compromised: Clinton, Bush and the CIA* (New York: SPI Books, 1994). The key to deciphering Reed's testimony is yet to be found in the role played by CIA agent Felix Rodriguez, a close associate of then-Vice President George Bush. Reed claims that a highly placed Israeli source told him Rodriguez was a double agent working for the KGB. In this context, the alleged CIA-connected drug trafficking into Arkansas under Clinton's regime gives us the specifics of the Red Cocaine operation outlined by the Czechoslovak major general, Jan Sejna, in Douglass's exposé, *Red Cocaine: The Drugging of America*. (Drug trafficking serves to assist Soviet agents in penetrating U.S. organizations, and in blackmailing U.S. officials.)

not to alarm the intended victim beforehand. Better to bide one's time and pursue other avenues of attack.) The employment of government sponsored organized crime syndicates is something the Kremlin leaders have perfected. Under the fake democracy of Boris Yeltsin, the party and KGB have fallen back on various secret structures (as Lev Timofeyev calls them),[7] which are associated with the idea of the "mafia." But we must recognize that this has long been part of a larger strategy of world conquest.

In this context it was fascinating to read David Remnick's Pulitzer Prize winning book, *Lenin's Tomb*, which nearly persuaded me that the Soviet collapse was something spontaneous, that the secret structures spoken of by Timofeyev were quite incidental. But just as I had resolved to change my views, in the last few pages of the book, I found the following passage:

> There is not a single field of activity, not a single institution, free of the most brutal sort of corruption. Russia has bred a world-class mafia. According to Luciano Violante, chairman of Italy's Parliamentary committee of inquiry into the mafia, Russia is now 'a kind of strategic capital of organized crime from where all the major operations are launched.' He said that Russian mob leaders have held summits with the three main Italian crime organizations from Sicily, Calabria, and Naples to discuss drug-money laundering, narcotics trade, and even the sale of nuclear material. Russia, he added, 'had become a warehouse and clearing house for the drug market.'[8]

This picture was anticipated by the Czech general, Jan Sejna, who was present when the Soviets began to organize the drug trade, building up their agent networks in the underworld.

> The Soviets reasoned that if they could successfully infiltrate organized crime, they would have unusually good possibilities to control many politicians and would have access to the best information on drugs, money, weapons, and corruption of many kinds. A secondary reason was to use organized crime as a covert mechanism for distributing drugs.[9]

---

[7] Lev Timofeyev, *Russia's Secret Rulers* (New York: Alfred A. Knopf, Inc., 1992), p. 88.*

Timofeyev writes: "But against whom was the ruling Party of our own country, which was essentially the government itself, waging war? Why would such an omniscient government need secret structures? From whom was it keeping secrets? After all, isn't the struggle between liberals and conservatives an internal Party struggle? Who is the external enemy, the battle with whom requires blood and death?"*

[8] David Remnick, *Lenin's Tomb: The Last Days of the Soviet Empire* (New York: Vintage Books, 1994), p. 537. Remnick has no idea of the significance of his statement regarding the mafia. Like nearly all Western journalists he is clueless.

The reader may have his doubts, but the testimony of Chairman Violante and the statements of General Sejna are suggestive. If President Clinton initially got his power from the movement of narcotics through Arkansas, as some have alleged, one needs very little imagination to connect the dots which form a larger, more alarming picture. In this case, the Third World War, as a clandestine war, may have already been won by the Russians. But this situation must give rise to further conflict, as the American people struggle to free themselves from secret structures now being put into place.

5. The Russian KGB defector, Anatoliy Golitsyn, is also aware of the organized crime angle. In his latest book he states:

> They [the Kremlin officials] will seek to exploit the new situation of 'openness' to send their own agent-running officers involved in criminal and economic activities abroad as illegals to build up their own networks along the lines of the Italian mafia which they know and understand. In this way they will seek to build up their penetration of and influence in the economic, financial and government sectors in the West. They will use this influence to assist their strategy of convergence with the West.[10]

The situation is quite serious, and it is only a matter of time before we learn the truth, one way or the other. Once the public is made aware of these operations, the country will arm itself. In this context, the American Left stands to lose everything it has accumulated over the last sixty years. The international situation would become incredibly tense.

6. Anyone interested in Soviet drug trafficking must read Joseph D. Douglass, Jr.'s *Red Cocaine*. General Sejna is Douglass's source, and according to his testimony the Soviets and their allies set up schools for drug traffickers. They put scientists to work on the types of drugs to be exported and the methods of processing to be used. The whole enterprise was elaborately organized, scientifically managed, and diabolically planned. Is Sejna credible?

Let us hope he isn't.

---

[9] Joseph D. Douglass, Jr., *Red Cocaine*, p. 11.

[10] Anatoliy Golitsyn, *The Perestroika Deception: The World's Slide Towards the 'Second October Revolution'* (London: Edward Harle, 1995), p. 216.

14

Additional Points for Consideration

... morality itself is a special case of immorality.
— NIETZSCHE, *Will to Power* #401

Lasting peace not only leads to enervation; it permits the rise of a mass of precarious, fear-ridden, distressful lives which would not have survived without it and which nevertheless clamor for their "rights," cling somehow to existence, bar the way to genuine ability, thicken the air and as a whole degrade a nation's blood. War restores real ability to honor.
— JACOB BURCKHARDT [1]

From the point of view of weapons, a third world war will be a *missile and nuclear war.* The massive use of nuclear weapons, particularly thermonuclear, will make the war unprecedentedly destructive and devastating. Entire states will be wiped off the face of the earth.
— SOVIET MILITARY TEXT [2]

1. However we try to understand the factors of the modern age, we must consider the war of mass destruction as something towards which many of these aforesaid factors conspire. In this context, destructive war also seems a likely bridge to an altogether new epoch. In the long run, few outcomes seem more elegant or comprehesive in the light of so many tangled conflicts. In terms of today's social algebra, the evils of a confused modernity stand on one side of our latter day equation, and mass destruction stands on the other. Or so it may seem to a gloomy sociologist. At the very least, the coming wars will signal a readjustment, a correction; not only of society, but of certain changes in the soul, and a balancing of the equation called man.

---

[1] Burckhardt, *Reflections on History*, pp. 217-218.

[2] *Soviet Military Strategy*, ed. V. D. Sokolovskii, trans. Herbert S. Dinerstein, Leon Gouré, Thomas W. Wolfe (Santa Monica, California: RAND CORPORATION, 1963), p. 313.

2. *As for what can be learned.* — When a way of life errs and becomes a fatality, it is only by meditating on that fatality and its consequences that we grow wiser. Before the fact, before disaster strikes, one cannot do this. One merely glides happily along, assured that all is right with the world. One cannot successfully explain an error to someone who lives the error; unless, of course, that someone possesses foresight, which is unlikely insofar as foresight requires moral vision, and that is precisely what is wanting. Instead, we march behind our latter-day mandarins to *the suicide of impossible ends.* Here, morality is conceived in political terms as something that brings utopia closer to earth. But if one considers this formulation, one is struck by the fact that good politics has always opposed utopia. Heaven and earth are opposites that cannot be conjoined. Taken in one sense: If Heaven is a metaphor for the spiritual world, and if earth is a metaphor for the material world, the formula "Heaven on earth" is nothing but the mixing of metaphors. And if it is ridiculous and unseemly to mix one's metaphors in speech, how much more so to mix one's metaphors in *action.*

3. After this, if we put all the blame for the coming catastrophe on the Soviet long-range strategy or strategic deception, we would merely be evading our own responsibility. For *we ourselves* have systematically, and over a period of decades, built up the forces of destructionism at home and abroad; encouraging them, tempting them, and even fortifying them with aid and trade until the twisted threads of history's fabric have become so hopelessly tangled that everything resolves itself into a Gordian knot, made ready for the man who will not hesitate to cut it—to slash it asunder with one tremendous thermonuclear stroke.

4. This fateful event, so near at hand, is also suggested to us by the vast nothingness that looms immediately ahead. Tomorrow appears to us as a blank. Where once we saw the future reflected in the past, we now discern, however vaguely, an absolute discontinuum. And because of this, the more we attempt to pierce the veil of futurity, the more dubious, tentative, and anxious we become.

It was not so long ago that we believed in progress, in the idea that each day would be better than the one before. Prior to that we believed time was cyclical, that the seasons alternated in succession. But now the weather falls out of season and a spirit of gloom, coinciding with the hollowest of hollow optimisms, begins to make itself felt. It is not merely that we have left the Age of Magic, that we have finally grown weary of science and machinery, but that we have entered into a realm of chaos. New phenomena, unknown to previous history, are visible

----

through the mists. We find no guidebook, no voice from Heaven telling us what we should do. And here, in this darkness, we find ourselves trapped by two great man-eaters: one is the Bomb and the other is the totalitarian state; each is possessed of an uncanny affinity for the other, reflecting an ominous interconnectedness in symbiotic twofold malignancy. Our presidents, poets, philosophers, and strategists all shiver when they attempt to work out the significances here unfolded. Even our greatest social thinkers are panicked to extricate themselves from this latter-day Scylla and Charybdis. Everyone is careful not to pursue the matter too far. Rather than growing more intimate with the evil forces of our age, rather than confronting the Bomb and dealing with it, rather than facing down totalitarianism with strength and moral fortitude, our political and intellectual leaders have distanced themselves. And with each passing year these ravenous monsters have become crazier, meaner, thinner, sharpened by our negligence. Even now our Scylla and Charybdis are gathering their energies, silently and steadily. The world might have profited by knowing something more, by acquiring a better appreciation for this frightening pair. But the world says with Hamlet: "I am pigeon-livered and lack gall." And so we are persuaded by glasnost and perestroika and the "Commonwealth of Independent Mush" that a dictatorship is a democracy and the Bomb is a peacekeeper.

5. Because we Americans have no sense of history, and because the future has become an enormous blur, any statement which suggests that world war is imminent automatically elicits our jeers. We think that humanity has outgrown world wars, that world wars no longer make any sense. Saddam Hussein,[3] as well, makes no sense to us. And yet, there he is: a living anomaly, haunting the thick peripheral fog of our semi-conscious, herd animal brain. We do not crack the egg of Hussein's meaning because we do not think he has any meaning. We do not *think*. We go along. And for the time being, we get along. But again, I can assure you, that the world war is coming. It is coming like the light of a distant star. It is out there, far in the distance, not yet visible. But rather than suspecting that such a light is on its way, our eyes remain fixed on stars that are already cold and exhausted. We see their light, and even though they are dead, we still believe in them. But oh how disaster shall come in the midst of our pleasures, our careers, and our all-encompassing obliviousness.

Of course, we do not want to believe that death and destruction are about to overtake us. We would rather think that the breakdown of

---

3 Saddam Hussein's secret 1973 agreement with the KGB included the reorganization of the Iraqi secret police in accordance with Soviet specifications, and the training of Iraqi security personnel in KGB and GRU schools. See Samir al-Khalil, *Republic of Fear* (New York: Pantheon Books, 1990), p. 12.

Western civilization is merely an interesting topic—not to be taken seriously. Many in America entertain an extraordinarily childish notion, that we are somehow safe, sacrosanct, and invincible.

What?! The world revolves around us? History is convenient for us?

6. When the voices of destructionism are so loud in the world, when the means of destruction are so prevalent, when the wise and the just have given way to the noisy and the shallow—can you honestly accuse the prophet, the predictor of "apocalypse now," that *he* is crazy and *you* are sane? You assume no more than he does, but he has facts on his side: thousands upon thousands of hydrogen bombs, and tons upon tons of anthrax, and intercontinental rockets, cruise missiles, supersonic bombers, submarines, nerve and mustard gasses in the hands of criminals, fanatics, and treaty-breakers.

Yet the prophet of mass destruction: *He is the crazy one.*

7. Then it is the end of the world—doom and gloom. And so you ask: What good is that? We cannot do anything with doom and gloom.

Quite right. It does not appeal and it will not sell.

But how about this? *It is the beginning of a new world. It is a bright unexplored horizon. New challenges and new tasks appear before us.* With these terrible events come wonderful opportunities. With destruction comes a chance, a hope, an opportunity to build something new and elevate something noble.

8. But how can we explain the West's insensibility in the face of this brightest of dark futures? If it is true that the West has failed to confront the problem of the Bomb, and has failed to face up to the meaning of totalitarianism, then what explanation shall we offer?

In the West, following the Second World War, we find the improbable advent of the United States as the West's military bulwark.

Yes, that is right, I used the word *improbable* to describe America's military ascendancy. And here is the reason: Few world powers in history have been as unwarlike and disinterested as the United States. This is because the United States did not attain its world-importance by policy. The United States became the world's foremost power by accident, unconsciously, and without forethought. We did not build and scheme. We did not maneuver for years, as did Imperial Japan or Soviet Russia. We merely blundered our way to ascendancy via Pearl Harbor. For those American leftists who imagine that they are living in the land of fascism, imperialism, and wage slavery, it will not sit well with them to acknowledge that America, through most of its history, disdained the maintenance of a standing army, despised military preparations, and loved peace as no other nation before. Even during the Cold War there remained a general and all-pervasive suspicion of the military establishment. And this is only natural because the business of America has ever been business. America does not like war. America does not trust the principle of unified and definitive authority that goes hand in hand with militarism. It likes comfort and well-being. It prefers that capitalist *thing*—that phrase in the Declaration of Independence—"the pursuit of happiness." But happiness is not the stuff of empires. One does not found a military bulwark on the pursuit of happiness. Up until now, every world power *with a future* has denied the importance of comfort and the pursuit of happiness. Hitherto, every world power has been compelled to cultivate hardness and stoicism, to emphasize duty and self-sacrifice. But this is inconsistent with our consumer orientation. For us there is something disturbing about Cicero's "Dream of Scipio," in which the ghost of the elder Africanus says: "all those who have preserved, aided, or enlarged their fatherland have a special place prepared for them in the heavens, where they may enjoy an eternal life of happiness." But no. We want to have our happiness *now*. Why should we wait? Why suffer for our country and for its strategic position? It is big enough to get along without us. And thus it becomes appropriate to ask whether the United States is a polity or a picnic.

Given all of this, it is logical to assume that one has, in the American superpower, an illusion of power: a weak-willed and poorly led giant; a klutz respected for its grotesque size and its sheer fiscal weightiness; a big baby that refuses to grow up. In the final analysis America is a temporary star, a passing phase, a misunderstanding that gives forth embassies and makes treaties until, at last, it is understood and sinks away. For how can comfort rule when the comfortable are unqualified to rule? How can comfort defend when defense is the antithesis of comfort?

What is most interesting about this bourgeois colossus and its *Pax Americanus* is the way in which consumerism, careerism, and convenience lead to its denouement. One marvels at the comedy of it. Entirely new concepts—in war, diplomacy, and espionage—are now blandly annunciated. However puerile these seem to observers from other countries and future times, it is clear that the vantage point of America cannot recognize any puerility in them at all. This is due to the odd historical conditioning of America's political unconsciousness.

9. Wherefore this geopolitical immaturity on the part of America? It is due to the fact that Anglo-Saxon institutions have been shaped, in the British instance, by the English Channel, and in the American instance, by the Atlantic and Pacific oceans. Separation by water is a blessed condition. Because of this, in Britain and America the aspiring tyrants

invariably found themselves unjustified. King Charles I of England was denied his claim to absolute monarchy and lost his head. Cromwell could never legitimize his dictatorship. Finally, after the mild reign of Charles II, King James II was unceremoniously replaced by a sovereign who clearly accepted the limits of royal power. As for King George III, he might have taxed and bullied the American colonies to his heart's content if only the French and Indians had still been scalping settlers and burning towns. Under such circumstances the colonists might even have thanked him for "instilling discipline." But as it was, with the defeat of France in North America, the colonies had become a second England, an island without any need of large armies or a powerful king.

It is a marvelous fact indeed, that the last pitched battle on English soil happened in 1685. As for the United States, it has not been invaded by foreign troops since the War of 1812. Thus geographical privilege has made the English-speaking countries the spoiled children of history. And though the spoiled child is the "lucky" child, he is also the child who never quite learns the important lessons. One cannot say the same for France, Germany, or Russia. With these continental countries a very different picture emerges; for example: when the unintentionally ironic French people overthrew and beheaded their king, but were compelled by invasions from abroad to enthrone and legitimize a military dictator named Napoleon Bonaparte, whose authoritarianism in the name of liberty, far from being ridiculous, was unavoidable. Since 1789 France has seen four republics, two monarchies, and two empires collapse. As odd as it seems to Anglo-Saxons, the French are currently living under their Fifth Republic. And if one supposes that the experience of France is unique, one need only turn to Germany. Here we find the trampled, burned, and pillaged theater of the Thirty Years War, the playground of Napoleon, an anarchic feuding medley of petty principalities entering late onto the path of nationhood, doomed to defeat and execration in the First and Second World Wars. Germany's first experiment with republican government lasted thirteen years and ended with the dictatorship of Adolf Hitler. The current period of liberty and prosperity now enjoyed by the Germans has only been made possible by the conquering Anglo-American armies and by American hydrogen bombs. As we can see, the German experience, like the French, smells of gunpowder. This is also true of the Russians, who over countless battlefields, over millions of corpses, have advanced to nationhood despite the enmity of Mongols, Swedes, Turks, Germans, French, English, and Poles. The land of Russ was often invaded by Europe's foremost warmongers: Charles XII, Napoleon, Mussolini and Hitler. The Russians were battered by the Japanese at Mukden, stung by Britain and France in the Crimea. And finally, with the overthrow of the czar, while the country was being invaded by the Central Powers, a shift occurred and the country was invaded by the Allies. To understand Russia's communist dictatorship as a mere manifestation of eight hundred years of historical conditioning would be a mistake. But it would not be as great a mistake as attributing the communist dictatorship to communism alone. Things do not give rise to themselves, but arise from previous states or conditions.

Such is the contrast between the political experience of the continental peoples and that of the Anglo-Saxon archipelago: a contrast which explains the latter's optimism, utopianism, and other "luxury" attitudes. America's political immaturity, therefore, arises partly from its island status. Nations are as mature as they have to be. The impolitic treaty-making and military fiascos of the United States are explicable by the fact that America, unlike other countries, has a forgiving history which has afforded it every latitude in stupidity, bungling, and naiveté. The essence of this forgiveness is found in the fact that America is far away, historically peripheral, unmolested, rich, and safe. If one sees to the bottom of this Anglo-Saxon experience, one realizes how shallow it is; giving rise to a mentality that is incapable of crediting the notions of Billy Mitchell or the warnings of Anatoly Golitsyn. It is a mentality which can never seriously entertain, regardless of evidence, the idea of another world war. It is a mentality poorly suited to cope with new vulnerabilities, dangers, and headaches. It is especially unable to cope with the appearance of nuclear-capped intercontinental rockets, which have taken away our island status by eliminating distances, overcoming natural barriers, and thereby transforming American invulnerability into a dangerous illusion. With the advent of the intercontinental rocket America has become continental, and continental sociology now applies. Therefore American history now teaches us the wrong lessons. We must learn from the Russians, who have been playing this game for more than five hundred years. We must learn from the French and the Germans. America's much trumpeted moral superiority, peaceableness, and economic productivity, are things of the past. Whatever peace and security we see before our eyes today is mere historical momentum: the unspent energy of bygone days transmitted to the present; a thrown rock still flying upward from the nineteenth century, but nevertheless doomed to fall as twentieth century gravity begins to assert itself.

10. *To summarize the aforementioned points.* — The current crisis consists in the fact that an incompetent political entity, misled by its own history, now manages a "world order" which coincides with Russia as superpower *plus* the Bomb. What we have is a maliferous conjunction of sociological determinants prefiguring an inevitable war of mass destruction. Communism is not dead and the Bomb will not go away. These are the facts—whether we like them or not.

----

11. It is important to understand that bourgeois dishonesty is not limited to white-collar crime and shoplifting. Our predisposition to cheat is not limited to the filing of income tax returns. Hedonistic selfishness soon leaves the sphere of wife swapping. It escapes the confines of sodomy. It leaps out of the "idiot box" and enters the brain of the secretary of state.

12. Oh, my friends, few of us realize how near we are to nuclear war. The barriers to it have been slyly broken down, even unto the forts of reason.

15

Elements of Strategy

Exchange models usually assume that in any nuclear war between the United States and Soviet Union, the USSR will strike first. This assumption is realistic. U.S. strategic doctrine is retaliatory. U.S. forces have most of their capability concentrated on slow-flying or slow reacting-systems, bombers and submarines, and so are clearly designed for retaliation. Official Soviet military writings, despite public disavowals of preemption, indicate that Soviet military doctrine stresses surprise attack and striking first. Soviet strategic forces have most of their capability loaded on fast-flying, quick-reacting systems—ICBMs— that are clearly designed for a nuclear first strike. Exchange models tend to produce military outcomes favoring the USSR because they posit a Soviet first strike. The strategic advantage that accrues to the Soviet Union from striking first in wartime far outweighs any alleged equality or slight U.S. superiority in the peacetime balance of forces.

— PETER VINCENT PRY, CIA analyst[1]

1. Five hundred years after Columbus, and we again find ourselves crossing over to a new world. This time it is not through circumnavigation, but through weapons and ideologies of mass destruction, which give rise to a tremendous and fearful struggle. To confound Karl Marx, this is not a class struggle, but a struggle without classes; a struggle, instead, as the means to new social structures. The first step: to make out the approaching storm; next, to weather that storm; later, to develop an economy based on salvage. Condition of the human spirit? Exhilaration rather than demoralization—because there's no end of the world. No sudden falling off.

2. If you know human nature in its modern mode, then you also know what the Bomb signifies: as the greatest eraser of bad grammar, the most uncompromising editor of unfit material, the ultimate pruner of overgrown and gnarled branches. The world shall grow larger, more horrible, younger, closer to God; but most of all it will become, for the first time in centuries, *less theoretical*. At long last we come to the end

---

[1] Peter Vincent Pry, *Nuclear Wars: Exchanges and Outcomes* (New York, 1990), pp. 82-83.

of academe and the scholastic mind. Fresh air—especially when laden with fallout—drives out musty air and musty men. The wars of mass destruction shall bring an end to all these parasites.

3. On 18 January 1977 General Secretary Brezhnev denied as "absurd and totally unfounded" the idea that the Soviet Union was positioning itself for a first strike against the United States. In this vein he advanced two critical propositions: Nuclear missile superiority is politically and militarily unusable; and the Soviet Union is not after unusable nuclear missile superiority.

It was strange, indeed, when General Secretary Brezhnev later acknowledged that the Soviet Union had attained, by some accident or other, this aforesaid unusable nuclear missile superiority.

4. According to Soviet Field Marshal V. D. Sokolovskiy and his staff of writers: "The rapid deployment of the [intercontinental] missile is due to its extremely advantageous characteristics. This weapon has unlimited range, enormous speed and high trajectory, great accuracy and maneuver of fire, and can carry a nuclear warhead of any yield. Ballistic missiles, employed en masse, are still practically invulnerable to existing means of air defense, and their employment is almost independent of weather conditions."

In the next paragraph they write: "These properties give missiles first place among all other instruments of war."[2]

5. For the Soviet strategist nuclear war is not merely an exchange of nuclear strikes, but a military operation involving huge masses of infantry, tanks, and ships. The key to victory in such operations is: exploit, exploit, and again, exploit. The idea is to use one's missiles to make huge holes in the enemy. Next: move rapidly through those holes before the victim can recover.

6. In the event of a nuclear attack on the United States our strategists do not intend to defeat the Soviet Union. They intend to set a good example by fighting as they did in Vietnam and Korea, only on a larger scale, and with weapons of mass destruction. It seems that we have abandoned the idea of victory in favor of the reestablishment of the conditions which inevitably led to war. This is known, in official circles, as "intrawar deterrence." The idea is to hold back and wait for the enemy to stop attacking, and then threaten him with retaliation if he renews his attacks. As one might guess, the Soviet generals, when they found out about this new "imperialist" strategy, were baffled. But as

---

[2] *Soviet Military Strategy*, p. 298.

they began to understand their enemy, it suddenly occurred to them that intrawar deterrence wasn't very baffling at all. The Americans are idiots.[3]

7. There are many important Soviet "internal" publications on nuclear war. One is *Soviet Military Strategy* and another is *The Nuclear Revolution in Soviet Military Affairs*. They are among a series of books written for the Soviet officer's library. There also exists a Soviet military journal—*Voyennaya mysl'*—the official organ of the Soviet General Staff. Five thousand pages from it have been translated and made available through the Library of Congress. In the 1970s the work of A. A. Sidorenko was also translated. Sidorenko's book, *The Offensive*, is a characteristic Soviet work about the nuclear battlefield. It describes the strategic rocket as a mere progression in the ever increasing efficiency of the artillery arm. In contrast to Western military literature, the Soviets seriously discuss the mechanics of winning a world nuclear war. Western strategists were, at first, baffled by Soviet writings of this kind. But after a while it was concluded that the Soviets could not be so stupid as to believe in this sort of rubbish.

8.   I quote from a leading Soviet Authority, Colonel General Makhmut Al. Gareev:
"The assertion that nuclear war will not be a continuation of politics is completely fallacious."[4]
Soviet theorist A. S. Milovidov agrees with this when he writes: "There is profound error and harm in the disoriented claims of bourgeois ideologues that there will be no victor in a thermonuclear world war." Milovidov explains that nuclear war has not ceased to "be an instrument of politics, as is claimed by the overwhelming majority of...anti-war movements in the bourgeois world." Says Milovidov about anti-nuclear pacifists: "[Theirs] is a subjective judgment. It expresses mere protest against nuclear war." Other Soviet strategists, V. D. Sokolovskiy and M. I. Cherednichenko, say that: "The Armed Forces of the Soviet Union and the other socialist countries must be prepared above all to wage war under conditions of the mass use of nuclear weapons by both belligerent parties."[5]

9. Let us consider the following quote taken from Sidorenko: "It is

---

[3] For further details, read Edward Zuckerman, *The Day After World War III* (New York: The Viking Press, 1984).

[4] Makhmut Al. Gareev, *M. V. Frunze — Military Theorist*, p. 24.

[5] Joseph D. Douglass, Jr. and Amoretta M. Hoeber, *The Soviet Strategy for Nuclear War* (Hoover Institution Press, 1979), p. 7.

believed that nuclear weapons, as the main means of destruction, will be employed only for the destruction of the most important objectives."[6] Please notice what is being said. The Russian generals will not use nuclear weapons when they can neutralize a target with infantry or tanks. Nuclear weapons are special, and they are very expensive. Therefore, nuclear rocket weapons are reserved for strategic, time-sensitive targets that cannot be effectively neutralized by other means.

10. Sidorenko emphasizes that only at the start of a war are you likely to have good intelligence on enemy deployments and plans. After the war begins, things will be much more confused and uncertain. Therefore, it is logical to initiate the largest strikes at the outset of a war. Sidorenko, in this context, wrote: "If the attack succeeds in destroying the defender with the very first nuclear volley, he will no longer be able to offer resistance to the attacker with either nuclear or conventional weapons."

Therefore, "Preemption in launching a nuclear strike is considered the decisive condition for the attainment of superiority over him and the seizure and retention of the initiative."

To further clarify: "It is believed that the side which first employs nuclear weapons with surprise can predetermine the outcome of the battle in his favor."[7]

11. There is a Soviet book called *The People, the Army, the Commander*. It is about global nuclear war and how it can be won. It uses the concept of "correlation of nuclear forces," which consists in secrecy, surprise, leadership, and psychological readiness. These are the decisive elements. Contrast this to the American position, mentioned earlier, of "intrawar deterrence."

12. How does the United States stack up to the Soviet Union in terms of the "correlation of nuclear forces"? In terms of secrecy, we are unable keep secrets because ours is a free and open society. In terms of surprise, as should be obvious, we are averse to making surprise attacks against other countries. Besides this, growing fiscal constraints have undermined our military readiness. In terms of leadership, our leaders are utterly exposed to a first strike and are not likely to survive the first five minutes of a war in which the Soviets have both secrecy and surprise. In terms of psychological readiness? Congress will want to extend the debate.

---

[6] A. A. Sidorenko, *The Offensive*, trans. United States Air Force (Washington, D.C.: U.S. Government Printing Office, Stock Number 009-070-00329-5, Catalog Number D301.79:1), p. 113.

[7] Ibid., pp. 109-137.

13. Captain First Rank V. Kulakov writes: "In a war against a strong enemy, with extensive territory enabling him to use space and time for the organization of active and passive defense, the maneuver of forces and the mobilization of reserves—a single attack with strategic rocket nuclear weapons is not enough for complete victory."[8] Contrary to popular misconceptions, world nuclear war could last many years. The Soviets, therefore, have established two vital principles for waging such a war: First, that the enemy *must* be destroyed or conquered; and secondly, that the ultimate Soviet objective is total victory and not mere survival. In keeping with this, Soviet operations aim at defeating the enemy's military power, seizing strategic areas, installing socialist governments, and ideologically converting the survivors. Thus the destruction of America's nuclear capability is merely the first step in a complicated series of steps leading to a Soviet world government.

14. How will the Soviet rocket weapons be targeted? Colonel M. Shirokov explains to his Soviet military readers that: "Not only the enemy's armed forces, but also the sources of his military power, the important economic centers, and also points of military and state control as well as the areas where different branches of armed forces are based, will be subjected to simultaneous destruction."[9]

15. For further corroboration we make note of a Soviet defector, writing under the pseudonym of Viktor Suvorov, who tells us that the standard Soviet approach to the problem of nuclear war is something called "the Axe Theory" in which you use your most horrible weapon first. The idea? To kill your enemy before he can kill you.[10]

16. The Soviets think that all combatants will attempt to recover from their losses in the event of world nuclear rocket war. Therefore *oil*, the element most essential to recovery, must be targeted and re-targeted.
"And on to Chicago if we have to!"

17. The Soviets carefully analyzed the effects of strategic bombing during World War II. They concluded that allied strategic attacks against German cities actually increased Germany's determination to resist. The Soviets are careful, however, not to draw the conclusion that nuclear bombing would have the same effect. But then, with weapons of

8 Douglass and Hoeber, p. 12.

9 Ibid., p. 16.

10 Viktor Suvorov, *Inside the Soviet Army* (New York: Berkley Books, 1982), pp. 185-96.

mass destruction, there is the chance that the other side might *sleep forever.*

18. The Soviets [now Commonwealth of Independent States] have already decided who the dictator of occupied France will be. He will be the commander of the Carpathian Military District. Non-Soviet armies will be prohibited from operating in France for fear of "fraternizing." The mayors, judges, police officials, and political commissars will all be Russians, that is, *in France.* The Warsaw Pact (which is supposedly disbanded) has already printed *millions* of ration tickets, proclamations, posters, and orders of the day in all European languages. Approximately ten thousand arrest warrants have already been written out for occupied Germany. "Former" Soviet combat units currently contain military courts intended to try Western war criminals.   All prominent representatives of the bourgeois system have their names written down, and their future crimes predicated. Some of these persons are to be shot. But the majority will be sent to the East, as conscript labor, to sort through Russia's post-war rubble.

With so much Soviet manpower and equipment moving West, there must be something to fill the boxcars moving East.

A functioning locomotive is a terrible thing to waste.

19. Item, 23 April 91: The *Los Angeles Times* has reported that over 1,000 Soviet and East European targets have been deleted from the Pentagon's revised nuclear war plan, including Soviet military bases, steel mills, tank factories, and unstaffed alternate command headquarters.[11]

20. The Soviet strategic literature indicates that chemical and biological agents will be used against "unsalvageable" populations, even after they have been disorganized and disarmed. As the communists define it, an unsalvageable population is thoroughly and irredeemably bourgeois. Such people are past the point of benefitting from any sort of reeducation. Therefore, all unsalvageables will be subject to a Kremlin-inspired "Final Solution," probably by way of biological attacks.

21. According to informed sources, there isn't enough serum in the United States to protect five hundred people from anthrax.[12]

22. The people of the United States stand a good chance of being

---

[11] "In Review," *Los Angeles Times* (23 April 1991), H5.

[12] Joseph D. Douglass, Jr. and Neil C. Livingstone, *America the Vulnerable* (Lexington: Lexington Books, 1987), p. 38.

----

treated from the outset as "unsalvageable." The reasons are not far to find. Soviet naval transport and manpower are finite. Even after massive nuclear strikes the economic power, manpower, and willpower of America is bound to be considerable. A Soviet-led invasion is likely to be irregular, prolonged, and costly. Resistance by an armed population in the interior could cost the Soviets millions of casualties. The Soviets have, in consideration of these points, built up their long-range air transport capabilities and their merchant marine fleet. Nevertheless, the invasion of a continent the size of North America constitutes a blind leap into an abyss. The repeated use of biological agents could shrink this abyss into a mere mud puddle. The idea here would be: if you can't beat 'em, exterminate 'em.

23.   The Soviets see any future war in terms of a period of THREAT. Their objective during this period is to steal a march on the Americans.   Once the THREAT stage has been triggered, a CONCEALED stage begins during which Soviet forces covertly position themselves to attack. Any number of ploys might be used to cover such preparations. For example, they might attack their own forces with submarine-launched rockets—especially as a diversion and pretext for later strikes against the United States. This would also provide them with an excuse for mobilizing reserves and putting people in shelters. Soviet leaders could also, by this device, deny any aggressive intentions in the midst of aggressive preparations. They might say to us: "Dear American brothers: Please remain calm. Soviet mobilization is merely a precaution. Refrain from initiating a countermobilization. This would be provocative. Provocation leads to war. War is the end of the world. Act rashly and everyone dies. Don't worry, our intentions are good. Go back to sleep."
The West would then abandon its own mobilization out of fear of triggering a war. The U.S. Congress could never hope to piece anything together in the remaining seventy-two hours. Therefore, it is quite probable that the Soviet government could shelter its population and bring its armed forces to a very high state of readiness while avoiding an American preemptive strike.

24.   Other potential smoke screens behind which the Soviets could conceal preparations for an attack on America include: military exercises, civil defense drills, a phony nuclear confrontation with China, a war in the Middle East or between India and Pakistan, or an apparent civil war inside the Soviet Union.

25.   After the CONCEALED stage comes the initial period of the war. This will be the DECISIVE phase. Just as in conventional war

there emerges an early air superiority of one side over the other, there will be a struggle for nuclear rocket superiority during the DECISIVE stage of World War Three. After the first strikes there will follow whole sequences of strikes, until one side uses up its forces or is effectively neutralized by: (1) liquidation of the top leadership and administration by decapitation; or (2) the destruction of its military power by counterforce attacks.

According to the Soviet theorists: once nuclear rocket superiority is achieved, the war is much easier to win. All that remains is conventional military operations, the extermination of unsalvageables, and the occupation of enemy territory.

26. *Why "launch on warning" is not practical.* — The guidance systems of nuclear missiles can be adversely affected by x-ray pulse detonations above the stratosphere. Therefore, it would be pure rashness to launch our missiles when enemy launches are detected. Also, the electronic ground equipment that launches the missiles might break down under the stress of attack. A fifty megaton range of force at an altitude of sixty miles can stop all ordinary ionospheric radio communications 2,500 miles in every direction. This technique can also blind the Ballistic Missile Early Warning System of the enemy.

The Soviets tested weapons of these extreme yields in the 1960s. They then rushed to foreclose parallel U.S. testing by means of nuclear test ban agreements.

27. Russian military technology is simpler than ours. This is a virtue not to be underrated. We cannot ignore the possibility that after the bomb, the very simplest weapons and military techniques may prove to be the decisive ones. Napoleon conquered Europe with mules, horses, and human sweat. Given the logic of nuclear war, old ways might again return. It is entirely possible that the sophisticated weapons of the West cannot be maintained or refueled in the post-nuclear environment due to the collapse of complex technical and economic infrastructures. A more primitive generation of weapons might, in fact, be more suitable.

28. America has built an array of highly sophisticated fighter planes. But such planes can be obliterated at their refueling stations by rockets. In other words, the Soviets have found another way to skin the cat. Therefore, the decisive component of the next war will not be the fighter plane, but the rocket. For it is the rocket that gives the edge to one's forces and removes countless obstacles to victory. It is the rocket that dictates the character of modern strategy. Yet America boasts about her fighter planes, even though there's no way that the fighter plane can

survive against the rocket. As Soviet Major General K. Stepanov has said: "Superiority in nuclear-rocket weapons is the decisive factor of military technical superiority."

29. The Soviets have never let us take inventory of their strategic stockpiles. Even if they did, we could never be sure that we were seeing everything they had. Soviet internal literature implies that Soviet silos can be reloaded, that there are vast undetected reserves of rocket weapons. The Soviets are convinced that hidden reserves gave them victory in World War II. They are convinced, therefore, that hidden reserves can also win World War III.

30. In 1968, Marshal Sokolovskiy's strategists claimed that the creation of new strategic rocket forces under conditions of the threat of nuclear attack require "profound scientific elaboration." This implies the pre-construction of thousands of strategic rocket kits. Such would enable Soviet work crews to assemble new rocket batteries in the midst of war, ensuring decisive firepower superiority over the long term.

31. All Russian forces which are visible to us should be regarded as the "first strategic echelon" only. For there are other echelons—secret depots, warehouses, and hidden bunkers throughout the "former" Soviet Union harboring second, third, even fourth echelons of armed might.

32. The Russians have stockpiled military supplies so that if industries are annihilated the logistical situation of the Soviet armies won't become untenable. They have also concluded that successful economic support of the armies in war involves the maintenance of rationally sited factories which are underground and that the United States is thoroughly outclassed in this respect. The concentration of industries in certain areas is a characteristic of capitalism, and though it is cost effective for profit making, it is nonetheless strategically unsound.

33. The Soviet strategists realize that most Russian industry will be destroyed in a nuclear war. But this is far from fatal. For there are other industries in the world, which are much better than Russian industries. The Russian people can easily take control of such industries when the smoke clears. In this context, one is reminded of Friedrich Nietzsche's prophecy that the overlords of the future will "employ...Europe as their most pliant and supple instrument for getting hold of the destinies of the earth, so as to work as artists upon 'man' himself."[13] For Europe contains great concentrations of wealth, know-how, and industry.

It is with this in view that one must evaluate the current Soviet

---

[13] Nietzsche, *The Will to Power*, #960.

attempt to make Europe into a nuclear free zone. Already we learn, by various Pentagon leaks, that the "former" Warsaw Pact countries and the Soviet forces deployed there are no longer targets in America's nuclear war plan (because the Warsaw Pact has supposedly collapsed). The Soviet generals should congratulate themselves, as they now have sanctuaries from which to operate against France, Italy, and Great Britain. After the anticipated nuclear exchange with the United States, the surviving communist troops, backed by the threat of ballistic missile weapons, will emerge from their sanctuaries in Eastern Europe and sieze Western Europe. In this way the Soviets are prepared to write off the Motherland of Socialism as one might write off a horse that has been lamed after carrying its rider over a great distance.

As all these notions are integral to the Soviet long-range strategy, the Kremlin began curtailing investment in its own economic infrastructure around 1975. Up through the Ninth Five Year Plan (1971-75) Soviet investments for capital goods grew at around 41 percent. Then, all of a sudden, for the Tenth Five Year Plan (1976-80) growth was cut to around 25 percent. Under the Eleventh Five Year Plan the growth rate was intentionally slated for a mere 10 percent. Western analysts, like Richard Pipes, conclude that this failure to invest in new factories is due to the Kremlin's inability to choose between guns for their arsenal or butter for their people. One wants to ask Pipes: When, in the whole history of the Soviet Union, has the ruling Communist Party ever chosen butter over guns? But Pipes' framing of the issue is itself a confusion, because the failure of Soviet reinvestment is not merely a failure to invest in a future military economy. It is a failure to invest in a future civilian economy too. The actual explanation, for which Pipes lacks the courage, is that a strategist preparing for nuclear war doesn't want to retool an industrial base that may be demolished. It is much more efficient to use up one's capital goods entirely and allow the enemy's rockets to destroy factories that are already worn out. It is much better to invest in armed strength over the short term, so that by sudden conquest the long term might take care of itself. In the final analysis: if Pipes could overcome his bourgeois sentimentalism he would immediately recognize that the collapse of Soviet reinvestment is indicative of impending world war.[14]

34. A recent Cuban defector has revealed that Russia maintains nuclear bombers in Cuba. Such planes can fly below radar and reach time-sensitive targets such as missile bases, command and control centers, and naval facilities.

In 1990 nuclear material and advanced MiG-29 fighters were

[14] Richard Pipes, *Survival Is Not Enough* (New York, 1984), pp. 119-120.

---

moved from Russia into Cuba. On 25 April 1991, U.S. spy satellites discovered at least one, "and possibly several," SS-20 missile batteries. The SS-20 has a range of 3,000 miles, MIRVs up to three warheads, and is highly accurate. The presence of Soviet missiles in Cuba is a direct violation of the 1962 Kennedy-Khrushchev agreement and the 1987 Intermediate Nuclear Force (INF) treaty.

35. The strategists in the United States entertain a bizarre concept: That restraint in attacking command, control, and communications assets will be reciprocated by the Russians during a nuclear war. This is a corollary of the aforementioned strategy of intrawar deterrence.

The destruction of the Russian leadership and their command-posts should be central to any U.S. strategy because the Russian leadership is the *real* enemy and not the Russian people. If the top leaders of Russia were killed or cut off from their forces the entire Russian military system might collapse. Yet the American strategists oppose direct attacks on the Russian leadership because, subsequently, the Russians might be expected to show a like-minded restraint, or perhaps even a willingness to negotiate a peace which could not otherwise be arranged.[15]

36. Herman Kahn, who was with the RAND Corporation until the early 1960s, said that the defense intellectuals at RAND were "dangerous as hell, especially for people who don't know what's going on." The reason? People believe in what defense intellectuals say, while such intellectuals possess little more knowledge than those they advise. Kahn believed that the general incompetence of these new up-and-comers would be little suspected. He said that people with credentials could get away with all kinds of "crap" because "this is a field where it is very easy to be illusioned, biased, or stupid." And besides, there is nobody policing your work.[16]

It is interesting to note that Herman Kahn left RAND because of his nuclear war research. His ideas on the subject precipitated a three-year running fight with the president of RAND, Frank Collbohm. It seems that Collbohm was, like those in the United States Air Force, opposed to civil defense, while Kahn said that civil defense was essential. We cannot be sure about the Air Force, but Frank Collbohm had reasons for opposing civil defense. It seems he had been director of civil defense at

---

[15] And why would anyone want to kill such wonderful people, who think of nothing but peace, and who talk of eliminating all nuclear weapons by the year 2000? To be sure, those *other* wonderful people, sitting at the opposite end of the conference table, haven't any wicked plan in mind. We know from history that this type of wickedness doesn't anywhere exist, except in the minds of paranoid right-wingers who, quite naturally, exist only in the minds of paranoid left-wingers!

[16] Paul Dickson, *Think Tanks* (New York), p. 110.

Douglas and, in Kahn's words, "had done some very stupid things." But this can hardly be surprising.

37. The Soviets will give "instructions" to their communist allies in the United States prior to an attack. The instructions will say: "Hide in the country. Build a fallout shelter." After the initial destruction, these leaders will then emerge and attempt to create pro-Soviet institutions, offering Soviet "fraternal assistance" as a carrot to collaborators. Mexico, Cuba, and Nicaragua would be important bases for furthering the process of internal collapse of the American resistance. It is important to recognize that psychological warfare does not end with the dropping of the first bomb, but continues.

38. To demonstrate how lax our national security is, Joseph Albright, a reporter with the *Atlantic Journal and Constitution* decided to test it. He writes: "As an imposter I talked my way past the security guards at two highly secret Air Force nuclear weapons depots last month and was given a tour of the weak links in their defenses against terrorist attacks."[17]

Also in 1978 the *Omaha World-Herald* reported that the SAC Headquarters at Offutt Air Force Base was easy to penetrate as well.

39. Soviet war plans call for the division of the United States into military districts; i.e., into zones of occupation. This fact merely emphasizes, once again, that the Soviets intend to conquer the whole of North America.

40. The Soviet leaders have estimated that they might lose between 5 percent and 8 percent of their population in a war. They would not mind 20 percent casualties if victory were assured. Remember—It does not matter how you play the game as long as you win.

41. The best evidence for the effectiveness of Soviet strategic deception is the fact that many leading American analysts believe Soviet deceptions never succeed. To state categorically that one has never been fooled is nothing but an admission that one is fooled on a regular basis.

---

[17] "Nuclear Security: How Secure?", *Atlantic Journal and Constitution* (8 January 1978), pp. 1-A to 16-A.

16

War and Its Aftermath

> There is no reconciliation in history. He who believes that there is must feel perpetual horror at the mad dance of events, and he only deceives himself if he believes he can ever stop it through covenants. There is only one end to perpetual strife — death. Death of the individual, death of a nation, death of a culture.
>
> — OSWALD SPENGLER, *Aphorisms* #135

> Then said I, Lord, how long? And he answered, Until the cities be wasted without inhabitant, and the houses without man, and the land be utterly desolate.
>
> — ISAIAH, 6:11

> With all this radiation we assume,
> That many men will sink into their doom;
> And as we watch the progress of the Bomb,
> We only find destroy'd what must be gone.
>
> — ANONYMOUS

1. *There are news flashes.* — We watch as communist rebels conquer the Congo. We learn of South Africa's anniversary as a "progressive" state under that old communist, Nelson Mandela. We read of continued fighting in Afghanistan, where a "former" Soviet general, Rashid Dostum, continues to advance *with* air support from the "former" Soviet republic of Tajikistan. NATO countries announce loans and treaties with a "reformed" Russia. Former Warsaw Pact countries enter NATO. America uncaps her missiles, melts down her ships, and employs her army on "peace keeping" missions around the globe. And why not? It is peace in our time.

But communists continue to advance around the world.

What!? A coup d'état in country X? A successful insurgency in country Y? Dictator T gobbles countries Q, R, and S?

The newspapers announce that the Russians have violated the

START Treaty, the Biological Weapons Protocol, the Conventional Forces Agreement, and the Chemical Weapons Ban. In response to this: a huge and vaporous yawn wafts skyward, a yawn which smells of brainwash. Don't trouble us with trifles. A new and exciting sex toy has just been marketed. The Movie Channel is playing something hot. A new type of ice cream, without sugar or fat, which can safely be eaten by the gallon, occupies our evenings. Are the Russians keeping some of their rockets in violation of the arms pact? Have they allied themselves to China? Well, so what? Let them have their silly rockets and alliances. What the Russians really need is food. And food arrives by way of America. So they'd better not nuke us, or they'll be sorry.

The West has the money and, therefore, has the POWER.

Yet nobody reckons that money merely talks, and cannot shoot, cannot explode, cannot obliterate its enemies. The fact is: money without resolve, without intelligence, without integrity—is only fancy paper on which the lie is inscribed, In God We Trust. One could more truthfully say, In (the former) communists we trust.

2. Numerous are the pigs, squealing and wallowing, grunting and snorting, enjoying these, our last days—like the last days of Sodom and Gomorrah. And *who* will deny that we deserve what is coming? For aren't we all Benedict Arnolds—hiding, keeping our mouths shut, blending into the crowd?

Who me?

Yes, YOU. All of you. Benedict Arnolds. Selling your country for a few years of fun. Traitors, betrayers, Judases! The fact of nuclear war has been before your eyes for fifty years. But you did not want to acknowledge your responsibility, your citizenship; you did not want to exert any effort, make any sacrifices, give up any so-called "freedom." So you became traitors.

"I didn't know," is what you'll say when the missile war begins. *But it was your responsibility to know.* The fact is: You didn't want to know. The fact is: You wanted to collect your thirty years of peace and plenty, so you betrayed your country.

3. A whole generation of Americans has grown up to believe in nuclear deterrence; a theory which suggests that nuclear weapons will always deter aggression—regardless. It is a magical formula, an accepted truism, a grand-strategic faith. But nobody stops to think about the psychopaths who, without batting an eye, have starved, shot, and worked to death many millions in Africa, Europe, and Asia. Nobody has the courage to see that the Kremlin still houses the same old bloodthirsty pack: men who have no scruples. —No

scruples, yet tens of thousands of nuclear warheads! From men like
these one cannot escape. One can only fight, and beforehand dig
shelters and build anti-rockets. But nobody seems to be doing so.
Nobody can face such an abominable, horrid, ugly task. All is a
dreamy never-never land, where "Smiling Mike" Gorbachev, like the
Cheshire Cat, disappears except for his disarming communist death-
grin. How soothed we are by the "collapse" of the Soviet Union.
Ah! What a fair façade for the thousands of city-smashing rockets
whose targets are New York, Seattle, Los Angeles, Boston, St.
Louis, Kansas City, etc. The underlying objective behind both
Russian and Chinese politics is: *war to the death against America.*

    4. And because we are soft, we evade the horrors of *this* reality
by any means we can: ideological or chemical; with food stamps
and video circus, with liquor and cocaine, with false sciences and
false religions; denial oozes from a gutless culture that worships
comfort and fashion. The idea of nuclear war is dismissed as
unworkable and undoable. People who discuss civil defense are
ridiculed. "Shelters do not work," we say to ourselves. In this way,
we contrive to evade, for just a little longer, that horror with heat-
shield and a payload, the mere thought of which is proscribed.
Therefore, the future too is proscribed, while many facts and
estimates are necessarily distorted. The typical citizen of today,
during the commercial break, gives a grunt and perhaps a thought:
"I cannot admit of such things. I can do nothing about them anyway.
I don't want to live without *Monday Night Football.* Besides, if I
dig a bomb shelter my neighbors will laugh at me."
    That's us in a nutshell. We are optimists, yes, but we are
optimist out of weakness.
    Our government, which is "of the people," reflects this optimism
quite readily. And the educated? The elite? What of them? They
are nothing but sentimentalists and naively egocentric children;
envious professors, bloated success-stories, frivolous-befamed under
a regime of philistine fashions. In the last analysis they do not
deserve their privileged status, and so they will lose it.
    Meanwhile, fortunes are amassed by panderers, clowns,
scribblers, and dope pushers; who divert, distort, and frazzle a
national intelligence made diabetic through a gluttonous absorption
of intellectual, chemical, and polemical junk. Homosexuals
militantly establish the first disease with "rights." History is
replaced with minority studies and feminist rant. Ingenuity goes to
the moon to play golf and cart rocks through the interplanetary
vacuum. Condoms substitute for chastity, television replaces books,

rehabilitation passes for justice, noise for music, spastic jerks for dancing, and badly welded garbage for sculpture. On and on it goes until we reach the political sphere, where foreign enemies are obsequiously courted and allies left in the lurch. Our ideas of politics and war are contaminated by an unctuous quack-fed boobery. All is of a piece, and so the fatal day arrives.

5. In 1997 the Russian nuclear forces go on permanent alert. Russia's rockets are brought to a high state of readiness.[1] America watches and shrugs. *There is no alarm.* The Russians explain that their early warning systems are not working. Since they cannot see if America is preparing to launch an attack, Russia must put its forces on a hair-trigger.

This flash of paranoia from the East passes without comment. The president does nothing. The generals sit on their hands. Meanwhile, inside Russia, America is blamed more and more for existing problems. Trouble develops in the world economy. Small wars break out. Unrest might occur in the United States. A crisis begins. But this crisis will be a diversion. It will facilitate further Russian mobilizations. Once the mobilizations are complete, at a predesignated instant, the Russian rockets will be launched. America will have no warning.

6. A few hours before dawn, on the day of the attack, a black van pulls into an empty alley in Washington, D.C. Three men open the van's doors and out rolls the fuselage of a small remote-controlled aircraft which takes off toward the White House. Within minutes an explosion rocks Pennsylvania Avenue. The residence of the commander in chief has been bombed. At 6:00 a.m. the normal television networks are simply cut off. The vice president of the United States gives a brief speech. He says that military officers have tried to seize power. He asks all military personnel to refrain from carrying out orders because these might be issued by traitors.

Normal television coverage resumes. But now there are reports claiming that the vice president was killed by terrorists an hour before his appearance on television. Others say that Russian commandos have taken hostages in New York.

Then, all radar signals and radio traffic experience a total and inexplicable interference. The generals at NORAD and ADC turn pale and curse. A thinned contingent of strategic bombers rumble across runways, crews tensely studying their contingency orders— old B-52s, controversial B-1s and B-2s. Perplexing seconds pass, voices rising against voices, alarms following alarms, with our

[1] This is what happened, as reported by major newspapers in August 1997.

----

missiles still in reserve. Then the American bombers begin exploding on their runways. Sirens are heard. *We are under attack. This is not a drill."* Small arms fire is reported around several Air Force bases.

The generals are wringing their hands. They are not sure what is happening. Then the line to D.C. goes dead. The lines to sixteen near-coastal Air Force bases follow suit, as well as submarine pens and other strategic sites. Everyone's hair stands on end in an atmosphere of disbelief, unreality, and continued cursing. There are further rumors of a military takeover. Yet nobody can confirm anything. The principal concern, says a leading expert at NORAD, is seismic activity. If we are attacked by Russian missiles then our seismic sensors will register the detonations. But somebody suddenly discovers that the sensors are not working. The commanding general grimaces. For him, *that does it.* "We're being attacked. There's no question." Frantic orders sally from four-star throats—"Launch!" at which instant, NORAD and ADC are impacted by direct hits. The generals are dead. An airborne headquarters takes command.

From Great Falls to Davis-Monthan, from Little Rock to Warren—silos are shaking, rattling, and exploding skyward in jumbled mountains of dirt, preemptively struck, falling for several hours afterward as bits of poisonous debris over the neighboring districts. Of three Russian rockets sent to dispatch Ellsworth, South Dakota, one explodes on launch, another misfires and falls into the Pacific, yet another makes the flight and proves a dud, rattles windows, wakes farmers, disturbs cattle. Russian (nay, Soviet!) technology fails in three critical instances. The Ellsworth ICBM fields, unblasted, analyzing the situation, open fire against Russian air bases and rocket silos. Much dirt and falling rock in the Central Siberian Uplands causes wild speculation in nearby labor camps. But Ellsworth's gloryday is short lived. Noticed by Russian reconnaissance on the following morning, it receives a series of direct hits and is now a pockmark that fills with water when the rains come.

At sea, bushwhacks and ambuscades with nuclear-capped torpedoes and rockets. Pearl Harbor without the harbor. The American aircraft carriers are struck simultaneously with megatonage. Of course, not everything works according to plan. The Russian fleet takes its lumps. A duel of submarines ensues, but the Americans are outnumbered.

Meanwhile, the Europeans and the Japanese do nothing.

----

7. On the fateful morning, minutes before dawn (Pacific Standard Time) Dr. Martin, a West Coast surgeon, is preparing breakfast when the electricity fails. Then his pager begins to beep. He fumbles around for the phone. But there isn't any dial tone. Dr. Martin goes out toward his garage through the north-facing back patio and, glancing skyward, he involuntarily drops his keys on the brick walkway. In the dark blue of the pre-dawn sky, beyond the earth, strange stars are visibly moving, by the hundreds. Stars he has never seen in this or any other sky. Stars which reflect borrowed light from a sun that in this hour hovers over Eastern Europe. The doctor raises a pair of trembling hands to his face. What does this mean?

He again scrutinizes the moving points of light as they grow nearer and nearer. Finally, Dr. Martin knows what he sees; knows that they are rockets rounding the poles, arching up through the edge of outermost space, then MIRVing down to earth, en route to many buildings and persons not long for this world. Doctor Martin realizes that life as he knows it is over, that a new life, totally alien to all his prepossessions, is about to commence.

The northern sky flashes white and rumbles with thunder. The distant harbor is struck with multiple blasts. Many miles from Dr. Martin, amidst flames and fallen houses are people; crying for help from beneath flammable soon-to-be-inflamed debris, feeling the first pains of broken bones, confused, staggering, burnt here, unburnt there, dazed, bedazed; a world come crashing down. The shock wave rolls gently, or not so gently, over the intervening forty miles and rattles the windows. Martin, blinded by the flash, blinks, rubs his eyes, but even so, he cannot see. So he feels his way back to the house, and then to the bedroom where his wife lies fast asleep.

"Honey?" His wife opens her eyes.

"God help us!"

His wife senses that something is wrong when she sees him groping his way across the room.

"It was a very bright light," he says.

8. "When you see a night illuminated by an unknown light know that this is the great sign that God is giving you that he is going to punish the world for its crimes."[2]

9. From beneath the rubble-heaps of countless American cities come the anguished cries of the victims. Smoky skies contain the ashes of those cremated and their belongings—photographs, gardens, family homes, amenities and keepsakes, all consumed, rising

---
[2] Words of the apparition at Fatima.

upward, blotting out the sun. At the same time deadly particles drift across America carried by the wind; odorless, invisible, death-dealing fallout, accompanied by an assortment of biological agents sent to infect survivors, disabling or killing millions more. People escape underground in droves; they crowd into shelters, basements, sewers, storm drains, subways. Rich and poor, old and young; every survivor, with dazed disbelief, descending into a cramped underworld of stench, thirst, and sweat. Food is scarce, water is of dubious quality, and basic services have broken down.

10. Through all this, who will count the dead and rescue the wounded? To remain above would be fatal, would save no one. So the anguished cries continue unanswered across the shattered bricks and twisted girders of the cities; no firemen come to check the progress of the flames. New York, San Francisco, and Seattle are burning; and in the District of Columbia, Potomac waters rapidly fill the giant holes where once a city stood.

11. Some urban areas are not attacked. There is nothing of immediate military-political value in or near them. In these places a panicked citizenry stampedes the supermarkets. Men begin digging shelters and forming militias. Hysteria grips the unrocketed in Miami, Portland, Green Bay, and other places; while the rural population remains somewhat calmer.

12. Russian reconnaissance aircraft are seen in the skies. Rumors circulate about parachutists descending in the night. These are the men of Spetsnaz: experts in impromptu torture, terrorism, and assassination—the first Russian troops on American soil. Many will come in uniform. Some will speak Midwestern English, wearing bluejeans. They are the vanguard of Russian Military Intelligence. And indeed, they reconnoiter and report, to the satisfaction of their superiors, that America has been "neutralized."

13. Western Europe begins to buzz. *What* has occurred? Nobody knows. America isn't answering her telephone calls. And there are rumors that Russia has been bombed.
The Russians make an announcement: "American militarists initiated a general nuclear war yesterday, at 6:30 p.m., Moscow time. Our forces quickly responded with a devastating riposte. We are awaiting further information on the extent of casualties."
The Europeans are relieved that they have been spared. Thank goodness. But the Russians make a further announcement: "Many

of our cities have been badly damaged, though civilian casualties have been kept to a minimum. Even so, we are confronting an unprecedented economic crisis and request emergency assistance."

Next: Russian paratroopers begin falling, like rain, over Western Europe. Russian tanks suddenly plow across Poland and Germany. "Blitzkrieg" is the old word for it. And for their next act? Ready the cattle cars for the European cattle. Ship them east! to new addresses: Camp 101, 102, 103, and so on. Russian generals begin moving into the best houses in Paris. It is not surprising that with so many houses in Russia destroyed one yearns to have a nice Parisian house, a Belgian apartment, or a British flat. This is known as "time-sharing" in America. You live in my Russian tent for a while and I'll live in your four-bedroom house. Fair is fair.

14. Bloody fighting erupts in Japan as Chinese forces attempt to invade. Resistance is heavy, so the invaders resort to a new kind of nerve gas. Consequently, millions of Japanese are killed and Japan is subjugated. Meanwhile: Taiwan has fallen, and North Korea finishes off South Korea. Vietnam blitzes Indonesia.

15. The Special Australian Envoy, kept waiting in a Foreign Ministry anteroom, is finally allowed to see the Chinese Premier. The premier's eyes are half closed. He is smoking a cigarette. He blows smoke in the Australian's face while an aide translates the words "unconditional surrender."

The room grows dark, the furniture begins to move in a circle, then the ceiling appears.

The Special Australian Envoy has fainted.

16. *Rocket-day plus thirty. The Russian Marshal speaks: —*

"Comrade President, comrade ministers: The American rocket forces and air forces have been completely demolished. Russian and Chinese marines are positioned at the outlets of North America's most important waterways. The national leadership of the United States is either dead or lingering in holes, waiting to die. The Cubans control Florida and the Mexicans have agreed to our terms for alliance and occupation of the remaining United States territory. Fairbanks, Alaska, fell to our paratroopers yesterday. I am grieved to report, amidst so much good news, that there remains some difficulty with American attack submarines; but since they haven't any way to refit themselves, they will eventually disappear. Nevertheless, our convoys have been decimated by these lingering vestiges of imperialist seapower and we have delayed the transport of Russian Sixth Army and Chinese First.

"As for the unsalvageables in North America: the anthrax campaign began five days ago. We expect to liquidate nearly one million Americans each day for the next twenty days. By the end of winter there will be fewer than twenty million Americans left. Due to this, our soldiers will have little trouble occupying the United States in its entirety. Already the mayors of various American towns have been begging us to accept their surrender, but we don't have any way to feed or accommodate these people; and then there's the question, which is quite upsetting, of what to do with all this excess anthrax." [mixed laughter from the Russian leadership.]

17. *A doctor's diagnosis.* —

Here lies a little girl, covered with bruises, her hair fallen out. She stares up at Dr. Martin, lifelessly. What is the cause of death, sir? Tell us, please. Is it the radiation sickness again?

But the doctor trudges on, as he has trudged on, through town and country, day after day, a witness to radiation, anthrax, famine, firing squads, lynchings, sieges, battles, seditions, and conspiracies. He passes over the particular symptoms and now draws his diagnosis from the broad entirety of the scene.

Here lies a baby smoldering amidst the burnt planks of a house; and there a police officer squats, frozen in death, who blew the back off his own skull with a service revolver. And beyond the fence we see a wagon heaped with corpses, bellies distended; and yonder lies an emergency field hospital, like thousands of other field hospitals— a sea of prostration.

From these and many scenes like them Dr. Martin does not draw a simple or immediate diagnosis. He takes his time and gathers every tidbit of relevant data. At long last, turning to a few attentive acquaintances in a hungry plaza crowd, he suggests that a Bad Conception has infected the world and has collapsed civilization.

His acquaintances don't comprehend. So Dr. Martin curls his lips in disgust, scowls at their ignorance of ideologic disease: "Of course, there are other contributing factors, but the decisive cause of death is a conception which, having gotten out of hand, moved the world toward certain, necessary, predictable consequences."

Beleaguered and rocketed remnants of men, seeing this Latest-Testament Prophet, protest that it cannot be. Conceptions cannot collapse civilization: "For what sort of thing is a conception, after all? It is a ghost, a phantom; harmless and practically useless."

"And yet," says the good doctor, "a conception has laid waste the circle of the earth."

Ragamuffins scrunch up their dirty faces in perplexity: "But a conception is an incorporeal thing. It cannot be touched, smelled, heard, tasted, or seen. How can it destroy? How can it trigger the Four-Fifths Death? How can something nebulous give birth to so much that is palpable? No, no, we are sure that ideas do not matter."

"One must learn to see with the mind's eye," says the doctor.

"What sort of thing is that?!" black fingernails scratch lice-infected heads.

Dr. Martin replies: "It is the faculty which scrutinizes the conceptions of the world."

Scrutinizes?! What a funny man he is, and he uses such funny words!

"And without a mind's eye," says Martin, "you won't see past your nose."

But then, as befuddled survivors rub their chins, Chinese soldiers bring prisoners into the plaza to be shot. Spies and other grumblers have an appointment with the firing-squad, being recently flushed out of cubbyholes by the "people's vigilance." And so our good Dr. Martin, husbanding his many griefs, slips away; a one-time curiosity for bedraggled spectators assembled accidentally at history's numb moment. He has, after all, recovered his sight; only to see that *everyone else* is yet blind.

18. Satanism is a real thing. What do I mean by this? That the Christian era inevitably gives way to a Satanic era. Carl Jung spoke of this in his book *Aeon*. In it he hypothesized that the unacknowledged metaphysical dualism of Christianity, stemming from the notion of God's absolute goodness, dialectically implies the rise of Antichrist, and a Satanic finale to the Christian era. What we now observe is the apparent verification of Jung's surmise; especially in the ascendency of Thanatos—as the will to universal destructionism, hate-mongering, and suicide; utterly the opposite of Christ's creative, loving, forgiving, and regenerating spirit. We see that Thanatos, at the close of the second millennium, seizes the world by the throat. The rebellion against God, reality, law, order, and life now declares itself victorious. All values are smashed. Now comes the enshrining of anti-values. Now comes the hour of total destruction. This is modernity's Satanism. This is the story of Antichrist. His appearance on earth has already occurred. The demonic energy of political fanaticism is *his* energy. The destruction of whole peoples, nations, and races is *his* destructionism.

"And there was war in heaven: Michael and his angels fought against the dragon; and the dragon fought and his angels...."

19. A Russian general, his conscience troubled, poses the following dreadful question to himself: *If the end justifies the means, then what will justify the end?*

20. To be sure, there comes a moment—but only a moment— when most Americans believe that surrender is the *only* option. Resistance appears pointless. Thus begins America's brief flirtation with defeatism. But it passes quickly. For defeatism invariably provokes a reaction against itself, out of which emerges men of energy, undazed by the Great Calamity. These are the diehards who are determined to resist in defiance of all odds. They are at first visible *in contrast* to the listlessness around them. And in the long run, their example is contagious.

21. The circumnavigators of the thermonuclear ocean suddenly discover that the world is spherical instead of flat. Now they feel contempt for the notion of a sudden falling off. The globe does not freeze into a cosmic ice ball, the earth is not forever contaminated, the crops soon grow again, the rains fall, the winds blow. *Life goes on.* Those exaggerated "end-of-the-world" stories, designed to benumb and misinform the slumberland of pre-rocketed America, have lost their credibility.

22. In the meanwhile: Desperation and panic take hold. Law ceases to function. Transportation and communications have broken down. The continent-turned-graveyard is now conscious of approaching winter: the coldest winter in American history. As the will to resist solidifies: tribunals of rough justice are convened against traitors, shirkers, looters, collaborators, and spies. Hangings, shootings, stranglings, have begun and continue unabated. In Chicago, which still stands untouched by Russia's Rocket-Socialism, yet rusted and ruined by a domestic kind, the mayor is assassinated by his own police. In the rubble of cities Y and Z hundreds are executed by National Guardsmen. Lists are drawn, suspects rounded up, whole schools of social science are denuded. Certain actresses and actors run to the Cuban lines in the south, to Soviet Alaska, or to Mexico. It is the terror of counter-revolution: an ideological purification without mercy. Nobody objects that civil liberties are suspended. The U.S. Supreme Court drifts with all the other stratospheric dust. The President is a charcoal shadow upon a submerged concrete slab, and Congress is a scattered remnant of discredited "November criminals," whose last acts laid the country open to devastation..

23. A nuclear war against the United States, if it is to end in total Sino-Russian victory, must eventually resolve itself into a war of attrition. And the determination of the American survivors to resist can only be bolstered by the fact that the nation and all its people must either perish or prevail; that no other alternatives exist in the wake of unprecedented Russian criminality and Chinese bloodthirstiness, in the ongoing merciless slaughter of innocents. And while the top American leadership, composed of the softest and least reliable human material, will be killed in the first days of any nuclear war, there will be new leaders, made of sterner stuff.

In organizational terms: America possesses auxiliary institutions in the form of municipal and county governments. The Russian generals might spend thousands of bombs to destroy the state and federal administrations; but they cannot, for lack of weapons, do away with school boards, city councils, and thousands of grassroots political organizations. Therefore, it is the fact of local self-government that makes the subjugation of North America such a difficult task, especially because a self-governing people can reconstitute the national authority and rapidly reorganize the country on the most solid foundation imaginable.

In the wake of nuclear rocket war, throughout North America, I see committees of correspondence mediating between the counties and municipalities. These committees would organize secret congresses to establish a new national military command. Under a cloud of fear and anger, with all thoughts of partisanship temporarily suspended, the men at such congresses would think and speak with one voice. The slightest sign of selfishness would be fatal to anyone who showed it. A true spirit of patriotism would be found at these assemblies. A new nation would thus be born from the ashes — with the hardness of tempered steel.

24. The mass murderers in unscathed, unrocketed Moscow wait for the surrender and collapse of becratered America. But alas, craters do not surrender. And now, from the bottom of a bodyheap of slain leaders there comes a voice, first heard in the Rockies. An orator speaks directly to the soul of America; expresses with eloquence the longing of every heart, of every newborn patriot. A mutter-ripple spreads from the Great Divide; across the Mississippi, Appalachia, up through the dens of the poor freezing Canadians. "We are not defeated," it says. "We are still alive."

25. Not everybody in America has been caught unprepared. Various societies, churches, and clubs had stockpiled food, fuel, and

other supplies. Various persons had secretly armed themselves. Once upon a time we sneered at these people as "survivalists." But now all those with food, with guns, and with intact organizational infrastructures, find themselves at the helm. In Montana there arises The League of Bastions, and in Utah, The Mormon Defense Council. They contribute disproportionately to the leadership of the secret national congress. Some of their members also belong to surviving National Guard units. Out of these emerges a military fire-eater. The new National Congress grants him dictatorial powers for the waging of war and for the defense of the continent. After this there follows a call for experts, for guns, for troops, for gold, for sacrifices of every kind. Plans are laid to build new factories. Committees of Defense are established in every district. Military conscription begins. Bomber aircraft, found hidden in the underbrush, are pulled out and repaired. Tunnels are dug under a pulverized U.S. Air Force base to recover unspent hydrogen bombs. Laboratories are established for the manufacture of biological weapons. America is recovering her balance.

26. Trouble with the French Canadians? The new American dictator takes things in hand. He descends upon Quebec like a wolf. There are executions, there are confiscations, there are gun-battles. Finally, after further nonsense, he encircles the leadership of the opposition and slaughters them. With these first victories the national congress heralds him as "archgeneral."

27. But what of the Russian leaders? *They are ecstatic.* And now, in the light of day, they reaffirm communism. Yes, communism. They begin to speak of the long range strategy. They gloat, they chuckle, and they enjoy themselves. Communism never collapsed. It was a trick. So communism has triumphed just as Lenin and Marx had predicted it would. Nothing can stop them now. They have won. And soon Latin America will be blackmailed into joining the "socialist fold." Only North America, driven to madness by its defeat, seems determined to offer resistance.

28. But something very strange begins to happen. Europe and Asia suddenly run short of capital goods. Food and fuel are becoming scarce. All the world's currencies have collapsed and international trade has ground to a halt. In Western Europe and Japan the plans for food rationing have degenerated into corruption and confusion. The KGB discovers that the Russian Army is dealing in the black market. The Party decides on a purge. Seventy-five

hundred Russian officers are shot in January.

29. In Africa and Asia there are unprecedented plagues and famines. Ninety million people are expected to die by June. Another two hundred million might die before the end of August.

30. Sixty-eight Russian cities have been demolished by America's nuclear counter-strike. Though most of the inhabitants were protected by blast shelters, they are now without housing, and conditions are growing unspeakably worse by the day. The Soviet Army begins transporting these homeless people to France for resettlement. But this sparks a violent counter-reaction. In early February, while the weather is still cold, French "bandits" initiate a nuclear terror campaign.

31. *Inside the Russian Defense Council.* —
President: Comrade General, we won't tolerate this blundering.
Gen. Demyanov: Comrade President, if there is any blundering it is to be found in the KGB.
KGB: The French terrorists got their nuclear weapons from the Army. The Army is therefore to blame.
Gen Demyanov: Then why didn't you put a stop to it?
KGB: Because your officers misled us.
Gen. Demyanov: That, of course, is possible. The KGB and the Army are rival organizations. But the KGB has the policing function and *this* is a police problem.
President: But how do you explain this inexcusable breach of security, General? Do you merely brush it off by blaming the Army's rivalry with the KGB?
KGB: I have told you, Comrade President, that the state of the Army in France is deplorable. Discipline has utterly broken down.
Gen. Demyanov: Discipline is bad, I admit. But this is due to the general demoralization of the Army. And the KGB hasn't helped.
President: But isn't there a connection between discipline and morale?
Gen. Demyanov: Of course. The men have lost faith in our cause, and have lost faith in the leadership. Therefore any attempt to impose discipline by means of threats or punishments only deepens the underlying rage which threatens to explode into a general uprising in the ranks. The troops have become increasingly sympathetic to the civilian population which has cleverly ingratiated themselves with the soldiers. The food situation is so severe, and the suffering of the civilians is now so extreme, that our people cannot

help drawing certain conclusions. What do you do when women and children come weeping to your encampments, begging the soldiers for food. Our men are not heartless.

KGB: And why, general, did you allow this to occur in the first place?

Gen. Demyanov: I had no idea what was occurring until it was too late.

President: General, you are relieved of command.

32. April, in the armies of Central Europe: a serious plot against the newly empowered Communist Party is discovered. Particularly alarming is the involvement of elements from both the Army and the KGB: — two institutions which are meant to keep watch on one another. Even more disturbing is the complicity of Communist Party officials charged with overseeing the KGB. The vulnerability of the regime is now understood. Things have not turned out as rosy as the October analysis had supposed. From now on: a Reign of Terror and a purging of the Communist Party of the revived (and expanded) Soviet Union.

33. *When your goose is cooked.* —
Where now dear communists? You have lived off the timid complacency of an overabundant capitalism for decades, with never-to-be-paid-back loans and stolen technology, with a massive reliance on Hammer Concessions, lend lease arrangements and other items of largesse. You have eked out your drab totalitarian days in tedious squalor, morbidly building your tanks, rockets, and submarines for that one glorious hour of fireworks. But now, the plutonium whirlpool sucks you down into History's most treacherous undercurrent. You have destroyed your credit by killing your creditors; you have blockaded your own harbors by closing the harbors of the free world; you have killed or ruined your best customers, your readiest suckers. Yes, dear socialists, dear parasites: the goose which laid the golden egg is cooked—nay, it is burnt. The world market has been sunk by the torpedoes of the Red Banner Fleet. Trade ceases, industry falters, crops rot in the fields, populations melt into skeleton piles, armies rebel, generals have to be shot, commissars wax independent, grumbling is ubiquitous.

The alleged capitalist exploitation, with which you justified your aggression, is reduced to black-market and post-thermonuclear barter. Capitalism withers, shrinks, and almost dies. Its stunned remnant wander amidst the ruins. Its great creative powers now utterly inconspicuous. The stuffed scarecrows of Soviet socialism imagine that they have nothing to fear. Ah! If they only had brains they'd realize that socialism is barren, having only the virtue of efficient destruction.

Poor dilapidated scarecrows of socialism; your gulag economy has, at long last, yanked itself from the apron strings of Western Civilization, there to flounder, to wither, to descend into the last awful stage of true communism: that is—cannibalism. Yes, how lamentable; especially in those numerous, unlucky, unrocketed parts of the world where the hideous experiment has begun. Here is a new rule, a new political economy, which works after the following fashion: Those who produce may eat, while those who cannot produce must eat those who can.

But what happens when you've cooked your goose—when you've nuked or raped the last productive economy in the world? What will you do then? Is this what Marx meant by the "withering away of the State"?

34. *The Era of Global Democratic Peace.* —

A Party mannequin, bouncing jerkily forward, announces that: "The Era of Global Democratic Peace is here. —Thank God."

But thanks due only to our glorious leaders: Comrades X, Y, and Z. We thank these, the new gods, makers of a thoroughly atheist cosmology. Imagine it! Never again "Our Father who art in Heaven," but "Our comrades who art in Moscow." Never again "God's wrath," but "the wrath of the Central Committee of the Communist Party Soviet Union." Never again "priest," but "Party Commissar." Never again "Heaven," but "Fully Developed Communism." Never again "Satan," but "Enemies of the Party."

35. For the Americans: defeat in the first phase must be accepted. But the second phase is altogether up for grabs. The enemy believes himself victorious, though he isn't. The war has only begun. Of course, it's true that America as a great power is effectively neutralized. Two hundred million Americans are probably dead. Millions of others are injured. The Soviet Air Force has dusted America's crops with rice blasts to kill the rice, and wheat rusts to rust the wheat. Every lethal and semilethal disease imaginable, from Japanese encephalitis B to anthrax drifts across the American hinterlands, carried by the wind. Armies of the glorious Socialist bloc have overrun Alaska, seized Florida; while thirty crack motorized divisions stand loaded on ships, soon to reinforce the beachheads. The war, from every superficial appearance, is over. But this is an illusion.

Eighty million Americans remain. They have learned in the

heat of the moment how to protect themselves from fallout, how to survive a biological attack, how to utilize gas masks, how to aim a rifle, how to hide a jet bomber in the underbrush, how to hunt up a nuclear bomb. With each passing day North America becomes more deeply entrenched. Though three-quarters of the capital goods in America are destroyed, a quarter remains. This quarter, by itself, has more economic potential than the entire pre-war Soviet economy. One must also consider the psychological reaction of the Americans. They are angry and are convinced that they have nothing to lose by fighting. In order to win, therefore, the Soviets and their allies must exterminate the Americans, and reduce the land area under American control. This will take a great deal more than thirty additional motorized divisions. It will take a great deal more than what remains of the whole Soviet nuclear arsenal. It was easy, of course, to kill Americans when they weren't expecting to be attacked. It was, in other words, a simple matter to kill the first two hundred million people. But the remaining eighty million—dispersed over a wide territory, carefully rationing their food and living off existing stocks, possessed of shelters, armed and angry into the bargain—will be hard to kill.

36. Already, as the war of extermination continues and the Europeans are themselves stuffed into cattle cars bound for the East, there dawns the realization that the world is dying and communism is the disease. After all its depredations, how few are those who yet believe in the triumph of communism?

And there's that stupid Soviet marching song: *"On to Chicago if we have to."* Well, *you have to*, dear comrade soldiers: dodging bullets at every step. It won't be nice. The children, the old women, the young women—everyone—will be trying to kill you on this "picnic" of yours. Young communists! Prepare to die! We are sending you to the North American Front. "Oh no, oh please don't send me there! Send me to Brazil, send me to Australia, send me to that godforsaken hole called Africa—but don't send me to North America. Please comrades, have mercy on me. I have three little children."

Everyone agrees that the Russian soldier is tenacious. But comrades, have you ever seen eighty million diehard "reactionaries" with nothing whatever to lose? The secret of America's previous weakness was that she was clinging to her prosperity, desperately hoping to keep it. And the communists used that against her. That was smart. But now what have you got? You have a breathing, hating, hundred-and-sixty-million-legged war machine. The new American soldier isn't some poor kid moving forward under threats from above. He's fighting because he wants to: *him*, personally. He wants a piece of the enemy. He doesn't want to kill some Chinese peasant you've whipped into an "instant" soldier. He wants to put a bullet through one of those *real* communists; the ones with the ridiculous formulas, the ones with revolutionary consciousness. That's who he wants to kill. Oh, you think that's funny? "All reactionaries are paper tigers"? But no! Not so at all! The twenty-first century "reactionary" is a marvelous achievement and let me be the first to congratulate you on creating him. Though I can't help asking: Did you really believe in communism? In that stuff about changing human nature? But that's not the way to change human nature; *not* with propaganda and ideological rhetoric. You change human nature with bombs. You kill a man's way of life and destroy his country, and you move in to finish him off — that's how you change a man! For in doing these things you give him his manhood and his sense of self-preservation. In doing this you set his priorities straight. And his first priority is to *kill* you.

37. *The smoke clears.* —

President: Comrade General, we are anxious to hear your report.

Gen. Gronski: Thank you Comrade President, comrade ministers: It is a privilege to serve the reborn Soviet Union, and it is especially good that we can engage in frank discussions of this kind. Last September military operations went better than expected. But recently our position has deteriorated.

President: Excuse me, Comrade General, but this sounds like pessimism.

Gen. Gronski: I am merely speaking of complications that might kill the patient.

President: Are *we* "the patient"?

Gen. Gronski: The Americans are reorganizing the interior of their country. We are entering into a war of attrition with them. We have tracked aircraft, believed to be B-1 bombers, on two occasions. We suspect that they have several nuclear weapons left. There is reason to think they retain a limited nuclear striking capability.

President: But this goes against everything you've told us before!

Gen. Gronski: Not entirely.

President: Why can't you merely locate these bombers and destroy them?

Gen. Gronski: These bombers can land on any freeway in America, and can be towed into the brush and camouflaged. We cannot easily find them; and there may be other military forces, also hidden in the underbrush.

KGB: Excuse me, comrades, but the intelligence reports say that the United States cannot project its power beyond North America.

Gen. Gronski: Perhaps that is true for the time being. I do not dispute the truth of our intelligence reports, as far as they go. What I dispute is the simple-minded interpretation that America is beaten.

KGB: Who is being simple-minded?

Gen. Gronski: I think we've all been simpleminded.

President: What are you saying, General Gronski?

NAVY: Comrade President, the Army has constantly spoken of America's recuperative powers, and the rest of us have refused to listen. Now it turns out that the Army has been correct in its assessments. Therefore we can no longer delay the seizure of the European and Japanese commercial ships.

President: That is a complicated situation, Comrade Admiral. The Europeans may be provoked into an uprising and the army of occupation is currently unreliable. To make such an announcement now would endanger our whole position.

KGB: The food situation is bad.

President: Very bad.

Gen. Gronski: We're getting off the subject, comrades. If I could redirect your attention to the question of America. Our forces are only sufficient for holding down the key coastal positions, Florida, and Alaska. Any attempt to advance inland could result in serious losses. The Chinese, of course, plunge ahead because of their numbers. They have swamped the Western states. But their logistical position is hopelessly overstretched. We dare not follow their example.

KGB: But there are no large American forces to oppose you, comrade general.

Gen. Gronksi: The latest military intelligence, which my secretary is placing before you, shows that the Americans have a loose defense, consisting of widely deployed platoons of self propelled guns with tactical nuclear and chemical capability. The critical roads and passes are protected. Advancing into the interior of the country is not by any means an affair of a few hundred thousand troops. The Americans have formed partisan groups, they are dispersed over an enormous territory.

KGB: This is sheer timidity. To keep these divisions idle on the inland waterways is stupid. They should be advancing to occupy the country and flush out the defenders. With all that has been sacrificed up till now, one cannot possibly lose very much in comparison.

Gen. Gronski: Comrade President, with all due respect to the chairman of the KGB, I cannot order my troops to occupy a hostile territory of several million square miles in the middle of winter. I must remind the KGB that I have only eighteen motorized divisions that are already stretched perilously thin.

KGB: You have a quarter of a million Cuban troops.

Gen. Gronski: The Cuban troops are sick and starved. Their food supplies have been ruined.

KGB: What about living off the land?

Gen. Gronski: This is a nuclear war, comrade, not Sherman's March. In January the Seventy-first Motorized Rifle Division sustained 7,300 casualties while "living off the land" in the Portland area.

President: I didn't hear about this.

KGB: Yes, I told you. These were the poisonings.

President: Poisonings?

KGB: Yes, Comrade President. The Army requisitioned food from the local population and most of it was poisoned.

President: They ate food given them by the Americans?

Gen. Gronski: Given to them by the mayor of the town.

KGB: A regimental commander was negligent. A minor matter.

Gen. Gronski: This is not a minor matter. The same incident has repeated itself elsewhere. Our troops haven't enough to eat. The commanders are desperate. The countryside is stripped. Much of what we confiscate from the local population has been tampered with. Those people are very angry and—

Navy: He's going to blame the Navy, and say it's the Navy's fault for not coming through with sufficient food supplies.

Gen. Gronski: I'm not concerned with blame. But the Navy has been unable to provide supplies to the expeditionary forces on a regular basis.

President: What is the reason for this?

Navy: Several American attack submarines are still operating, Comrade President; and our convoys are extremely vulnerable.

KGB: The Navy is timid like the Army.

Navy: We lost three hundred ships in one week! Is that timid? The man is besmirching the good name of the Navy! Since October we've almost lost a ship a day. All our harbors are demolished, our heavy ships cannot meet their yard periods. British and German ports are centers of sabotage and counter-revolution. The Navy is *not* timid.

President: We appreciate the heroic sacrifices of the Navy,

Comrade Admiral, but we must not shrink from further sacrifices if they are needed. The KGB Chairman is correct. I have seen too much caution in our military leadership. We mustn't forget that this is a revolution and we are on the point of accomplishing it.

Gen. Gronski: I agree. And that is why the Army must be given maximal support.

President: General Gronski is a clever man, and we will do what we can for him. I think we will try another anthrax campaign.

Gen. Gronski: This is not advisable, Comrade President. Our stockpiles are dwindling and our nuclear stores are not replenished. India and South America are rapidly arming themselves and breaking all their obligations to us. The Mexicans cannot be trusted. The Cuban morale is very low.

President: Surely, Gronski, you paint too dark a picture, trying to scare us with India and Latin America. These countries count for nothing, and couldn't oppose us with any strength. I'm really dismayed at this sudden pessimism. Everything couldn't be *that* bad.

Gen. Gronski: No, Comrade President, everything is worse.

KGB: Would you rather switch places with the Americans?

Gen. Gronski: Of course not. They aren't even a world power any longer. But even so, our position is much weaker than you believe. The Army in Europe is demoralized. The soldiers are saying that the war isn't over and the worst is ahead. Our shipping of thirty million Russians into Western Europe has galvanized anti-Soviet sentiment. We cannot feed the occupied countries. There are rumors that half of Europe will be dead of starvation in a year.

KGB: Sheer propaganda!

Gen. Gronski: This is not propaganda. It is fact. I have seen the situation. In Europe nothing works, nothing moves, and passive resistance is everywhere. One only needs a spark, an incident, a hint of weakness and the people are ready to let themselves be killed in large numbers. We must defeat the Americans quickly and convincingly. The morale of our people depends on it. There cannot be any more setbacks.

KGB: That is pessimism, Comrade General. I want to remind you of the scientific basis of Marxism-Leninism, which teaches that the forces of history are on our side.

Navy: Yes, obviously. Let us turn to the classics.

General Gronksi: But gentlemen, Lenin was not a determinist. He was a realistic thinker.

President: All we can ask of you, Gronski, is to do your best. We have great confidence in you. You've done fine work. Perhaps you are fatigued and temporarily discouraged. Take a month of vacation. The weather is still cold and nothing much can happen until the spring.

KGB: Yes, that's an excellent idea. The man is used up.

Gen. Gronski: But comrades, the situation is critical.

President: We order you to take a vacation.

38. *The fighting spirit.* — The International Expeditionary Force consists of Soviets, Mexicans, Chinese, Cubans, Vietnamese, Angolans, and assorted others. They are coming. They are soon upon us. First, we withdraw into the interior. Second, we ambush them with tactical nuclear weapons. Third, we encourage their troops to desert. Fourth, we poison their drinking water. Fifth, we cut their supply lines.

39. *The Soviet strategic error?* — To believe in communism: that is the worst mistake imaginable. That the communists are sincere damns them without appeal. For in the game of strategy only the realist can be master.

40. *What is to be done?* — The strategic position is like this: a Grand Communist Alliance invades the United States. Meanwhile, the world is starving. Economic activity has ground to a halt. The only plan the Central Committee can think of is: exterminate the Americans. Exterminate them before communism experiences a genuine collapse. Dump more anthrax on them. Use up the rest of the nuclear stockpile. Send more armies, more tanks, guns, and planes.

The Central Committee of the Communist Party Soviet Union meets to decide population issues in Western Europe. Old Bulganin rises and speaks in favor of a severe bread ration for France. He ends his speech by saying: "And furthermore, America must be destroyed."

They meet to discuss the Cuban plan for reorganizing Brazilian agriculture. Old Aleksandr Bulganin rises and speaks in favor of abandoning all luxury agriculture. At the end he interjects: "And furthermore, America must be destroyed."

The Portland Convoy is butchered and Russia's 27th Army finds itself isolated. An emergency meeting is held in Moscow. Old Bulganin rises and speaks in favor of an airlift without regard for costs. Then he calls for an anthrax campaign against Canada, and ends his speech with the familiar refrain: "And furthermore, America must be destroyed."

41. If communism were true, if it worked, then who could stop it? After all, communism has the means to defeat its enemies, but, in the final analysis, it cannot win any friends. It cannot accomplish any positive program. It is only able to destroy, to sweep away the old world and make room for something else. It cannot, by its very nature, do more, though it may rule the world for the next thousand years.

42. America can survive if: (1) part of the U.S. nuclear stockpile remains after the initial attack and is dispersed into secret locations for later use; (2) stealth bombers are kept hidden and operational; (3) an ad hoc military dictatorship promptly organizes the survivors into a cohesive national unit; (4) American attack submarines hinder the massing of large invasion forces in the months immediately following the first large-scale missile strikes.

43. The Sino-Russian conquest of the world is entirely possible if we fail to organize ourselves, and if we fail to take a few simple steps. This book, for example, is one of those steps. Whatever small mistakes it contains, it is a first step. For those with a future: *this is your cue.* Take it. Do something with it. Prepare yourselves. The smallest pre-war contribution might prove critical. We cannot know which man, or group of men, will be called upon to save the country on a given day: a single pilot, a submarine captain, the owner of a local radio station, a farmer, a teacher, a mother. To survive we will need new heroes and new heroic thoughts. Begin cultivating them now.

44. *Lenin's last sarcasm.* —Machiavel Lenin was sarcastic, and thus he remains, even in death. Though men infrequently appreciate the mummery of Marxism-Leninism, they may now appreciate the mummy of Lenin. Rather than irony mocking a gaudy world, irony itself becomes gaudy. Here, in the atheist's crypt, we find the ironic oxymoronic, the iconoclastic icon, the godless deified, the corrupt made incorruptible. Here lies Saint Vladimir Ilyich, the choleric opportunist and apostle of Karl Marx, enshrined like the true jawbone of Saint Peter.

On 21 January 1924 Lenin dies. On 23 January he comes to Moscow, still dead. He lays in state four days, perforce un-resurrected (and not even a stone to be rolled away). In Red Square the cardboard skeleton of Lenin's pyramid begins to rise. Then, Vladimir Ilyich, rotten (as in life) but not decomposed, is whisked into a laboratory and mummified by secret chemical witcheries. Abracadabra! And at last we recognize, once and finally, a Lenin more alive than all the Living.

In this manner—stuffed and displayed—Lenin gives us his last sarcasm, which slyly confounds superstition and scientific socialism by way of taxidermy. The Red Tutankhamen, Vladimir Ilyich, lies mummified within his tomb, his mausoleum. He, the graven image of the East, pickled in pseudo-formaldehyde, animates the life of Party and State. He symbolizes the aspiration of all working people. Cosmonauts carry his baby pictures into outermost space; women, children, and vulgar tourists queue up to gawk at his devilish goatee. The philosophic pilgrim, peering deeper into Lenin's chemically preserved face, may discern therein an authentic ember of the October Revolution; which ember is now responsible for setting Western Civilization ablaze, and for dispatching Eastern barbarism into a whirling abyss. Yet, even as Communist Antithesis seems to triumph, to gloat, to chortle, and as Capitalist Thesis staggers in its death throes, old Lenin turns purplish, with flesh sagging, curling, flaking; a strange and horrible sight for the viewing public. Imagine! Lenin's body giving way to dialectics, giving way to its antithesis. Alas, we fear that even the true jawbone of Saint Peter must lose a tooth now and again. And in the light of this: certain dogs (or certain cynics—as cynic means "dog") wonder if Marxism-Leninism might be finished. Some begin to suspect that history is not Thesis against Antithesis, Proletariat against Bourgeoisie, Haves against Have-nots; but, rather, ideological fantasy and objective reality locked in mortal combat; with fantasy losing, fading, dying—as all fantasy must.

And to think that Purple Vladimir never worried that *his* fantasy would succumb to reality. As realist and cynic he should have known better. Think, old holy mustachioed corpse, what a decrepit tool your ideology makes during the Four-Fifth's Death, under Rocket Socialism, Anthrax Socialism, Firing Squad Socialism—under a world-wide anti-capitalist malproduction, malnutrition (exempting, for the moment, a well-fed cannibalism). And now, when people need their pacifier, their security blanket, their icon, their Lenin more than ever—Behold! You, Vladimir Ilyich, begin to undergo disconcerting changes. The reflective Russian, even drunk, may justly begin to inquire: When comes Utopian Synthesis to the Great Revolution? When comes the Withering of the State and the life everlasting promised by the Apostles, the Disciples, and by Marx himself? Or are they, too, sagging and purple? What becomes of Socialist dreams when Lenin—at long last—turns a bluer shade of red?

The omen presages ill. The superstitious soul of Russia winces,

cringes, and fears the worst. Old Lenin turning purple? What could
it mean? The Politburo meets in emergency session. The General
Secretary demands that Lenin be removed from view.

"But won't this raise suspicions?" asks Comrade X.

Indeed! The peasant whisperings will overshadow the land.
Then shall come the famines. People will draw a parallel between
the decomposition of Lenin and the decomposition of Rocket
Socialism. Oh unfortunate coincidence!

But what can one do? Lenin is turning purple, and it can't be
helped.

Funny, choleric Lenin. His sarcasm remains, even in death.

45. Remember this phrase: "The point of absolute cynicism."
And what does it signify? Our moment of opportunity. The moment
at which the besieged and beleaguered North Americans can strike at
the heart of the enemy with decisive effect. It refers to the day when
communist morale collapses, when even the true believers lose their
faith. · For in the end these communists are merely men, and men
have limited endurance, especially as they are atheists without a God
to lend them strength. As much as they may bolster themselves with
names like "Josef Steel" and "Iron Shurik," they are but flesh and
bone. The grave is the end for them, with nothing beyond it. Thus
the failure of communism for a communist is an absolute and final
failure. It means that the human race is irredeemable, that history is
senseless, mankind an abortion, and life an absurdity.

But *when* will this authentic collapse begin?

When the communists see that the whole human race would
rather die than obey. Then will communism come unraveled like a
cheap sweater. And all America, rising in a body, will strike down
the enemy and relentlessly exploit the sudden collapse of entire
armies, fronts, and nations. For when the communist reaches his
point of absolute cynicism there is nothing left for him but to
become utterly and entirely selfish. And when a critical mass of
communists attain to this point of absolute cynicism, communism
will fly apart and disintegrate into the dog-eat-dog existence which
lies not far beneath its ideological surface.

46. The paradoxical red monster, writhing in its death agony, at
last expires. In defeat victorious and in victory defeated.

17

Refounding Fathers

> He who hath grown wise concerning old origins, lo, he will at last seek
> after the fountains of the future and new origins. —
>
> O my brethren, not long will it be until *new peoples* shall arise and new
> fountains shall rush down into new depths.
>
> For the earthquake — it choketh up many wells, it causeth much
> languishing: but it bringeth also to light inner powers and secrets.
>
> The earthquake discloseth new fountains. In the earthquake of old peoples
> new fountains burst forth.
>
> And whoever calleth out: "Lo, here is a well for many thirsty ones, one
> heart for many longing ones, one will for many instruments": — around him
> collecteth a *people*, that is to say, many attempting ones.
>
> Who can command, who must obey — *that is there attempted!* Ah, with
> what long seeking and solving and failing and learning and re-attempting!
>
> Human society: it is an attempt — so I teach — a long seeking: it seeketh
> however the ruler! —
>
> — An attempt, my brethren! And *no* "contract"! Destroy, I pray you,
> destroy that word of the soft-hearted and half-and-half!
>
> — NIETZSCHE, *Thus Spake Zarathustra*, 56: 25

1. To destroy communism we must be willing to risk our lives. If
we are unwilling to do this, then we won't survive. The Red Dictatorship
will triumph. Cruelty, war, famine and distress will rule the earth. Then,
truly, would come the end of history—and a world where *The Gulag
Archipelago* sings its woeful tune, like some broken record, through all
posterity.

In the previous chapter I took an optimistic view. But in all honesty
the evidence points to an altogether different outcome. For why should
communism falter in its moment of triumph?

But I hear a voice from above. It is my editor. He says: "You have
told your quota of truth. Now it's time for sweets, for happy endings,
cotton candy and lollipops."

Therefore, I venture a shred of hope. Though a shred of hope from

me might yet appear a rung of Hell.
And so I begin. —

2. *Doctrine of the Fourth World War.* — Another war is
vouchsafed to us by virtue of numerical progression, as in counting: one,
two, three, four, etc. The necessity of sequence, in this case, signifies
inevitability and cuts the floor out from under all those who preach "the
end of history."

3. Ah, sweet Progress! She was a seductress. Didn't you see her
(but a short time ago) luring us to the craters of the moon, calling us to
the ravines of Mars and the volcanoes of Venus? Didn't you see her in
the floorless vault of heaven beckoning us to the stars? And now that
we've shot our rockets at ourselves she laughs at us, throwing back her
head—so gay, so amused at her little joke.

4. A famous barbarian once explained: "I feel something within me
that compels me to burn Rome."

5. Man is territorial, even about his ideas. That man should kill for
ideas is therefore to be expected. But in the twenty-first century ideas
will not merely be seen as things worth killing for, but as weapons *in
and of* themselves. For ideas, too, will be drafted into the wars of mass
destruction — to justify, to dupe, to soften, to bloat, to tear up the very
souls of men and make conceptual cripples out of them, or enslave them
to a new kind of tyranny. In fact, the whole realm of ideas will be
represented to the masses as a minefield that can only be entered by the
most serious people. And as such, a great deal of the unseriousness and
cowardice that previously crept into our thinking will be driven out.

6. The ideology of bureaucratic organization, reaching its upper
limits, now succumbs to gravity, begins to fall, tearing away the myth of
the modern state as it goes. One must realize what an unnatural and
contrived bit of machinery a modern state is. One finds, behind the thin
veneer of paternal helpfulness, a hodgepodge of bureaus staffed by
nonentities. These small and hopping insects of the hour are only useful,
and only know their place, while a powerful idea, a willful aristocracy, or
a great man towers in the background. As history shows, bureaucracy is
a hollow shell that cannot rationalize its power except that something or
somebody lends it support. For bureaus are merely hunks of machinery
which may be built up or broken down, and which possess very little of
their own. Bureaucrats can be dismissed, replaced, threatened, or shot.
If a strong political swell mounts up before him, the bureaucrat must
either ride it or be drowned by it. All our fears concerning the power of

bureaucrats are therefore misplaced. What matters most is the animating force *behind* the officials. That is the thing worth worrying about. The myth, for example, that the "functionary" Josef Stalin was an epiphenomenon of the Soviet bureaucratic system, rather than an ultimate and necessary product of Marxian communism, is best debunked by noticing that communists are everywhere Stalinistic even as they denounce Stalin. Under no other bureaucratic regime does one encounter this situation. The brutality of communism is not, in any single case, an idiosyncratic byproduct of the administrative staff of particular communist countries, but comes from the communist idea itself. And this is true, whether one considers the millions starved to death in Cambodia, the tens of millions worked to death in the gulag, or the hundreds of millions killed in nuclear wars. Those who would propose that bureaucracy itself is responsible for these crimes have no idea what they are talking about. For bureaucracy is a tool, a machine. Its good and evil qualities are determined by forces outside of itself. The bureaucracy, in every instance, is only an empty vessel ready to be filled by the *real* power, flowing directly from the charisma of certain men or ideas. It is marvelous to consider that a man or an idea might suddenly excite the human imagination to such awe, that deeds once thought impossible would suddenly be performed, and commands once unthinkable would be readily obeyed. Here one finds that the state machinery is necessarily dependent on a higher-level phenomenon, which is moral and spiritual in nature—not mechanical, routine, or formalistic. Here we find the true source of the power and energy on which every bureaucracy in the world depends. It is a kind of energy which gives rise to a feeling or an expectation, and which cannot be produced by rationalized functionaries.

7. *In the world of the future:* — The bourgeois oligarchy, which hasn't been very clean or upright, will be turned out of power. This is because the bourgeois oligarchy, which seemed so humane and promising, has helped to bring about the worst catastrophe imaginable. For the bourgeoisie, as a ruling class, has been from the outset unable and unwilling to uphold economic freedom, Christian values, and good government—which are essential to the continuation of the bourgeois way of life. In all of this, the bourgeoisie has proven itself to be, paradoxically, a propertied class against its own kind of property, overseeing the development of monopoly capitalism, the welfare state, and paper money. *So* self-destructive is bourgeois capitalism that even its nemesis—socialism—is largely the product of bourgeois "thinking." And communism, as it developed from its Russian base, could always count on the capitalists to "sell it the rope."[1]

8. In an age of mass destruction aggressive military action has built-in advantages. When weapons can depopulate entire continents, a first strike may be the last and only strike—winner take all. Circumstance itself therefore dictates an ideology of attack, an ideology of palpable objectives like those advocated by Hitler in *Mein Kampf.* In other words, the voice of history itself becomes perverted and favors the monster, the devourer, and the preemptive imperialist. Whereas in the First World War the weakness of offensive arms led to a repudiation of imperialism and militarism, in the Fourth World War the weakness of defensive arms will dictate that every ideology become imperial, or perish.

9. *Perspective.* — War as a vital, life-giving, life-affirming and meaning-intensive activity, perhaps the highest, most exalted and ennobling activity for man.

Item: The specific units of war, the plans of war, and the effects of the weapons now dictate a new type of government (the survivalist state). The weapons of mass destruction have become primaries. Consequently, a new militarism, a new law, and a stronger social order—*by necessity.*

Item: Reciprocity between the tools of war and the society which produces those tools, leading to a new rationale for authority. The shallow theory, once prevalent, that the superstructure of society determines how weapons will be used, is defunct. Every community now discovers that the weapons of mass destruction determine and justify the superstructure. Authority can now demand greater sacrifices, more horrible punishments, stricter discipline and clearer ideas. For one has received, out of the hellish transmission belt of history, a new standard: in life and death. Or shouldn't we call this an old standard, as in ancient times, when war took center stage and was the determining human activity? Once again: cities and nations will put walls around themselves. They will dig down and sleep with weapons by their bedsides.

Item: The brutality of the situation will contribute toward a new illiberalism of tone. On the devastated periphery of the great communist power system there will arise social-political mutations, that is, new states and ideologies. Direct contact with demolished cities and depopulated towns, empty fields and fallen bridges, will give these states a new feeling about the world. The unconventional tendencies of survivalist political and religious groups indicate a certain potential for

---

[1] Lenin said: "Comrades, don't panic, when things get very tough for us, we will give the bourgeoisie a rope, and the bourgeoisie will hang itself." Karl Radek asked: "Vladimir Ilyich, but where are we going to get enough rope to hang the whole bourgeoisie?" Lenin replied: "They will sell it to us themselves."

civil strife or even civil war. Nevertheless, as a new and necessarily
ruthless authority emerges, an increase in concern for community, for
posterity, and especially for history, shall also emerge. Expressions of
belief in God will once again pepper daily utterance with constant
prayers and exhortations to heaven, while atheists—taken for
communists—shall often swing neatly from the end of ropes.

A further idea: That the future of the warmongering spirit looms
large and glorious, never before such wars vouchsafed to us. A new
martial spirit rises up, not seen since Medieval times, born of a constant
comradeship with Death. It will be a spirit disdainful of capitalism,
socialism and democracy.

Tied up with all this: the notion of a ruling class, of privilege, of
aristocracy, of superiority and inferiority based upon qualities of intellect
and character which serve the survival of the community.

What monsters of the deep shall surface at the dawning of this new
world we cannot tell, though we may, at our leisure, work toward a vague
outlining of the twenty-first century's most serviceable themes.

10. *The Hereafter.* — Snapshots of the future, as one takes
photographs at a wedding, of the kiss, the crying mother, the envious
sisters, etc., with the difference being the bridegroom as Grim Reaper.

Point of initial departure: the end of a civilization.

Midpoint: a reborn Soviet Union in crisis, the crisis of totalitarian
machinery attempting to adapt to the world *as hurricane.*

Endpoint: a great personality rises up, attracts followers, annihilates
foes. The dawn of a new era, a new mystique, a new political seduction
and ruthless brutality, noble lies at its beck and call, a certain philosophy
carried forward in this process, and a wagon-train of scribes, pharisees,
theologians: high churchmen to the twenty-second century.

11. There is coming a new class of heroes. People with grating
voices and big sticks. People without much education but with a great
deal to teach. For example, we observe the ambitious North American
Archgeneral:

He delivers a speech to the Academy: "Political science is a
general science. What the twentieth century tried to do was make it into
a series of useless specialties. Political knowledge then became
impractical. It became stupid. Therefore, political science's utter failure
to have any positive effect on world events."

After he slaughters the Mexican prisoners: "I'm not disturbed
when people say I'm evil. That's as it should be. If I smiled sweetly at all
hours of the day I'd be the dupe of somebody who prays to hell."

After he marries his daughter to a Russian General: "There's nothing more contemptible than a man who lets his wife berate him. Women can smell weakness and never leave off an opportunity to dig their claws into ready prey. Now take my daughter, for example."

After the liquidations near Lake Superior: "Why so many people are shot is a question I cannot answer. The rules are clearly posted, the consequences for breaking them are unequivocal. I guess you'll have to ask the people we're shooting why they're so anxious to be shot. I've nothing against them. But a decree is a decree."

After sacking Executive Department C: "When four or five billion people are dead due to a world war, I think it's rather petty to bemoan as tragedy the sacking of a few hundred insolent time servers."

12. The question of the Archgeneral, the Caesar, the dictator, is one of great importance. For the character of the Archgeneral shall imprint itself on the politics of the future. Will he be a restorer of classes or a servant of masses? By necessity he might be restricted to certain choices. Perhaps after the Nietzschean fashion he must be a breeder of new classes and races. Exactly how crude he will be—how bloody, how wise—remains in question. We only hope he will be a good republican, that he will fashion himself as a second George Washington, a refounding father in the true Federalist mold.

But that is almost too much to hope for.

13. *Nomadism.* — Something must be said about nomads. We mean to speak of all restless, shifting, mobile peoples, especially since history is so inconvenienced by them: pouring in, pouring out, exacting tribute here, inflicting butchery there. Tiresome people, these nomads: marauding, looting, committing atrocities against their domesticated brethren. Through many centuries the clans, tribes, nations, hordes and confederacies have left their bloody legacy: Huns, Tatars, Mongols, Turks, Cossacks. Little, nasty, bowlegged horsemen.

Somewhere in my notes there must be something about the mentality of nomads, something about their attitudes and their culture. For a new kind of nomad, with some of the old nomad habits of mind, shall follow in the wake of nuclear rocket war. Whole peoples shall suddenly take to the road, uprooted and hungry, looking for empty lands. Pressures shall be exerted from this people onto that people, huge chain reactions commencing, as when Hun pressed against Ostrogoth and Ostrogoth upon Visagoth, and everybody down upon the Romans. Ah, the swirl and the medley of violent moving forces, kicking up dust across the plains, deepening the mountain passes with the constant traffic of horsemen, displacing rivers with stones, picking cities clean, seizing slaves and booty.

----

14. Savages possess less bodily strength and smaller nervous systems than civilized men. They reach physical maturity earlier. Puberty comes, perhaps, at age seven. Herbert Spencer called the primitive man irregular, capricious, and vain. "The Fuegians," wrote Spencer, "are affectionate towards each other; and yet in times of scarcity they kill the old women for food."

15. "I take the following approach," says the Archgeneral. "The wise men cannot agree, so therefore the armed men must fight. Have rights become problematic? Rely on us, the armed men, to make them unproblematic. Are people confused about the law? Don't worry, ours is an unmistakable practice of 'training through punishment'—on the gallows or with the lash. The task now is one of simplification. Simplify, simplify, and again, simplify. For we have lost too many facts to immerse ourselves in the useless complexities of logic. All that remains is the promise of the armed man. Therefore, only one question matters. And that question is: *Which* armed man?"

16. And what shall become of the total state? Let us make a calculation. The total state brought us total war. It resulted in near-total destruction by way of a perfectly unrestrained fight to the death. We only had to have a silly, bookish, Marxian rationale, and off we went. But a total war, bringing near-total destruction, might undo the total state. Then again, there is the chance of total victory followed by total peace.

17. *From Archgeneral Smith to the world. —*
As the blood has barely dried on my besplattered boots, people hanker after some tidbit, perhaps for a lock of hair from someone's shrunken head. So I tender this: my war of destruction against philanthropy, pacifism, and liberalism, against humanitarianism and equal rights. And why do I declare such a war? Because these ideals seek the improvement of humanity where humanity is not amenable to improvement. For if one improves X, then Y worsens. Improve Y, then Z worsens, and so on *ad infinitum.* Therefore, due to repeated frustrations, idealism becomes angry, bitter, and misanthropic. The Christ who promises heaven on earth turns into a mass-murdering Antichrist, filled with rage at the world's imperfections, waging war against the very foundations of the universe, sweeping away everything in favor of a utopia which cannot exist. But this is only a general criticism. To take the aforementioned idealisms one at a time, and explain in greater detail my objections to them, I will start with pacifism which gave us all these wars in the name of peace, disarming the noble to the advantage of the ignoble. The sad fact is, peace cannot kill its enemies. Therefore, it cannot preserve itself. War is bound to triumph.

Thus do I make war on pacifism.

Then there are the liberals. They have vouchsafed to me my dictatorship because they are too weak, too moral for writing their authoritative tomes in blood. Thus do I make war on liberalism.

The humanitarians, in their turn, impoverished us with their war on poverty, with their welfare state and their dream of universal affluence. Thus do I make war on humanitarianism.

And next come the egalitarians who destroyed social harmony in the name of harmony, who robbed the poor man of his dignity and the rich man of his innocence, who gave us license, injustice, and moral relativism in the name of love, justice, and morality. Thus do I make war on egalitarianism.

Say good-bye to the world then, you would-be messiahs and other mock-crucifieds. *You are finished!*

18. Parable: from a tale of science fiction about a planet which achieved perfect bliss.

—How the people of this planet were thereby degenerated and made ready for slavery.

—How the most barbaric and least "comfortable" element enslaved them.

Lessons to draw from the parable?

One must avoid achieving perfect bliss. For the regime of perfect bliss is not sufficiently rigorous. It makes weak. It makes stupid. It makes lazy. Only a morality which preaches to the muscles, which develops the moral muscles, has any future in it.

19. *The case against economic hedonism.* — America's calamity has to do with the doctrine of progress conceived as the development of sensual bliss instead of moral muscles. Under this doctrine: rather than exerting one's powers in the cause of self restraint, one always gives in to desires. The spirit, placed in this situation, quickly loses its masculine aspect. It grows flabby, weak, and incapable of thinking painful thoughts. Ergo, it loses the power of self-examination and self-rectification. In fact, it becomes incapable of any genuine thought whatsoever. Therefore one achieves, in all actuality, a regress and a downgrading of human character, where people become immoral as well as stupid.

Sadly, after this fashion pre-holocaust America gradually became stupid and immoral. An almost constant decline in I.Q., in academic test scores, and in overall cultural development was apparent from 1950 onwards. Likewise crime rates—especially theft—give us some indication of the moral picture. It would be interesting to speculate what the course of further American degeneration might have brought if nuclear war had not intervened. It is always difficult to know how far into degradation a nation can go before something snaps. Sometimes it is possible to escape the consequences of immorality if a society has clever leaders. But America was a democracy, and the combination of widespread immorality and stupidity cut off all hopes that immorality could find a cunning solution. That the immoral are, under the sensualist regime, anything *but* cunning, is absolutely fatal to the whole notion of sensualist progress.

20. Rule: The determination to do good does not follow from right reason, but from rightness of will.

21. Alexis de Tocqueville once said that democratic nations "care but little for what has been." Notice, then, how democracy so little serves a nation with something that it cannot possibly forget.

22. Our greatest leaders, Washington and Lincoln, believed in Providence. This belief was part of their greatness. And as we learn of such men, we begin to believe in Providence ourselves.

23. The meanness of Napoleon and Caesar has largely been missed by history. What we find in these two men is a loss of self-control as they became intoxicated by their own ever-increasing power. This intoxication took the form of a morbid lust for greatness that eventually destroyed them both. Caesar yearned to be deified, and was assassinated in the Senate; while Napoleon thought to conquer Russia, and was ruined. Each dreamt of world conquest; a dream which ended in the nightmare of ignominious death in one instance, and pathetic exile in the other. If we call these men "great," we would give them too much credit. For as they set out to conquer the world, as it turns out, they couldn't even conquer themselves.

24. Do you imagine that politics and morality are easy? Do you imagine that solutions to human problems ask no blood, or fail to demand the spitting-up of various and imaginary happinesses? And wasn't it Christ himself who paradoxically argued that the first shall be last and the last shall be first?—which is to suggest that men have always misconstrued the very essence of that which is good and desirable. It seems we cannot help asking for good things which are not really good. At the same time we avoid those necessary evils which lead us to suffer for a better end.

25. *The Archgeneral describes himself.* — And what am I, but the

instrument of a just Nature bringing matters round again? I replace the
impotent and stupid financiers who strutted upon this very stage forty
years ago. I sweep up all these sorry carcasses into the ashcan of history.
I alone grow strong and vigorous beneath the mushroom clouds.

And do I, answering yesterday's imperatives, talk of restoring the old
order? I ask you: What is the proper use of rotten timbers? Why should
I restore to life a thing that gave money to its enemies? I scoff at all
those choirboy MBAs with Ivy League lobotomies, riding corporate
escalators toward redundant vice-presidencies, tampering with things
they knew nothing about, becoming cabinet secretaries, senators,
diplomats—ha! Why should I restore zeros to political power? A system
which promoted a Robert McNamara deserves to die. So many of his
kind rot in unmarked graves. I dance upon these graves. For I found the
power of the world amidst a pile of corpses, dipped my hand into the
hungry maggot stream and made that power mine. Let the idiots have it
back? —Never!

The leaders of the Old Civilization should have battled until all their
enemies were dead or helpless. But then, that wasn't in their nature, their
breeding, their democratic-liberal moralism. Tell me: Who has ever
trembled at the sight of a liberal? For that matter, are not conservatives
merely liberals with a slower pulse, poorer digestion, and greater
patience? And this being the case, imagine how vast a void I fill? And
what sort of monkey would call itself man after another thousand years of
liberal and conservative?

But on this account, never call me savior, reformer, liberator. Call
me hammer, or that which breaks apart the last vestiges of the corrupt
and rotten. I am the antithesis of Jacques de Larosiére, the capitalist
hero. Does anyone remember him? His is a funny story. As managing
director of the IMF he propped up a failing financial structure. Alas, he
was no builder, but only an embalmer of dead things. His formula? New
loans would make bad loans good loans, make medium bangs into a big
bangs. I thank him. My soldiers thank him! Bravo, Larosiére! How
could the capitalists have loaned so much money to hostile countries if
not for foolish men like you? Wasn't it obvious, even then, that the
debtor nations would simply, one day, refuse to pay? Wasn't it clear that
the Soviets and the Chinese were building up their warlike capacities for
that one grand hour of fireworks?

Not only did the old order invent the weapon of mass destruction and
allow it to fall into enemy hands, but the old order enthroned the bungler,
the mediocrity, and the shiftless demagogue to stand watch over the
system. The capitalist bankers, stupid and dishonest as never before,
were living only for the present, never admitting to themselves that the
bombs and the generals were on their way. A new international order
based on guns was the only thing left to replace the one based on trust,

----

based on money — after trust and money had grown senile. Banks backed by governments and governments backed by banks, governments stealing from people and banks from governments. One generation of vipers, one day of mayhem and a tremendous "cashing in." Alas, 'tis my cue. Enter, Stage Right. Nature abhors a vacuum and these boots and spurs do fill it. A slight downturn in the world economy and then begins a chain reaction of default. If default, then crisis, if crisis, then Soviet plan B; if Soviet plan B, then war; if war, then me and my army. You see how it is? People ask me all the time where I came from? Out from under which rock?

I am a bill drawn on Nature's reality. I am the result of your spiritual, intellectual, political and financial bankruptcy. And once you've defaulted, you cannot reschedule me.

26. *Eternal Return.* — The liberal is merely an egg from which the social democrat hatches. The social democrat is food for the Leninist. The Leninist destroys industrial civilization and becomes, in turn, food for the war lords. Enter, once again, the Liberal.

27. The Archgeneral, who was still engaged in the wars, brought all the women together and spoke as follows: "Look to your children and stay at home. The world is for men."

And when they heard this, the women hissed at him.

Then the Archgeneral asked: "Shall we draft your maladapted and lumpy bodies into the army? Perhaps you would prefer to fight the wars while the men sit at home and grow breasts."

Some of the women complained that war is stupid.

"Ah!" said the Archgeneral, "then you won't mind if we let the enemy rape you, steal your children, take your belongings, and burn your houses."

The women were silent.

So the Archgeneral continued: "Also, take good care of your husbands. Treat them with respect. Honor and obey them in what is proper."

And a woman rose up from the crowd, saying: "We demand equality in politics."

"When you are equal in war," said the Archgeneral, "then you may be equal in politics. For politics and war grow out of one another. Unfitness for war means unfitness for politics. Be silent and look to your children."

After hearing this, the women went home.

28. On the next day the Archgeneral summoned all the men who

----

were on leave from the wars, and said to them: "Take care of your wives
and children. You may shortly die, but they shall carry on after you."

After hearing this, someone shouted: "We are bored with them."

"If you were not weak and fickle," said the Archgeneral, "your wives
would not bore you. And if you took care in your manners, they would
sing sweet songs. But since you are weak and slovenly, your wives
chastise you, that is, they encourage you to recall your better selves.
Therefore, be faithful to your wives."

Another man spoke up and said: "My wife has grown old and ugly.
Why should I be faithful?"

"Are you yourself not old?" asked the Archgeneral. "Might you not
grow feeble before your wife and need looking after? How will your
children love you then, and honor you, as you begin to stumble into old
age, having treated them so lightly, having behaved with so little dignity?
For as I am your neighbor, hearing of your present attitude, I would call
you a fool for sacrificing family affection to a momentary urge."

After this, the men went home.

29. Then the Archgeneral called everyone together at an assembly,
and said to them: "No nation can last where the children are spoiled.
Therefore, control your children so that they might control themselves.
Do not allow them to dominate the home. Spank them. Say no to them.
Be kind to them, but show a strong hand. Teach them proper manners
and set yourself up as an example to them. Give them dignity. Give
them right and wrong.

"To the children I say this: Often when your parents punish you,
there is wisdom in it. Your parents brought you into the world, and their
thoughts are far ahead of yours. Do not desire to be pampered or have an
easy time of it. All spoiled children are cursed. Nature curses them, God
curses them, and the state curses them. And parents, let us save our
harshest punishments for the spoiled child. Let us unspoil him.

"On the cult of youth I heap scorn. Let this cult be persecuted.
What we need is the cult of maturity. How can the folly of youth be
thought wonderful or beautiful next to the grandeur and dignity of years?
Let us shake our heads at the young as all the genuinely progressive
generations have done, that the young may follow the path of their
fathers in attaining full maturity.

"To unmarried adults I say the following: Sex without children is a
vile thing. Look at America before the Bomb. Were they not unnatural
monsters who slaughtered their own unborn? I warn you against
imitating them; for such are degenerates, having little reverence for life.
And then there are the social diseases which come with loose living. Do
we want to be spreading such things without concern for the ultimate
consequences?

"To all wastrels and libertines, who are but sick old dogs, I say: Now you shall be forced to take your medicine. For I have prescribed the pill, and all shall be compelled to swallow it. Beware the mood of the times; for this mood is against you. The world has become grave even as it becomes a graveyard. Soon, in regarding you, the people will say to themselves: 'What right does he have to an unthoughtful life?'

"Verily I say unto you, oh people of the new times: Who is so clever as to escape such currents as these?

"And to the publishers of dirty pictures: I shall make you drink from the gutters and eat from the garbage. I shall sink you in pits, and drown you in swamps. You shall no longer ply your trade among us. For we have need of strong families, which your type of propaganda strives to undermine.

"And you who are homosexuals: take hold of yourselves lest I take hold and use you as faggots for my campfires. What value are you, you dried up unfruitful branches? We do not care for your disease-ridden ways. Go back into the closet if you must. There is no place for you in a society based on self-control, that is, a society on the road to civilization.

"And for the rest?

"I warn all utopians: tend to the real world. Be good citizens and honest men. We gain more from this than from all your foaming at the mouth.

"To the greedy businessman I say: *Something for nothing is a disease.* And this disease is fatal to us all. Go out and make money if you must. But do right by every man, and keep your promises. Otherwise the socialists will return, and the world will be twice-burnt, and you shall be exterminated.

"As for the demagogues, I know them well and rebuke them. If they should enter the assembly and give out conceits I will expel them and have them flogged.

"To the potheads and the junkies: We have no pity for you. We do not acknowledge that you are sick, but that you are weak and cowardly. Further, we hope you will overdose and that you will do it soon. Of your kind we are tired. Doctors: You do us injury when you revive these prodigals, and when you fancy to give them clean needles. Let them keep their dishonor and die.

"And finally: How is it that I speak so harshly? And why do people applaud my sayings? Because after the holocaust men have a clearer notion of cause and effect, of truth and consequences. Our tolerance for false steps and soft words has disappeared. We who are hungry, decimated, and grim cannot feel as deep a sympathy for weakness as once we did when life was easy. Prosperity makes men sensitive to the pain of others, but while we suffer, let us not hear a chorus of whining in the background, especially when that whining might be silenced with a bullet to its brain."

30. Let hope remain, but as a shadow of its former self: hope — on a diet.

31. The builders of states have frequently taken on the taint of bad men. For to build is to destroy, and a founding is impossible without the crime of sacrilege against the past, which every founder must commit. Consider the saying: "Darkness before light." The builder of order begins with darkness. He trods a new path, confronting evil in others and in himself. His experiment is the most dangerous enterprise of all. For he is attempting to organize the power of a people. And one never knows what power, or people, will do. Therefore, the hero often finds himself surrounded by demonic forces. He must control them or they will control him. And much of the time he fails. It is a battle which requires all of his goodness and all of his wickedness. For he must be hard and ruthless, yet fair and humane. These are the paradoxical difficulties of the state-founding hero.

32. In the future great economic sacrifices will be required, even during peace, so that a nation might be protected against the fatal day when weapons of mass destruction are again unleashed. Because commercial democracy emphasizes an ethic of consumption, it will be necessary to limit commercial advertising. Values of conservation, self-sacrifice, and delayed gratification will have to predominate; and any propaganda which would unleash a flood of sensualism is certain to be considered dangerous, even subversive.

33. Consider the Archgeneral's formula: If there is no "down" then there cannot be an "up." Without an "up," we cannot ascend. If we cannot ascend, then gravity wins and we sink into the mire.

34. *In Cato's speech before the Senate against the conspirators.* — "Do not imagine that it was by force of arms that our ancestors transformed a petty state into this great Republic. If it were so, it would now be at the height of its glory, since we have more subjects and citizens, more arms and horses, than they had. It was something quite different that made them great—something that we are entirely lacking in. They were hard workers at home, just rulers abroad; and to the council-chamber they brought untrammeled minds, neither racked by consciousness of guilt nor enslaved by passion. We have lost these virtues."[2]

---

[2] Sallust, *Conspiracy of Catiline*, trans. by S. A. Handford (England: Penguin Classics, 1982), p.

35. The "ancients were by no means foolish" wrote Polybius. They acted wisely when "they introduced...belief in the punishments of Hades." Polybius thought that politicians who reject the necessity of religion are foolish and "take great risks." "The result is," he declared, "that among the Greeks, apart from anything else, men who hold public office cannot be trusted with the safe-keeping of so much as a single talent, even if they have ten accountants and as many seals and twice as many witnesses." As for the Romans, who were more religious than the other pagan peoples, Polybius tells us: "their magistrates handle large sums of money and scrupulously perform their duty because they have given their word on [religious] oath."[3]

Therefore even the atheist must admit the usefulness and grandeur of religion. And of religions, isn't Christianity the grandest of all?

36. The historian Jacob Burckardt once wrote that the state is a product of criminal and violent longings. But once firmly established, the state makes possible a society and an alliance of individuals with interests in common. From this there can begin a gradual movement toward justice and decency. And after that, toward liberalism and decadence.

37. Only profoundly conservative societies have produced great and lasting empires — or have survived the aggressive probings of the barbarian.

38. It has been said by more than one great thinker, that despotism has certain advantages over freedom. For despotism is capable of organizing the maximum external strength of a community in its struggle against other communities, and is able to demand great sacrifices from its subjects.

39. Jacob Burckhardt, in his *Reflections On History*, makes the surprising observation that culture, taken as a whole, "flourished more under durable tyrannies than in freedom."

40. Forgive us, Lord, for all the evil we have brought to this beautiful world. Life would be simple if only we could love one another. Show us, again, the life everlasting. Amen.

223.

3 Polybius, *The Rise of the Roman Empire*, trans. Ian Scott-Kilvert (England: Penguin Classics, 1984), p. 349.

41. What could it mean to profess conservatism in a society based upon a process antithetical to conservation—*capitalism*; adhering to a value system diametrically opposed to moral absolutes—*the market*; supported by political authorities against authority—*democracy*; grounded in a utilitarianism which gradually undermines the institutions of greatest utility—*family, motherhood, and church?*

42. There will be a new aristocracy. It will define itself in terms of service to the nation in war. It will claim special political privileges because of its indispensability. It may become corrupt with power.

43. Raw plutocracy is dead. Why? Because it has failed history's most crucial test. *It has proven itself unwarlike.*

44. Despotism cannot become tyranny as long as there are aristocrats to hold it in check. Aristocrats cannot become oppressors while the people maintain their right of veto. The people, in their turn, cannot grow lawless while the rulers are strong and watchful.

45. It was the great social thinker, Vilfredo Pareto, who denied any truth to the ideology of progress. For him, history was the stuff of non-logical human activity. He also said that society would continue to be ruled by the few; that force and fraud would always be big determiners in history; that violence "has supreme value in and by itself" and "remains superbly alien to the values which it is supposed to serve."

46. Let us take a lesson from Machiavelli: In every great crisis *choose sides.* In other words: take the lesser of two evils. Then, after several thousand years, there might appear upon the earth something genuinely good. This I call the evolutionary or conservative approach to politics, which opposes itself to political utopianism.

47. There is a cloud, a reason to worry, and a tremendous pang of doubt hovering over us. Will a critical and over-rationalizing spirit, stoop-shouldered and weak, take us by the throat as we emerge from the womb of these great wars and upheavals?

48. We must remember that Rome fell because of gravity; because of a universal force of nature which pulls ever-downward. *That still pulls,* even now, continually.

49. Joseph Schumpeter suggested that liberalism was only made possible by its feudalistic "protective strata." Therefore when liberalism

finally enforced its ideals consistently (which meant destroying the feudal remnants), it was committing suicide.

50. *From the generals to the sociologists, present these:*
War is so much more certain than sociology. What, in the final analysis, can sociology solve? At most, it bores the casual observer, or titillates the bookworm. Meanwhile, we — the generals of war — can remove whole cities, divert rivers, empty lakes, and blast mountains into valleys. The new weapons make us into history's engineers while you sociologists are merely dreamers. You chatter about demographic trends while we make them. As Leon Trotsky once said: "All through history, mind limps after reality." *You* are mind, *we* are the reality.

51. The Archgeneral says: I am not a fascist. Fascists have ideology. I only have instincts. Consequently, I do not argue. I shoot.

52. The Archgeneral continues: Am I a tyrant? Most "thinking" people say so. But then, it is consistent with the "enlightened" man's relativism to conclude that all authority is tyrannical. Yet if we can escape for a moment the narrow categories of liberalism, it is clear that I am not a tyrant. For I am cold, whereas a true tyrant is invariably hot. I am respectful of law, whereas the true tyrant is lawless. I am patient and reasonable in my dealings. A tyrant is consistently capricious. Who, then, dares to say that I'm a tyrant?

53. It is the end of the Fourth World War. The Archgeneral goes to meet the senators at Ford's Theater. And there is Brutus, and John Wilkes Booth, and Cassius, and Lee Harvey Oswald, and the tribunes. Since the war is over, they haven't any need of Archgenerals. So Casca strikes the first blow, followed by the others. They hack at the stunned dictator. And he falls — a gash-ridden corpse at the foot of Pompey's statue.
"*Sic semper tyrannus!*"
"Liberty! Freedom! Tyranny is dead!"

54. People can say whatever they want about the Archgeneral. Yet words are empty. Only deeds count. But even deeds cannot do very much against an Archgeneral. Therefore, I would warn all those would-be assassins, that they cannot alter the social need for a strong national leader by eliminating a contingent human being. The principle of the unity of authority is favored by the times. Therefore, the spirit of the Archgeneral will live on after his assassins.

55. But let us pray, for the sake of liberty, that our jealous senators and tribunes are lucky; that the Republic *is* restored; that the people have become virtuous; that the people have become tough; that the age of mass destruction comes to an end. Let us hope that the Archgeneral, before his death, is a builder and not merely a leveler.

56. Religion shall be restored. There are two reasons for this: First, closeness to death often inclines people to think of God; second, prodigies, signs, and wonders may make themselves felt, as during other periods of great stress, leading mankind away from materialism back towards supernaturalism.

57. Aristocracy, by hurricane politics and hurricane politicians, returns. The egalitarian abyss of two centuries is abridged. Mankind is restored to rank order. The people, rediscovering eternal verities and inner lights, finally agree to self-limitation. No more reliance on liberal abstractions. Dead is the statecraft of pity; gone are the rationalist's Rights of Man and the moral pregnancy of the down-trodden. No hideous new births and revolutions out of men like Marx. Antichrist is finally cast down. A more mature spirit, of intellectual modesty, prevails. No more neurotic hankering after utopias. It is accepted that certain problems are forever with us. Poverty can breathe easier, becoming respectable again. War recovers its former place. Political authority no longer needs to make so many apologies. There comes an end to assaults on the foundation of order. At long last a political class of implacable senators and sturdy generals rises out of the human lowlands. And behold! Even the lowlands are raised.

In philosophical terms, it is the end of Platonic moralism, which is to say: *moral rationalism.* The manly virtues—which are real, worldly, and natural—return to the fore. It is not that justice has been usurped by brute strength (for that was the communist model), but that justice has come down to earth, at last becoming realistic: ending the slaughter, the madness and the stupidity of modern politics; while vouchsafing to us new slaughterings, madnesses and stupidities as yet undreamt of.

Index